VISUAL QUICKSTART GUIDE

VECTORWORKS 9

FOR WINDOWS AND MACINTOSH

Tom Baer

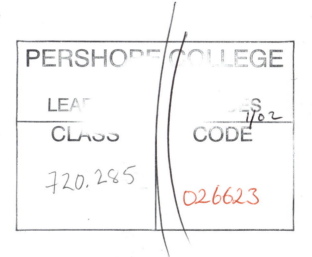

Peachpit Press

Visual QuickStart Guide
VectorWorks 9 for Windows and Macintosh
Tom Baer

Peachpit Press
1249 Eighth Street
Berkeley, CA 94710
510/524-2178
800/283-9444
510/524-2221 (fax)
Find us on the World Wide Web at: http://www.peachpit.com
To report errors, send a note to errata@peachpit.com
Peachpit Press is a division of Pearson Education
Copyright © 2002 by Tom Baer

Editor: William Rodarmor
Production Coordinator: Lisa Brazieal
Copyeditor: Sally Zahner
Compositor: Christi Payne
Indexer: Emily Glossbrenner
Cover Design: The Visual Group
Technical review: Dan Monaghan, Nemetschek North America

ISBN 0-201-70365-3

9 8 7 6 5 4 3 2 1

Printed and bound in the United States of America

Dedication

To my sister, Marjorie and to my wife, Susan, and my daughters, Lola and Cecilia, all of whom encouraged me when this project seemed inexorably beyond my grasp and all of whom were somehow able to grant me a measure of forbearance even when it it looked as though there might never be a light at the end of the tunnel.

Acknowledgements

I'd like to thank everyone at Peachpit, including worthy freelancers, for their help with this complex project. In particular, I'd like to thank production coordinator Lisa Brazieal for project management, editorial assistant Suzie Lowey for helping sort out the graphics, editors Sally Zahner and William Rodarmor for their scrupulous attention to my words, Christi Payne for compositing, and Emily Glossbrenner for a superb index. Many thanks, too, to Dan Monaghan, at Nemetschek NA, for his support, and to the many active and vocal participants on the VectorWorks listserv. Finally, thank you to Adam Aronson, Alain Boisclair, Alain Counson, Dave Donley, Matthew Panzer, Guy Rollins, and Gerrit Vanoppen, whose VectorWorks drawings grace the gallery pages of this book.

TABLE OF CONTENTS

TABLE OF CONTENTS

INTRODUCTION

Let us begin with, "What is CAD?" Literally the letters stand for computer-aided design, but nowadays that might apply to any number of applications. What distinguishes CAD programs from other kinds of design tools is that the two-dimensional pictures you create are not the final product—they're precision drawings intended to model an actual object, such as a building or a mechanism. They not only represent the object visually, they also contain information to enable someone to construct the object—part numbers and materials, as well as exacting measurements.

In the CAD market, Nemetschek's Vector-Works occupies a niche somewhere between the simple but surprisingly sophisticated design-your-own-kitchen packages and full-featured applications like AutoDesk's AutoCAD, Bentley MicroStation, and PTC ProEngineer, each of which costs thousands of dollars per workstation and requires extensive training. At less than $700, VectorWorks offers a balance of capability, price, and ease of use.

VectorWorks is most often used by architects designing buildings, but it's also suitable for other jobs, from designing mechanical assemblies to creating theater lighting. While AutoCAD remains the standard for large architectural projects, many designers consider VectorWorks the best choice for small to medium-sized projects.

What VectorWorks Does Best

VectorWorks can be used to draw and model just about anything. You can start with simple two-dimensional shapes and, using such techniques as *extrusion* and *sweeping*, create three-dimensional objects. The program provides stock 3D shapes like spheres, cones, and rectangular solids as ready-made *primitives*.

You can then add, subtract, and intersect these solid forms to define more complex ones. Solids can also be treated as 3D *meshes* that you can twist and pull into whatever form you need (**Figure i.1**).

What VectorWorks really excels at is architectural design. Its system of *hybrid objects* makes it easy to create 3D models of walls and floors and roofs while working in the 2D drafting environment. The package includes a large number of *plug-in objects* such as doors and windows that can be inserted into walls and individually custom-tailored. A library of ready-made objects—such as furniture and drafting *symbols*—saves you the time and effort of creating them anew for each project (**Figure i.2**).

VectorWorks supports other design specialties, too. It has a generous collection of nuts and bolts for mechanical designers, plants for landscapers, and desks and files for space planners. Some of these are static symbols, but others are flexible plug-in objects.

Unlike pencil and paper drawings, a single CAD file can contain all the information for the project; for a simple building, for example, that might include the floorplan, framing materials, plumbing, electricity, and so on. Imagine trying to look at all of that information at once—it would be an unintelligible tangle of lines and text. Fortunately, VectorWorks's *layer* and *class* structure organizes large numbers of objects and attached records so you can see and select only those you need.

Figure i.1 Using VectorWorks's simple 3D tools, you can generate some pretty complex shapes. This example was generated using Boolean functions to add and subtract solids.

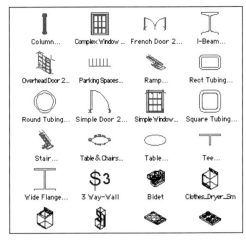

Figure i.2 Symbols can be 2D or 3D, or hybrids of both. They are easy to create and use.

	A	B	C	D	E	F
1	WINDOW SCHEDULE					
2	ID#	Size	Manufacturer / Supplier	Stock #	Color	Rough Opening
3						
4.1	RW1	21 1/2" W. x 38 1/2" H.	Velux	VS104	Copper	21 1/2" W. x 39" H.
4.2	RW1	21 1/2" W. x 38 1/2" H.	Velux	VS104	Copper	21 1/2" W. x 39" H.
4.3	RW1	21 1/2" W. x 38 1/2" H.	Velux	VS104	Copper	21 1/2" W. x 39" H.
4.4	RW1	21 1/2" W. x 38 1/2" H.	Velux	VS104	Copper	21 1/2" W. x 39" H.
4.5	RW1	21 1/2" W. x 38 1/2" H.	Velux	VS104	Copper	21 1/2" W. x 39" H.
4.6	W1	3'-1 5/8" W. x 5'-4 7/8" H.	Andersen	TW3052	Sandstone	3'-2 1/8" W. x 5'-5 1/4" H.
4.7	W1	3'-1 5/8" W. x 5'-4 7/8" H.	Andersen	TW3052	Sandstone	3'-2 1/8" W. x 5'-5 1/4" H.
4.8	W1	3'-1 5/8" W. x 5'-4 7/8" H.	Andersen	TW3052	Sandstone	3'-2 1/8" W. x 5'-5 1/4" H.
4.9	W1	3'-1 5/8" W. x 5'-4 7/8" H.	Andersen	TW3052	Sandstone	3'-2 1/8" W. x 5'-5 1/4" H.
4.10	W1	3'-1 5/8" W. x 5'-4 7/8" H.	Andersen	TW3052	Sandstone	3'-2 1/8" W. x 5'-5 1/4" H.
4.11	W1	3'-1 5/8" W. x 5'-4 7/8" H.	Andersen	TW3052	Sandstone	3'-2 1/8" W. x 5'-5 1/4" H.
4.12	W1	3'-1 5/8" W. x 5'-4 7/8" H.	Andersen	TW3052	Sandstone	3'-2 1/8" W. x 5'-5 1/4" H.
4.13	W1	3'-1 5/8" W. x 5'-4 7/8" H.	Andersen	TW3052	Sandstone	3'-2 1/8" W. x 5'-5 1/4" H.
4.14	W1	3'-1 5/8" W. x 5'-4 7/8" H.	Andersen	TW3052	Sandstone	3'-2 1/8" W. x 5'-5 1/4" H.
4.15	W1	3'-1 5/8" W. x 5'-4 7/8" H.	Andersen	TW3052	Sandstone	3'-2 1/8" W. x 5'-5 1/4" H.
4.16	W1	3'-1 5/8" W. x 5'-4 7/8" H.	Andersen	TW3052	Sandstone	3'-2 1/8" W. x 5'-5 1/4" H.
4.17	W2	2'-11 15/16" W. x 1'-5" H.	Andersen	AR31	Sandstone	3'-0 1/2" W. x 1'-5 1/2" H.
4.18	W2	2'-11 15/16" W. x 1'-5" H.	Andersen	AR31	Sandstone	3'-0 1/2" W. x 1'-5 1/2" H.
4.19	W2	2'-11 15/16" W. x 1'-5" H.	Andersen	AR31	Sandstone	3'-0 1/2" W. x 1'-5 1/2" H.
4.20	W2	2'-11 15/16" W. x 1'-5" H.	Andersen	AR31	Sandstone	3'-0 1/2" W. x 1'-5 1/2" H.
4.21	W2	2'-11 15/16" W. x 1'-5" H.	Andersen	AR31	Sandstone	3'-0 1/2" W. x 1'-5 1/2" H.
4.22	W2	2'-11 15/16" W. x 1'-5" H.	Andersen	AR31	Sandstone	3'-0 1/2" W. x 1'-5 1/2" H.
4.23	W2	2'-11 15/16" W. x 1'-5" H.	Andersen	AR31	Sandstone	3'-0 1/2" W. x 1'-5 1/2" H.
4.24	W2	2'-11 15/16" W. x 1'-5" H.	Andersen	AR31	Sandstone	3'-0 1/2" W. x 1'-5 1/2" H.
4.25	W2	2'-11 15/16" W. x 1'-5" H.	Andersen	AR31	Sandstone	3'-0 1/2" W. x 1'-5 1/2" H.
4.26	W2	2'-11 15/16" W. x 1'-5" H.	Andersen	AR31	Sandstone	3'-0 1/2" W. x 1'-5 1/2" H.

Figure i.3 Parts lists and window and door schedules can be displayed in the drawing or exported to other spreadsheet and database applications.

You can generate worksheets and databases directly from a VectorWorks drawing that can be used for parts lists and bills of materials or tabulated catalogs of doors and windows (**Figure i.3**).

VectorWorks is capable of rendering its 3D models in a reasonably realistic manner. Using Nemetschek's companion rendering program, RenderWorks, you can create sophisticated images with cast shadows, reflections, transparency, and texture mapping (**Figure i.4**).

Figure i.4 Supplemented by RenderWorks, VectorWorks can produce nearly photographic-quality renderings, with textures, reflectivity, and transparency.

WHAT VECTORWORKS DOES BEST

Presentations

When you're in the process of designing on the computer, you can use any method that suits you, but at some point it will be time to present your project. Often, the traditional top, front, and side views will offer an adequate presentation of your ideas for you and your client to look at and evaluate (see Chapter 10, "Worksheets, Reports, and Presentations").

Models can be presented in a whole range of ways, from wireframe to simple solids to solids with shadows on up to a fully textured model (**Figure i.5**). You can even import image files into VectorWorks and use them as texture details or backgrounds. VectorWorks has both *flyover* and *walkthrough* tools that work with its 3D models. A flyover moves the viewer through orthogonal space around the object; a walkthrough uses the illusion of perspective space to let you walk into a building and tour its interior spaces (**Figure i.6**).

At the end of the design cycle, you will want to release the drawings and other documents to production. VectorWorks's data management functions greatly simplify the paperwork that goes along with a project, automatically tabulating parts lists and *schedules*.

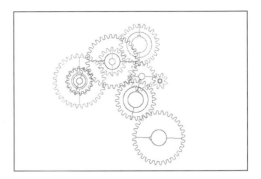

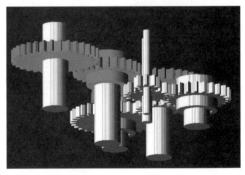

Figure i.5 Wireframe renderings are quick and easily manipulated, but it is often easier to visualize the object if you render it. Final renderings, with texture mapping and dramatic lighting, are more work to create and take longer to regenerate.

Figure i.6 The Flyover tool lets you quickly rotate a view and see your design from all sides. Walkthroughs are a little more difficult to navigate but can give you a sense of what the interior spaces of a building will be like.

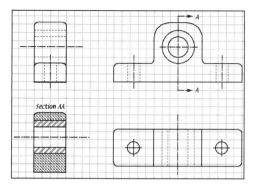

Figure i.7 You can use VectorWorks's drafting tools to draw quickly and accurately.

Learning the Program

VectorWorks is easy to learn. With minimal training, you can use it as an efficient 2D drafting program; its many handy tools make precision drafting nearly intuitive. As you draw, the pointer displays its alignment with other objects on the screen and snaps to key points not only on objects, but along lines projected off them as well (**Figure i.7**).

From there, it's only a small step to simple architectural drafting in two dimensions, and then on to 3D. In fact, when you use VectorWorks's hybrid tools to draw in plan view, you are really creating a 3D model to which you can then add windows, doors, and all the other details (**Figure i.8**). It takes a bit more training to model other 3D forms, but with a little practice, you will become comfortable in the 3D modeling environment and will be able to use the program's tools to design a variety of objects (**Figure i.9**).

This Visual QuickStart Guide will introduce you to all the basic concepts and operations you need to master to work competently in VectorWorks. Tasks are broken down into clear, step-by-step instructions, with ample illustrations so you can be sure you're on the right track.

After installing and initializing the software, you'll take a brief tour of the interface. Chapters 2 and 3 discuss creating and modifying 2D shapes. In Chapter 4, you'll learn to work with *constraints,* which, despite the forbidding name, are actually very helpful drawing tools. Chapter 5 introduces VectorWorks's very useful system of layers and classes, and Chapter 6 gives the low-down on 2D Symbols and plug-in objects. In Chapters 7 and 8, you'll learn how to create and edit 3D objects. Chapter 9 deals with a VectorWorks specialty, architectural applications. Chapter 10 shows how to generate the worksheets, reports, and presentations so other clients and coworkers can appreciate your designs and put them to use. Finally, check the book's companion Web site at www.peachpit.com for instruction on customizing the VectorWorks interface so you can tailor it to your particular working style.

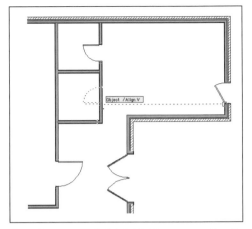

Figure i.8 VectorWorks's hybrid objects create 3D walls with doors and windows when you draw the floor plan.

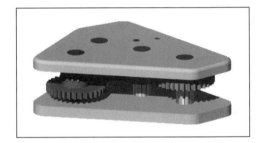

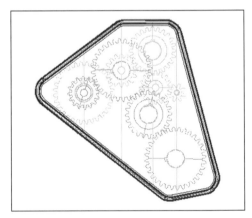

Figure i.9 You can assemble complex 3D models using VectorWorks's 3D tools.

Platform and System Requirements

VectorWorks 9 runs on both Mac and Windows platforms, and we note the few differences that exist in interface or commands. If no platform is mentioned, you can assume that the program works the same way under both operating systems.

Windows:

- Pentium processor or greater
- 64 MB RAM
- 110 MB hard-disk space for full install, 64 MB hard-disk space for basic install
- Microsoft 95(r) or Windows NT 4.0(r) or greater
- SVGA Monitor with 256 colors or more colors
- CD-ROM drive

Macintosh:

- Power Macintosh or greater
- Mac OS 8.6 or higher
- 64 MB RAM
- 110 MB hard-disk space for full install, 64 MB hard-disk space for basic install
- CD-ROM drive

PLATFORM AND SYSTEM REQUIREMENTS

A VectorWorks Art Gallery

You may already know what projects you have in mind for VectorWorks. To see what other VectorWorks users have achieved with the program, see the Gallery pages following this introduction.

BILO RESIDENCE, ELEVATIONS
Matthew G. Panzer

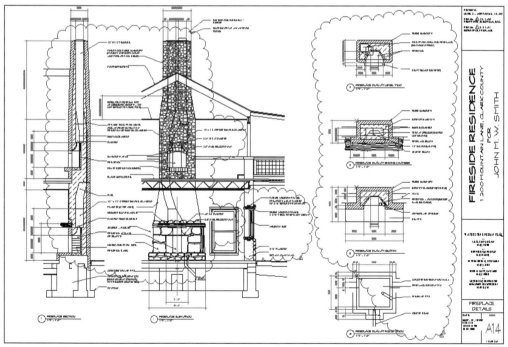

FIRESIDE RESIDENCE, FIREPLACE DETAILS
Guy Rollins, Architect, www.architx.com

CHURCH
AERIAL VIEW RENDERING
Matthew G. Panzer, William A. Smith, Architects

CHURCH
PERSPECTIVE RENDERING
Matthew G. Panzer, William A. Smith, Architects

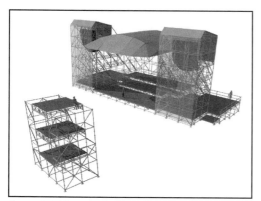

AIDS 2000
PERSPECTIVE
Alain Counson, GEARHOUSE, South Africa

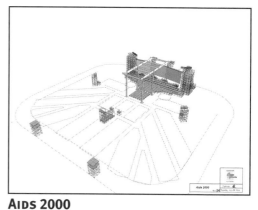

AIDS 2000
BIRD'S-EYE VIEW
Alain Counson, GEARHOUSE, South Africa

AIDS 2000
DAYTIME RENDERING
Alain Counson, GEARHOUSE, South Africa

AIDS 2000
NIGHTTIME RENDERING
Alain Counson, GEARHOUSE, South Africa

VALVE BODY
Alain Boisclair, CEP Forensic Engineering

GIJBELS PROJECT
Gerrit Vanoppen, Architect,
Bouwexterten, Moers & Vanoppen

DEPT. STORE, MERCHANDISING FIXTURE
Adam Aronson, 2www.coroflot.com/adam1

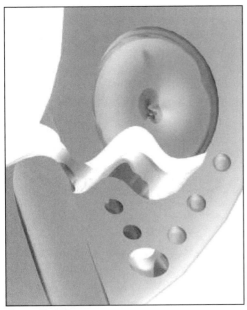

COOL SOLID
Dave Donley, Nemetschek North America

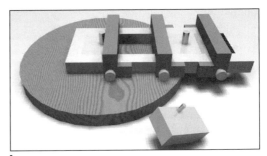

JIG
Dave Donley, Nemetschek North America

GETTING STARTED

This chapter begins with personalizing your copy of VectorWorks, then explains how to open a new drawing file and offers a tour of the VectorWorks interface. Finally, it lays out the fundamentals you'll need to grasp before you can start designing. Then we'll be ready to move on to Chapter 2, "Creating 2D Shapes," where we actually start drawing.

Personalizing Your Software

Installing VectorWorks is no different from installing almost any other application, except that you get to put your personal stamp on it.

To enter your VectorWorks serial numbers:

1. The first time you fire up VectorWorks, you'll be presented with a screen asking you to "personalize" the software (**Figure 1.1**). Fill in the blanks and click OK.

   The Serial Numbers dialog box opens (**Figure 1.2**).

2. In the Serial Numbers dialog box, type in the serial number that came with the software. Click Add. If you have installed the RenderWorks package you will be asked for its serial number as well (see Chapter 10, "Worksheets, Reports, and Presentations").

   The numbers are added to the VectorWorks Serial Numbers list.

3. Click Done to finish the installation process.

   A new drawing file opens in the default settings.

Figure 1.1 You need to personalize VectorWorks the first time you start it up.

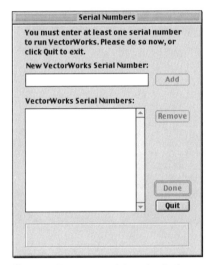

Figure 1.2 Type your serial number in the field in the dialog box. If you've installed RenderWorks, you'll need to add the serial number for it as well.

Figure 1.3 The Create Document dialog box offers you the choice of a blank document or one of your templates as the starting point for a new drawing file.

Figure 1.4 VectorWorks 9 comes with only four templates, but you can easily add to them.

✔ Tips

■ VectorWorks always uses a template to open a new file; the Blank Document option is just the bare-bones template.

■ You can open recent VectorWorks files by choosing their names from the bottom of the File menu.

Opening a New Drawing File

Once you've installed VectorWorks, you can create as many new drawing files as you like. You can always begin with the blank document option and construct the drawing environment as you go, but it is much easier to set up most of the underpinnings at the beginning.

Templates are the simplest way to jump-start the design process. When you open a file from a template, you have already set the page size, the scale, the grid, and the dimensioning standard, and have at your disposal whatever hatches, symbols, records, and scripts are included in the file.

Templates also often include font preferences as well as formatted borders and title blocks to ensure a consistent appearance for an office's work product regardless of who worked on the drawing. Creating templates that include libraries of key details and layers with the basic layout information for the project will also help make the design content consistent.

To open a new drawing file:

1. From the File menu, choose File > New. The Create Document dialog box opens (**Figure 1.3**).

2. Click the Create Blank Document radio button

   or

   Click the Use Document Template radio button and choose one of the templates from the pop-up list (**Figure 1.4**).

3. Click OK. A new document opens using the selected template.

To open an existing drawing file:

◆ Choose File > Open, or press Command+O (Mac) or Ctrl+O (Windows), and navigate to the name of the file you want to open

or

Click the File menu and drag down to select one of the recently opened files listed near the bottom of the menu (**Figure 1.5**).

To save a file as a template:

1. Choose File > Save As Template.

   The Save as VectorWorks Drawing Template dialog box opens (**Figure 1.6**).

2. In the Name field, type a name for the new template. Click Save to close the dialog box and continue.

✔ Tip

■ While it might seem like a good idea to create folders within the Templates folder to organize large numbers of templates, the Create Document dialog box finds only those at the root level of the folder.

Figure 1.5 Opening a recently used drawing file is as easy as dragging down the file menu and selecting its name from the list.

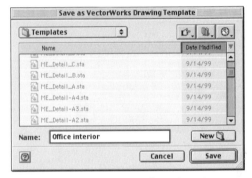

Figure 1.6 To add to your store of templates, just save an open file as a new template.

OPENING A NEW DRAWING FILE

The VectorWorks Interface

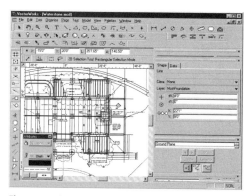

Figure 1.7 When all the palettes are open on and around the drawing area, there's not much room to work.

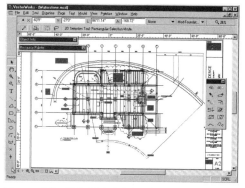

Figure 1.8 You'll find it helpful to close the palettes you don't use at all, zip up the ones you aren't using at the moment, and drag some others off to the side.

Once the document is open, the many functions that make up the VectorWorks interface comes into play. The center of the window, literally and functionally, is the drawing area. It is surrounded by the menu bar, the Data Display bar, the Mode bar, the View bar, rulers, and an array of palettes.

In this section, we will take a whirlwind tour of the interface. The function of each tool and command will be discussed in greater detail later in the book.

The screen can become awfully crowded if all the palettes are displayed, leaving very little drawing space in which to work (**Figure 1.7**). So by default, some palettes aren't displayed; others overlap one another. Luckily, you have a number of options to give yourself more elbowroom (**Figure 1.8**).

Managing palettes in Windows

◆ To open a palette, drag down to the palette's name on the Palettes menu and put a check by it (**Figure 1.9**).

◆ You can dock palettes at the sides of the drawing area by dragging them there. The drawing area shrinks to accommodate them. If you don't want them to expand at the expense of the drawing area, hold down the Ctrl key while you drag them over (**Figure 1.10**).

◆ You can zip up a palette to show just its title bar by double-clicking it; double-clicking it again unzips it (**Figure 1.11**). But if you zip a narrow palette that has no name in its title bar, you run the risk of forgetting which one it is.

◆ Double-clicking the title bar of a palette that is docked at the side of the drawing area moves it into the drawing area. To redock it, drag it back to the edge of the drawing area.

◆ You can close a palette by clicking the x in its upper-right corner or by dragging down to the palette's name on the Palettes menu.

◆ Palettes can be reshaped by dragging on their edges; when you dock a palette at the edge of a drawing, it automatically stretches out along that edge (**Figure 1.12**).

◆ The Object Information, Resources, Object Browser, and Working Planes palettes dock at the right and left but not the top and bottom of the screen. The Attributes palette doesn't dock at all.

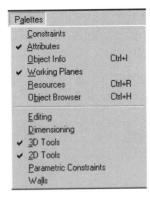

Figure 1.9 Closed palettes open when you put checks by their names on the Palettes menu.

Figure 1.10 In Windows, if you don't want a palette to jump into the gutter and push the drawing area out of the way, hold down the Ctrl key as you drag the palette toward the edge of the drawing area.

Figure 1.11 Zip those palettes and free up valuable real estate for the drawing.

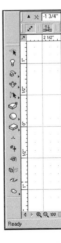

Figure 1.12 When you dock a palette along any edge of the drawing area, it stretches out to conform to the edge.

Managing palettes on the Mac

◆ To open a palette, on the Palettes menu drag down to the palette's name and put a check by it.

◆ When you bring a palette within a few pixels of the edge of the drawing area or another palette, it snaps into alignment.

◆ You can zip up a palette so that just its title bar shows by clicking the zip button in the upper-right corner. But if you zip a narrow palette that has no name in its title bar, you are left with just a blank title bar in your drawing area and you may not remember just which palette it is. Clicking again unzips the palette.

◆ You can also zip or unzip a palette by double-clicking its title bar.

◆ You can close a palette by clicking the x in its upper-left corner or by dragging down to its name on the Palettes menu.

◆ Settings for the Palette margins on the Session tab of the VectorWorks Preferences dialog box control how a new document aligns with the palettes on the desktop.

THE VECTORWORKS INTERFACE

The drawing area and the print area

In a VectorWorks drawing file, the print area floats within a larger area called the drawing area. This is a nice feature of CAD. Gone are the days when you suddenly realize that you should have started on a larger sheet or centered the drawing a little differently and are now out of luck. In VectorWorks, you can change the size of the print area at any time and move it to include parts of the drawing that would otherwise have fallen off the edges. If you're printing your D-size drawing to your desktop printer, VectorWorks will tile the sheet and display the page breaks (**Figure 1.13**). You can even set the print area to a single page and print out a detail for reference.

The menu bar

VectorWorks divides its interface between commands that you invoke from the menu bar and tools that are called from the palettes. The menu bar changes when you change workspaces; you can customize it in the Workspace editor. The individual menus (in their default configurations) are displayed collectively in the Appendix.

Rulers and grids

The VectorWorks workspace has rulers along its top and left edges; their units are controlled by the Units settings in the Page menu and by the magnification of the screen (**Figure 1.14**).

The Data Display bar

The Data Display bar is an interactive display along the top of the drawing area (**Figure 1.15**). Use it to read out the position of the pointer as you draw or—and this is an important feature of VectorWorks—to type coordinates into it to place a data point precisely.

Figure 1.13 Check Show Page Breaks in the Set Print Area dialog box to see how the print area will be tiled onto smaller sheets.

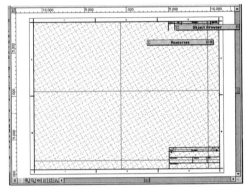

Figure 1.14 The grid is independent of the rulers; you can set up a grid in whatever divisions you like and rotate it to any angle.

Figure 1.15 You can use the Data Display bar to enter data points precisely, even overriding the settings on the Constraints palette.

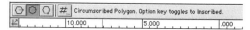

Figure 1.16 Use the Mode bar to choose among the functions a tool can perform.

Figure 1.17 The View bar is a shortcut to some commands that are also found in the menus—and some that aren't.

The Mode bar

Most tools operate in more than one mode. The Fillet tool, for example, has three modes of operation. Some tools also put in a Preferences button on the Mode bar that opens a dialog box so you can change certain parameters (here, the number of sides on a polygon) under which the tool operates (**Figure 1.16**).

The View bar

Way down in the lower-left corner of the window, you find the View bar, with eight buttons that give you a quick way to zoom in and out and recall earlier views of the drawing area (**Figure 1.17**).

The Tools

While you're working in VectorWorks, most of your tools are conveniently arrayed on the palettes in the drawing area. Different work-spaces have their palettes arranged differently, but they look enough alike that a view of the default palettes is instructive.

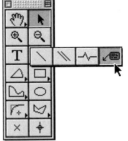

Figure 1.18 To save space on the screen, some tools are hidden under others on the palette until you hold down the mouse button. The flyouts are a little different on the Mac (left) and Windows (right).

✔ Tips

- To save space, VectorWorks sometimes stacks several tools at a single location on a palette. These are called *flyouts,* and you'll know there are additional tools hiding when you see a little arrow in the lower-right corner of a tool. Hold the mouse button down to expose the other tools; release it to select one (**Figure 1.18**).

- When you double-click some tools, they open a dialog box that lets you create an object by entering data from the keyboard.

Figure 1.19 The tools for creating 2D objects are grouped on the 2D Tools palette.

2D Tools palette

The 2D Tools palette contains the basic drafting tools along with tools for navigating around the workspace (**Figure 1.19**).

Editing palette

The tools in the Editing palette are mostly for use in the 2D environment, but you can use the Mirror, Rotate, and Duplicate Along Path tools for 3D objects as well (**Figure 1.20**).

Figure 1.20 Tools for editing 2D objects are on the Editing palette.

3D Tools palette

The 3D Tools palette is home to the tools that both create 3D objects and allow you to view them as if they were really 3D objects (**Figure 1.21**).

Figure 1.21 The 3D Tools palette has tools for creating, manipulating, and viewing 3D objects.

THE TOOLS

Figure 1.22 The Resources palette doesn't have any tools on it, but it lets you create new resources and import them from other files.

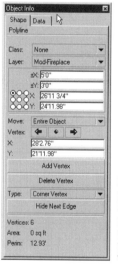

Figure 1.23 The Object Info palette, like the Data Display bar, is another place you can make precision adjustments to your drawing by typing values into the edit fields.

Figure 1.24 The Parametric Constraints palette sets up relationships between objects and constrains the modifications you make to them.

Resources palette

The Resources palette is the interface between your active drawing file and all your other ones. You use it to bring a variety of scripts, symbols, textures, and other useful stuff into the file, to create new resources, and to manage the resources within the document (**Figure 1.22**).

Object Information palette

The Object Info palette is a way to check the properties of objects in a drawing, but is even more important as a tool for changing those objects (**Figure 1.23**).

Parametric Constraints palette

The Parametric Constraints palette operates only in the 2D drafting environment, but it is a powerful kit of tools that lets you sets up dimensional links among objects while allowing you to move and modify them within the constraints you impose (**Figure 1.24**) (see Chapter 4, "Drawing with Constraints").

Dimensioning palette

The Dimensioning palette creates dimensions according to the standard you select in the Document Preference dialog box. You can associate dimensions with objects so that the dimension (with its numbers and lines) changes as you modify the drawing.

THE TOOLS

Walls palette

The Walls palette contains the set of tools that create and modify walls. Walls are *hybrid objects;* they—and the doors and windows they contain—are drawn according to the conventions of architectural drafting in plan view (**Figure 1.25**); but they are modeled as 3D objects in the orthogonal and perspective views (see Chapter 7, "Creating 3D Objects").

You use the Walls palette in its hybrid mode: Walls are presented as 2D objects in your plan but are 3D in the other views. Most of the wall tools require you to work in plan view (**Figure 1.26**).

Object Browser

The Object Browser is a special palette that lets you select and place symbols, editable groups, and plug-in objects in a single step. The Browser opens a set of graphic resources for direct application to the drawing. When you click on a symbol, for example, it is automatically activated for placement. (**Figure 1.27**).

Figure 1.25 The tools in the Walls palette create and modify hybrid wall objects.

Figure 1.26 The Dimensioning palette includes a variety of tools for dimensioning your drawings. VectorWorks 9 has *associative dimensioning*, which changes the dimensions as the object changes.

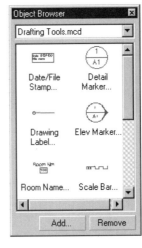

Figure 1.27 The Object Browser groups all kinds of insertable objects in one place: static symbols, plug-in objects, and modifiable groups.

THE TOOLS

Figure 1.28 The Attributes palette sets the appearance of the drawing objects.

Figure 1.29 The Constraints palette helps you draw quickly and accurately by forcing the cursor to key points relative to the grid or other objects in the drawing.

Figure 1.30 Use the Working Planes palette to store various working planes and more easily orient objects that do not lie comfortably on the Ground Plane.

Attributes palette

The Attributes palette controls the graphic attributes of drawing objects: line style and weight, patterns, hatches, fill colors, and so on (**Figure 1.28**).

Constraints palette

The Constraints palette provides a group of settings that you can use individually or in various combinations to streamline drawing one object relative to another (**Figure 1.29**).

Working Planes palette

To draw 3D objects in the correct orientation relative to one another, you need to set up a working plane in which they will be created. Once you have set one up, you can store it in the Working Planes palette for future use (**Figure 1.30**).

THE TOOLS

Workspaces

Workspaces, like templates, are ways of tailoring the application to specific purposes, but they aren't part of the document, and you can move from one workspace to another at any time during the design process. VectorWorks comes with a general-purpose workspace, but you can design new ones to meet your particular needs. Each workspace has its own arrangement of menu commands and tool palettes. Think of workspaces literally: You pick up your drawing and take it someplace else to get a different set of tools. Changing workspaces has no impact on the content of the document.

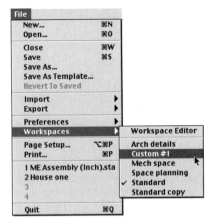

Figure 1.31 You can use a variety of workspaces to group functions for specific kinds of design work.

To go to another workspace:

◆ Choose File > Workspaces, and from the drop-down menu choose the workspace into which you want to move the file (**Figure 1.31**).

The palettes and menus change, giving you access to a new set of tools and commands.

✔ Tip

■ The first item on the Workspace sub-menu is the Workspace Editor. Use this command to modify one of the existing workspaces or to create a new one in which you arrange the commands and tools to your liking.

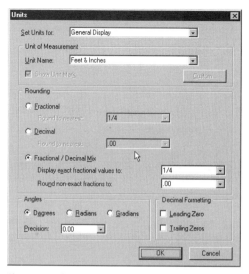

Figure 1.32 The Units dialog box sets up the units for both the dimensions and the display. The accuracy of the drawing file, however, is independent of these settings.

Setting Up a New Document

Once you have opened a new document, you may find that the template you used is just right and you can get down to the design work immediately. On the other hand, the template may need some adjustments. If you started with the Blank Document option, this will almost certainly be the case.

To set the measurement units:

1. Choose Page > Units from the Page menu. The Units dialog box opens (**Figure 1.32**). By default, the Set Units menu is in the General Display mode. The settings for dimensioning are discussed in Chapter 10, "Worksheets, Reports, and Presentations."

2. In the Unit of Measurement area, choose a setting from the pop-up menu, which offers the usual English and metric units. You can create custom units (such as rods, cubits, furlongs) if you need them.

3. In the Rounding area of the dialog box, select the Fractional, Decimal, or Fractional/Decimal Mix radio button.

4. Choose values for rounding from the menus.

5. In the Angles area, choose the Degrees, Radians, or Gradians radio button and then a setting for the precision of the display from the pop-up menu.

6. In the Decimal Formatting area of the dialog box, select the Leading Zero and/or Trailing Zeros checkboxes to display readouts with those options.

7. Click OK to close the dialog box and reset the display to the new units.

To set up a document for printing:

1. From the File menu, choose File > Page Setup.

   The Page Setup dialog box opens. The features of the Page Setup dialog box will vary according to the printer or plotter.

2. Configure the preferences according to the instructions of the printer or plotter manufacturer and click OK to close the dialog box.

✔ Tip

- In Windows, choose File > Print Setup to open the Print Setup dialog box.

To set the print area:

1. From the Page menu, choose Page > Set Print Area.

   The Set Print Area dialog box opens (**Figure 1.33**).

2. In the Set Print Area dialog box, choose a sheet size from the pop-up menu.

   The Pages display on the right side of the dialog box shows how the drawing will be tiled based on the Page Setup dialog box.

3. If you want the tiling displayed as a grid of gray rectangles on the drawing area, select the Show Page Breaks checkbox.

4. Choose the Move Page tool from the 2D Tools palette (normally a flyout from the Pan tool).

5. Drag the page outline to redefine the print area.

The Snap Grid sets up a grid of points to which the pointer will jump when Snap to Grid is selected from the Constraints palette (see Chapter 4, "Drawing with Constraints"). Grids are great tools for increasing productivity. You can change the grid size and angle to suit your needs at any time.

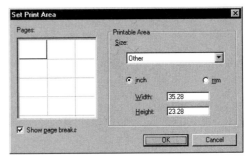

Figure 1.33 The Set Print Area dialog box defines what part of the drawing area will be printed and how it will be translated to the page size of your printer.

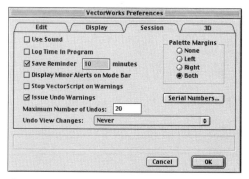

Figure 1.34 You can set VectorWorks to remind you to periodically save your working file.

Figure 1.35 The Save VectorWorks Drawing dialog box.

Saving, Closing, Quitting

When you're done working for a while, you will want to close your drawing file and maybe exit the application. VectorWorks closes up shop just like any other piece of software you own.

Saving files is likewise pretty routine. It's wise to do it frequently throughout the process; VectorWorks doesn't have an automatic save feature, and should your machine or the application crash, you will lose all the changes made since the last time you saved. The program will remind you to save your work at fixed intervals if you choose that option on the Session tab of the VectorWorks Preferences dialog box (**Figure 1.34**).

To save a file:

1. Choose File > Save or press Command+S (Mac) or Ctrl+S (Windows).

   If you haven't saved the file before, the Save VectorWorks Drawing dialog box opens (**Figure 1.35**).

2. Navigate to the folder in which you want to save the drawing file. In the Name field, type in a name for the file.

3. Click Save to save the file.

What if you're working on a file and have made significant changes that you want to save without losing what you had before? The best approach is to do a Save As, and create a new drawing file while leaving the original as it was when you last saved.

To use the Save As function:

1. Choose File > Save As.

   The Save VectorWorks Drawing dialog box opens.

2. Navigate to the folder in which you want to save the drawing file. In the Name field, type in a new name for the file.

3. Click Save to save the file.

To close a drawing file without exiting the application:

1. Choose File > Close or press Command+W (Mac) or Ctrl+W (Windows).

   If you have made changes in the file since it was last saved, a dialog box will open prompting you to save the changes, discard them, or cancel.

2. Click Save to close the file and save the changes

   or

   Click Don't Save to close the file and discard the changes.

To quit the application:

1. Choose File > Quit or File > Exit, or press Command+Q (Mac) or Ctrl+Q (Windows).

   If you have made changes in any open file since it was last saved, a dialog box will appear prompting you to save the changes, discard them, or cancel.

2. Click Save to close the file and save the changes

   or

   Click Don't Save to close the file and discard the changes.

3. Repeat Step 2 for as many files with unsaved changes as you have open.

   When you have done it for all the open files with changes, the application quits.

CREATING 2D SHAPES

2

In this chapter we will discuss what you need to produce 2D elements by drawing with the mouse, entering data in the Data Display bar, and working with dialog boxes—and by combinations of all three. In Chapter 4, "Drawing with Constraints," we will talk about ways to use constraints to draw more efficiently.

Our discussion will range from general drawing strategies to the specifics of drawing rectangles, circles, arcs and polylines.

There are quite a few ways of coming up with exactly the same object on the screen, especially if it's a simple shape like a rectangle, or a complex polyline. Which way you go often depends on personal preference—or habit— as much as anything else. But by the end of this chapter you should have a pretty good grounding in the art and science of object creation.

Attributes

The strictly visual character of a drawing, independent of its geometry, is determined by how you assign attributes to the objects that it contains. You might think of attributes as the uniforms the objects wear. They give a distinct esthetic to the drawing and help you identify which parts belong together. Some designers are often nearly as fussy about the line weights and dash styles in their drawings as they are about the design itself and the final product it represents.

Traditional drafting practice relies on lines and text alone to delineate the design, and many people are very skilled at visualizing a design just by seeing the top, front, and side views or from plans and elevations. CAD offers those of us with more limited imaginative abilities a wide range of options for displaying 2D shapes so they are more readily discerned and for generating models in a virtual 3D space to help us better see what we are doing.

The Attributes palette can be considered in two parts: a fill part and a pen part. The pen settings determine the appearance of lines both as objects in themselves and as the outlines of other shapes both two and three dimensional. The fill settings determine the appearance of the surfaces you create with the various tools at your disposal.

Figure 2.1 The Attributes palette packs the many settings for Line and Fill into a relatively small footprint.

Figure 2.2 Choose the kind of line you want from the Pen Style pop-up menu; you further define your choice using the other menus in the dialog box.

To set the default pen style:

1. Choose Palette > Attributes from the menu bar.
   The Attributes palette opens (**Figure 2.1**).

2. Click the Pen Style button to open the pop-up menu of lines (**Figure 2.2**).

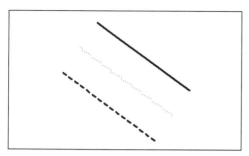

Figure 2.3 The pen style option you select sets the appearance of a line. Choosing None just sets the line's display width to o; geometrically speaking, lines don't have any width anyway.

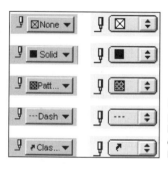

Figure 2.4 The pen style you have chosen is displayed on the Pen Style button.

 Figure 2.5 When you set the pen style to solid or dash, there is one color swatch. Choose the pattern option, and there are two of them to the right of the pattern display.

3. Choose a style for both line objects and the outlines of the objects with surfaces, as follows, from the pop-up menu:

"None" creates an invisible line (as opposed to no line at all).

"Solid" draws a solid line.

"Pattern" uses one of the patterns from the Pattern palette to define the line's appearance.

"Dash" draws a broken line using one of the default styles in the drawing file

"Class Style" sets the line to the Dash, Solid, or Pattern setting or to None as dictated by the settings for the active class in the Edit Class dialog box (see Chapter 5, "Using Layers and Classes") (**Figure 2.3**).

The selected style will be shown on the selection button (**Figure 2.4**).

4. Set the line color by clicking the swatch(es) below the Pen Style button.

If you have selected solid and dashed lines, there will be only a single rectangle displaying the color that will be applied to lines. For a patterned line, there will be two swatches, one each for the foreground and background colors of the pattern, to the right of the pattern display (**Figure 2.5**).

continues on next page

ATTRIBUTES

5. Set the line thickness by clicking on the Line Style button of the Attributes palette and doing one of the following (**Figure 2.6**):

Dragging down to the line thickness you want on the palette

or

Dragging up to Class Thickness. This will set the line thickness according to the settings chosen in the Edit Class dialog box for the active class

or

Dragging up to select Set Thickness.

The Set Thickness dialog box will open and you can type a value into the edit box and choose its unit of measurement by clicking one of the radio buttons (**Figure 2.7**).

6. Set the Dash line style by clicking on the Line Style button on the Attributes palette and dragging down to choose one of the dash styles from the pop-up menu.

Choosing a Solid or Dash style or the None option, you can override the choice you made in the Fill Style menu.

7. Click on the Line Endpoint (Arrow) Style button and choose a line terminator style from the Arrow pop-up menu (**Figure 2.8**).

8. Click the Start Arrow and/or End Arrow buttons to place arrow heads on line and arc objects.

If you click only one selection, the end of the line to which the arrow head (or other style terminator) is applied depends on the direction in which the object is drawn.

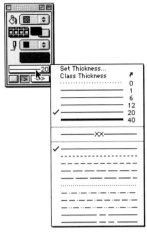

Figure 2.6 The settings for line thickness share a pop-up menu with those for dash styles.

Figure 2.7 The Set Thickness dialog box opens when you choose Set Thickness from the thickness/dash style pop-up menu on Attributes palette.

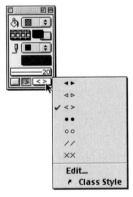

Figure 2.8 The Arrow Style pop-up menu.

ATTRIBUTES

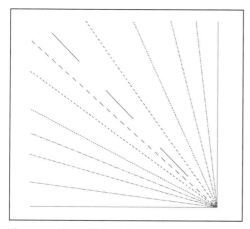

Figure 2.9 A line with its style set to pattern changes its appearance as you rotate it. Sometimes the changes are none too subtle.

✔ Tips

- The orientation of the pattern is independent of the direction of the line. This can be problematic, especially when the line is relatively thin. Choose dashed lines for the most predictable results (**Figure 2.9**).

- You can create custom dash styles by choosing Page > Set Attribute Defaults > Dash Styles (check companion website for "Customizing the Interface").

- Changing the line thickness defaults in a document sets the default thickness for the entire application but does not affect lines already drawn.

- You can edit the default arrow styles (temporarily and for the active drawing file only) by choosing Edit on the Line Endpoint pop-up menu. To do it more permanently and globally for the application, choose Page > Set Attribute Defaults > Arrow Heads on the menu bar.

- The line terminators for dimensions are controlled not by the default attributes, but by the settings in the Document Preferences.

ATTRIBUTES

To set the fill style defaults:

1. Choose Palette > Attributes.
   The Attributes palette opens (**Figure 2.10**).

2. Click the Fill pop-up menu and choose a fill style from the list as follows (**Figure 2.11**):

   "None" if you don't want any fill (including white) within an object.

   "Solid" if you want the fill to be a single color.

   "Pattern" if you want to select from the Pattern palette.

   "Hatch" if you want to select a hatch style from those available in the drawing file (see below).

   "Class Style" if you want the fill style (but not the colors) to be determined by the setting in the Edit Classes dialog box (see Chapter 5, "Using Layers and Classes").

3. Click the color swatch under the Fill Style button to open the drop-down color palettes, and choose a color for the fill when the Solid option is your choice.

   If you have chosen a Pattern option, you will see two swatches, one each for the foreground and background colors. Choose a color for each (**Figure 2.12**).

   Choose the Class Color option by clicking the bar at the top of the palette. This switches the colors of both the foreground and background colors to the setting established in the Edit Class dialog box.

   If you have chosen None, there is (obviously) no color option.

   If you choose Hatch, instead of a swatch there will be another pop-up menu listing the names of all the hatches currently in the drawing file (see below) (**Figure 2.13**).

Figure 2.10 The upper part of the Attributes palette controls the fills you can use to block in surfaces in your drawing to make them easier to pick out.

Figure 2.11 The pop-up menu for fill options opens when you click the button next to the paint bucket icon.

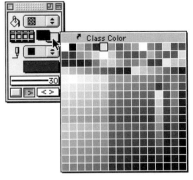

Figure 2.12 When a pattern is chosen to define either the pen or the fill, the overlapping swatches set the foreground and background colors.

Figure 2.13 The Hatch pop-up lists hatches available from the document's resources. You can import hatch settings from other files or create new ones. The active hatch is marked with a dot (Mac) or a check mark (Windows).

ATTRIBUTES

Figure 2.14 Click the first square on the pop-up Pattern palette to choose no line or fill. Click the second or third to choose a solid line or fill using the background or foreground color, respectively.

✔ Tips

■ The first three squares in the top row of the Pattern palette actually select non-pattern options. The first square sets the color to None, the second chooses the background color as a solid, and the third square sets the color to a solid using the foreground color (**Figure 2.14**).

■ If you have installed RenderWorks, you can apply textures—a more complex kind of attribute—to objects to render them photorealistically. They are assigned to objects from the Texture tab of the Object Info palette (see Chapter 10, "Worksheets, Reports, and Presentations.").

■ Using the Hatch setting for a fill attribute produces a very different result than using the Hatch command on the Tool menu.

ATTRIBUTES

Hatches: Associative and Static

VectorWorks has two distinct modes of filling objects with hatch patterns. Hatches applied from the Attributes palette are applied as *associative* hatches, while the hatches placed using the command from the Tool menu are *static*.

Hatches applied from the Attributes palette take their attributes from the definition that created the hatch when the hatch was defined as a resource. Hatches applied from the Tool menu take their geometry from the hatch definition and accept whatever attributes are assigned to them by the Attributes palette (including the class attributes of whatever class the hatch belongs to).

Associative hatches are like any other fill: Once they have been applied to a surface, no matter how you change that surface it remains filled with the hatch and you can change to another attribute setting from the Attributes palette (**Figure 2.15**).

Associative hatches also have the property that like symbols, they refer back to the resources of the drawing, and all instances of the hatch change when the definition is edited.

When you hatch an object with the Hatch tool, on the other hand, you create an independent group in the active class on the active layer that VectorWorks trims to the outline of the shape to which you apply it. You can even select several objects and hatch the area that they enclose. If you change the object, the hatch doesn't change with it (**Figure 2.16**). Scaling the hatch as a group changes its visual character as a fill (**Figure 2.17**).

You can also apply more than one hatch, or the same hatch positioned differently, to the same object with the Hatch tool to get crosshatch or other complex effects (**Figure 2.18**).

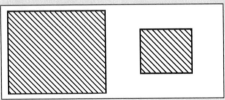

Figure 2.15 Scaling the rectangle on the left does not change the character of the hatch used to fill it if it is an associative hatch.

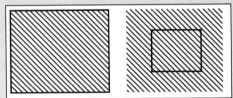

Figure 2.16 When you scale an object hatched using the Hatch tool (a static hatch), the object changes independent of the hatch.

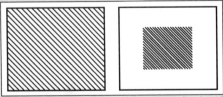

Figure 2.17 Scaling a group of lines originally placed as a hatch changes their visual personality.

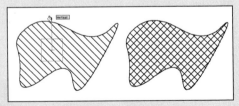

Figure 2.18 If you reselect a hatched area and add another hatch at an angle to the first, you can create a crosshatch (or an even more complex pattern).

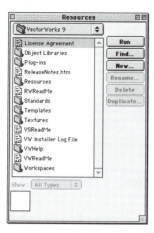

Figure 2.19
Hatches are imported from other drawing files by entering them through the Resources palette. You can also create new hatch definitions by clicking New.

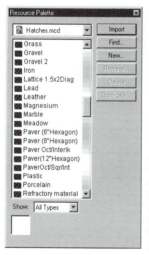

Figure 2.20 The set of hatch patterns that comes with the software is a good starting point. You can use them as-is or modify them to suit your own purposes.

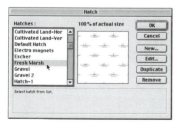

Figure 2.21 Once you have imported a hatch (or created a new one), it is available both as a static hatch (left) and an associative one (right).

Applying hatches from the Tool menu

The hatch patterns used by the Hatch command are selected from the same inventory of resources accessed by the Attributes palette. Static hatches, unlike associative hatches, use the geometric relationships but not the attributes specified in the Hatch dialog box. VectorWorks comes with a range of hatch patterns, and you can create as many new ones as you need (see Chapter 11, "Customizing the Interface").

To import hatches into a drawing file's resources:

1. If it is not already open, open the Resources palette by choosing Palettes > Resources, or by pressing Command+R (Mac) or Ctrl+R (Windows) (**Figure 2.19**).

2. Navigate to the drawing file from which you want to import a hatch.

   VectorWorks comes with a collection of ready-made hatches in the file called Hatches.mcd. You will find this file in the Resources folder included with the application (**Figure 2.20**).

3. Click Enter on the Resources palette or double-click the file icon.

   The Resources palette displays a list of all resources available in the file, including hatch definitions.

4. Select the hatches you want to import, and click Import

   or

   Double-click the hatch definitions you want to import into the active drawing file.

   The hatches are added to the resources of the file and are now accessible from both the Attributes palette and the Hatch dialog box (**Figure 2.21**).

To apply a static hatch to an area:

1. Set the pen thickness, line style, and color for the hatch in the Attributes palette. (Unless you want arrow heads in your hatch, be sure to deselect them; they're hard to get rid of afterward.)

2. Select the object or the set of objects that define an area you want to hatch (**Figure 2.22**).

3. Choose Tool > Hatch. The Hatch dialog box opens (**Figure 2.23**).

4. Choose a hatch from the list. Click OK. The pointer turns into the paint bucket.

5. Click inside the area you want to hatch at the point you want to set as the origin.
   A box with a cross appears.

6. Drag out a handle and rotate the hatch to the desired angle (**Figure 2.24**).

7. Click to apply the hatch.
   The Hatch is placed in the active layer and class (**Figure 2.25**).

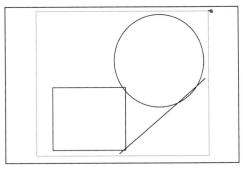

Figure 2.22 You can drag a marquee to select the objects that define the area you want to hatch, or you can select them by clicking.

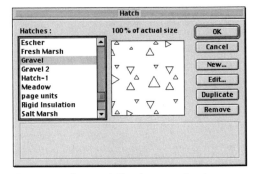

Figure 2.23 After you define the area to hatch, open the Hatch dialog box to choose the fill you want to place from the resources in the drawing file.

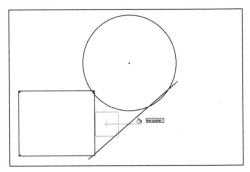

Figure 2.24 Whether you are hatching a surface enclosed by a single object or a set of objects, you click the paint bucket in the area you want to fill. Then drag out the handle to define the angle of the hatch.

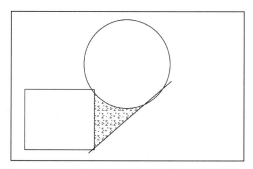

Figure 2.25 Set the angle and then click. The hatch is placed in the defined area.

To change the attributes of an object:

1. With the Selection tool from the 2D Tools palette, select the objects whose attributes you want to change.

2. On the Attributes palette, choose a new setting for the attribute you want to change.

Drawing Strategies

The most intuitive way to draw is to use the mouse. In the case of a rectangle, this means clicking at one corner and then at the diagonally opposite one. When you draw a circle, you can use one click to locate the center and a second to define the radius, two clicks to define a diameter, or three clicks to define a circumference.

Most of the other objects you will be called upon to draw are defined by a straight line (or a series of straight lines), so spending some time mastering this tool will help you in using the rest of the tools in the VectorWorks arsenal.

To draw a line with the mouse:

1. Select the Line tool by clicking it on the 2D Tools palette or by pressing the 2 key on the main keyboard (not the number pad). The pointer changes to a small cross and the Mode bar changes to Line tool mode (**Figure 2.26**).

2. On the Data Display bar, choose the layer and class into which you want to place the line from the drop-down menus.

3. On the Attributes palette, set the line's style, weight, and color.

4. On the Mode bar, choose either Constrained or Unconstrained. Drawing in Constrained mode limits the angle of the line as determined by the settings in the Angle Snaps dialog box (see Chapter 4).

5. Click in the drawing area to place the starting point of the line.
   The line previews as you move the mouse.

6. Click to finish the line.

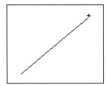

Figure 2.26 As you draw a line with the mouse, its tentative length and angle are sketched.

✔ Tips

- Fill settings don't affect lines. You can choose a pattern as a line style, but the effect depends on the angle of the line and usually ends up looking like an inconsistent dash.

- Select tools from the 2D Tools palette using keyboard shortcuts. The Line tool, for example, is activated when you press the 2 key on the main keyboard. (The 2 key on the number pad puts the active layer into front view, which has no effect when you are working in two dimensions.)

- If you are drawing in Unconstrained mode, you can still constrain the line to the settings in the Angle Snaps dialog box by holding down the Shift key as you draw.

- You can toggle between the modes, even in the middle of drawing an object, by pressing the U key.
  By default, VectorWorks draws in a two-click sequence: You initiate an action with one click and end it with another. If you prefer a different approach, go to the VectorWorks Preferences dialog box and select Click-Drag Drawing. Then you draw by clicking the mouse to initiate a construction, holding it down as you move it, and releasing it to finish the construction.

DRAWING STRATEGIES

Figure 2.27 The Create Line dialog box includes fields to both create and position a line.

Figure 2.28 Changing the option from Rectangular to Polar coordinates affects the parameters you use to create the line, but its location is always an *x-y* setting.

Setting the Segment or Box Position

To create objects with the mouse and/or the Data Display bar, you designate first a starting point and then an end point to define the shape and its location at the same time. When you create an object from a dialog box, you create the shape as a free-floating entity and then locate it either with a click or a by typing a coordinate location into the dialog box.

But you need to specify *which* point on the object will be your designated insertion point. Many object creation dialog boxes have a control feature that sets the *box position* or, for line objects, the *segment position* for the insertion (**Figure 2.29**). Click one of the little points on the control to choose which point on the object's bounding box will be identified as the insertion point.

Figure 2.29 The box position setting in the dialog box lets you select a corner or the center.

To draw a line using the dialog box:

1. On the Attributes palette, set the line's style, weight, and color.

2. Double-click the Line tool.

   The Create Line dialog box opens (**Figure 2.27**).

3. Choose the layer and class from the drop-down menus.

4. Click the Rectangular Coordinate button and set the length and direction of the line by entering its horizontal component of the line in the ΔX (Mac) / ±X (Windows) field and its vertical component in the ΔY/±Y field.

   or

   Click the Polar Coordinate button and enter values for the line's length in the L field and its angle in the A field (**Figure 2.28**).

5. Click one of the points on the Segment Position to select the center or one of the ends of the line as the point on the line that will be placed at the point designated by either a mouse click or the values in the X and Y fields.

6. Define the line's position with values in the X and Y fields and uncheck the Position At Next Click box

   or

   Check the Position At Next Click checkbox and define the insertion point with the mouse after you close the dialog box.

7. Click OK.

   The Create Line dialog box closes and, if you left the checkbox open, the line is placed. Otherwise, click to place the line in the drawing area.

DRAWING STRATEGIES

31

You may not have much cause to draw lines using the Data Display bar exclusively, but it is often useful to enter an object's starting point from the keyboard, or to constrain just a segment's length, angle, or its *x* or *y* value and then to complete it with a mouse click.

The Data Display bar works with the other drawing aids in VectorWorks. You can use it to accurately position a symbol or an object created in a dialog box. You can also use it in tandem with the Constraints palette to align one object to another while maintaining its distance or angle from a reference point.

Another reason to use the Data Display bar is to enter points in units other than the default ones; if you are working in inches. You type *mm* after the number you enter to specify millimeters, *cm* for centimeters, and *m* for meters. Similarly, if you're working in metric measurements, you can use ' for inches and " for feet.

For instance, a land survey with a known benchmark and a succession of bearings and distances can be reproduced in the drawing by entering the starting point and the angles and the lengths in the Data Display bar.

A Note About Coordinate Systems

Like most CAD programs, VectorWorks uses two coordinate systems, *Cartesian* and *polar*. Cartesian (aka. *x-y*, or rectangular) coordinates identify a point in the plane by its horizontal and vertical distances from a point of reference called the origin. Polar coordinates define a point by describing the line between the point and the origin by specifying its length (L) and its angle (A). Angles are measured counterclockwise from the 3 o'clock position (**Figure 2.30**).

You can switch between systems at will, using whichever is more convenient. Sometimes what's important is the angle of a line (say the slope of a roof); sometimes the distance above the floor (its ΔY value) is what needs to be defined.

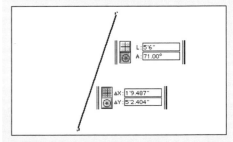

Figure 2.30 You can use either Polar coordinates or Cartesian ones to describe a line.

Figure 2.31 Pressing the Tab key highlights the first field in the Data Display bar. Press again to tab across to the others.

More on the Data Display Bar

While the easiest way to enter data points is by clicking the pointing device, sometimes you'll need to enter a point by typing it into the Data Display bar.

The keyboard not only allows you to enter exact values, it also allows you to override whatever constraints you have imposed, such as Snap to Grid, Snap to Object, or angular constraints (see Chapter 4, "Drawing with Constraints").

You might want to enter a point at a certain distance (L) and angle (A) from another point or at specific coordinates relative either to the page origin (x and y) or to the last point you placed (ΔX and ΔY). Or suppose you want to place a point at a predetermined distance from a specified point and on a particular x or y coordinate or perhaps at a certain height (ΔY) above another point and a certain distance (L) away. The Data Display bar is the generally the way you do it.

The values you type into the X and Y fields in the Data Display bar are relative to the page origin (the 0-0 point on the page rulers). Alternatively, VectorWorks permits you to choose a temporary reference point (the Datum) from which the values in the Data Display bar are measured.

The following is just an example. It sets the starting point of the line at a specified x-y location and then defines the end point by horizontal distance and angle.

To draw a line with the Data Display bar:

1. Click the Line tool in the 2D Tools palette.

   The cursor changes to a small cross and the Mode bar changes to Line tool mode.

2. On the Data Display bar, select the layer and class into which you want to place the line from the drop-down menus.

3. On the Attributes palette, set the line's style, weight, and color.

4. Press the Tab key to highlight the X field in the Data Display bar, and type a value for the horizontal position of the line's starting point. Press Enter to lock that value (**Figure 2.31**).

   The Y field is highlighted and a vertical dotted line appears at the specified value when the pointer is in the drawing area.

   continues on next page

5. Type a value for the vertical coordinate of the starting point and press Enter.

A horizontal dotted line representing the vertical coordinate intersects the vertical line (**Figure 2.32**).

6. Click the mouse anywhere in the drawing area.

The starting point is placed at the intersection of the dotted lines, and the lines themselves disappear The Data Display bar updates and now includes ΔX and ΔY (Mac) / ±X and ±Y (Windows) fields.

7. Press the Tab key again to highlight the ΔX / ±X field. The value in this field sets the distance along the horizontal axis between the starting and end points of the line.

8. Type a value and press Enter. The dotted vertical line for that value appears, and the ΔY / ±Y field is highlighted.

9. Tab across to highlight the A field, type a value into the field, and press Enter. The line is previewed.

10. Click the mouse anywhere in the drawing area to finish the line with its attributes.

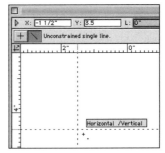

Figure 2.32 Once you have locked values for both X and Y, the unique point you have defined lies at the intersection of the two dotted lines.

Changing tools

You can always change tools by moving the mouse over to the tool palettes and clicking on a new tool, but there is an easier way: keyboard shortcuts. All the tools on the 2D Tools palette (except the Locus tool) can be selected by clicking a single key on the keyboard. You can change the assignments of keys to tools in the Workspace Editor (see Chapter 11, "Customizing the Interface").

You can temporarily summon up the Pan, Zoom in, and Zoom out tools without switching functions. This is referred to as the "Boomerang mode."

Imagine, for example, you are creating a polyline and you realize you should have zoomed in a little closer from the beginning. Instead of switching to the Zoom tool and having to start all over, hold down the spacebar, press C to call the Zoom in tool, use the mouse to draw a marquee around the area of magnification, and then release the spacebar to return to where you left off. (Or, hold down the spacebar and double-click the C key to zoom in 200%.)

DRAWING STRATEGIES

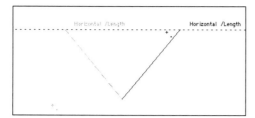

Figure 2.33 Both these lines are length L and end at value Y; use the pointer to choose between them.

More on the Mode Bar

Some tools operate in more than one "mode." The Regular Polygon tool, to cite an instance, has three different drawing modes: inscribed polygon, circumscribed polygon, and edge-drawn polygon. When you select the tool, the Mode bar displays a grouping with a button for each one of those modes. Click the button for the mode you want.

Some tools require you to set certain parameters and have a button that opens a dialog box. For example, when you use the Regular Polygon tool, you also have to set the number of sides the polygon has.

For some tools (the 2D Selection tool, for example), you use the buttons to turn options on or off rather than for switching among modes.

You can activate the buttons from the keyboard without interrupting your drawing: Press the U key to toggle among the first group of the buttons, the I key to manage the second group, and the O key for a third group.

✔ Tips

- For values, you can use either decimals or fractions in the Data Display bar. You can also enter values in a number of units other than those set as the document default.

- To unlock a field into which you have locked a value, highlight it and press Shift+Tab.

- Some pairs of values (y and L, for example) define *two* possible points, and you have to choose between them with a click (**Figure 2.33**).

- The $\Delta X/\pm X$ and X fields control the same coordinate; setting one automatically unlocks the other. The same holds for $\Delta Y/\pm Y$ and Y fields.

- Some pairs of constraints ask the impossible—an L smaller than the minimum distance to a locked y value or an A parallel to a locked coordinate. In that case VectorWorks will just ignore the first setting in favor of the second.

DRAWING STRATEGIES

Drawing Double Lines

Double lines are a quick way to draw things like walls in two dimensions. Unlike walls, double lines aren't hybrid objects with a distinct identity in 3D views; but they are easy to create and edit, and you can create them in any view, not just in plan view.

You can use the Double Line tool for a lot more than just drawing two lines, however. It can create various combinations of lines and polygons between the two principal lines (**Figure 2.34**). You can use these to represent such things as the internal structure of a wall in plan view or a roof in section (**Figure 2.35**).

The Double Line tool, like the Line tool, has both Constrained and Unconstrained modes. You choose between them in the Mode bar, which also contains four modifiers and a Preferences button specific to the Double Line function (**Figure 2.36**).

The placement of a double line is determined by a control line. The control line can be the upper or lower line of the double line, or you can place it anywhere in between (**Figure 2.37**).

✔ Tips

- By default, the Double Line tool is hidden as a flyout under the Line tool on the 2D Tools palette. To access it, hold down the mouse on the Line tool and drag to the Double Line tool (**Figure 2.38**).

- Although you draw Double Lines as a single object, once completed each line is independent of the others.

    The Wall tool is different, although a wall looks just like a double line in the plan view; walls transform as units until you ungroup them. And, as hybrid objects, they have a 3D component that comes into play when you shift into one of the orthogonal views (**Figure 2.39**.)

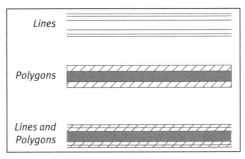

Figure 2.34 Choosing Lines, Polygons, or Lines and Polygons allows you to use the same double-line setup to draw three different sets of objects.

Figure 2.35 You can use the double lines to represent the framing of the wall and the materials on either side—in this case, brick veneer on the top and Sheetrock on the bottom.

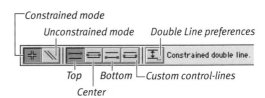

Figure 2.36 The Mode bar for the Double Line tool includes a pair of buttons for the Constrained mode, four more for the control line position, and a button that opens the Preferences dialog box.

Figure 2.37 Using the dotted line as the control line, these double lines were placed using (top to bottom) the Top, Center, Bottom, and Custom control line modes.

Figure 2.38 The Double Line tool is under the Line tool on the 2D Tools palette.

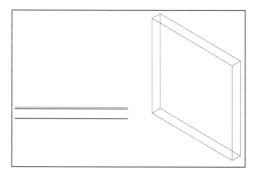

Figure 2.39 While double lines look just like walls in Plan view, once you move into a 3D view, the difference is clear.

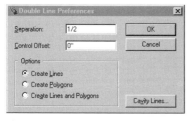

Figure 2.40 In the Double Line Preferences dialog box, you set up the double lines and their cavity lines and filled cavities, and choose which will be displayed.

To draw a simple double line with the mouse:

1. Click the Double Line tool on the 2D Tools palette.

   The pointer changes to a small cross and the Mode bar shows three button groups.

2. On the Mode bar, select either the Constrained or the Unconstrained mode button.

3. Select a Control Line mode from the modifiers in the Mode bar to define the relationship between the path delineated (in this case by the mouse) and the lines drawn by the Double Line tool.

   The usual modes are Top, Center, and Bottom, but you can set a Custom control line anywhere within the double line pair.

4. Click the Double Line Preferences button in the Mode bar.

   The Double Line Preferences dialog box opens (**Figure 2.40**).

5. Select the Create Lines radio button.

   (The other options, Create Polygons and Create Lines and Polygons, are discussed later in this chapter.)

6. Enter a value for the Separation between the lines. Click OK.

   The Double Line Preferences dialog box closes.

   continues on next page

DRAWING DOUBLE LINES

7. In the Control Offset box, type the distance you want the control line offset from the centerline of the double lines.

   This setting applies only in the Custom Control Line mode. The value can be no more than half the Separation; positive numbers lie above the centerline, and negative numbers are below.

8. Define the starting point of the double lines by clicking in the drawing area.

   What you are doing here is creating an invisible control line parallel to the double lines. Its position relative to the line pair is defined by the settings in the Data Display bar.

9. Click again to complete the double line.

   If you have chosen the Click-drag option in the VectorWorks Preferences dialog box, you will release the mouse to complete the line.

✔ Tip

- You can use the Data Display bar to precisely delineate the Control Line just as you would an ordinary single line.

DRAWING DOUBLE LINES

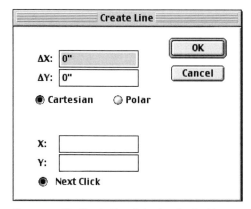

Figure 2.41 The Create Line dialog box for double lines has fewer options than the one for single lines.

To create double lines with the dialog box:

1. Set up the attributes for the double line as above using the Mode bar and Preferences dialog box.

2. Double-click the Double Line tool to open the Create Line dialog box.

   It's different from the one for single lines. The dialog box for double lines has no provision for defining the insertion point of the lines—it's always the starting point of the control line—or for setting the layer and class of the lines within the dialog box (**Figure 2.41**).

3. Define the length and direction of the double line in one of two ways:

   Click the Cartesian radio button and type the value for the horizontal component of the line into the ΔX/±X field and for the vertical component into the ΔY/±Y field

   or

   Click the Polar radio button and enter an L value for the length of the line and an A value for its angle.

4. To set the starting point of the control line for the double line, enter its x and y coordinates

   or

   Select the Next Click radio button to position the line manually with a click of the mouse after closing the dialog box.

5. Click OK.

   The dialog box closes and, if you chose the first option above, the line is created. Otherwise, click the mouse where you want to place the starting point of the control line.

DRAWING DOUBLE LINES

Cavity Lines and Filled Cavities

The cavity lines between double lines are often used to represent the structural elements of a wall, like the framing and the thickness of Sheetrock. Add areas of fill (filled cavities) within a double line, and you get a nice graphic image of the wall section (**Figure 2.42**).

You ordain the geometry and the attributes of the cavity lines and filled cavities in the Cavity Setup dialog box. The principal lines themselves are drawn with the attributes currently active in the Attributes palette.

Use the Filled Cavity option to create additional filled polygons when you choose one of the polygon creation options of the Filled Line tool.

To add cavity lines to a double line:

1. Click the Double Line tool on the 2D Tools palette.

2. Click the Double Line Preferences icon in the Mode bar.

   The Double Line Preferences dialog box opens.

3. Click Cavity Lines.

   The Cavity Setup dialog box (**Figure 2.43**) opens.

4. Click New Cavity.

   A line is displayed across the middle of the preview window.

5. In the Offset field, enter the distance you want the line offset from the centerline as either a positive number, putting the control line above the centerline, or a negative number, putting it below.

   Click the preview window to show it in its new position (**Figure 2.44**).

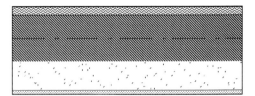

Figure 2.42 Set the fills and hatches in the double line to simulate a section of a wall.

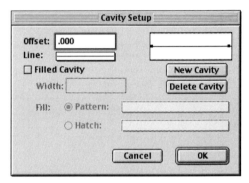

Figure 2.43 The Cavity Setup dialog box handles both cavity lines and filled cavities.

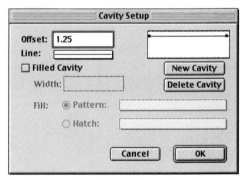

Figure 2.44 Set an offset for a cavity line to move it up or down from the centerline.

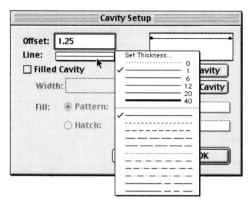

Figure 2.45 There's a drop-down menu for line style and thickness.

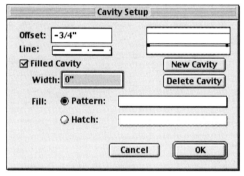

Figure 2.46 Checking the Filled Cavity box gives you access to the areas of the dialog box that set the fill for the selected cavity line.

6. Click the Line menu and select the line style you want from the drop-down menu (**Figure 2.45**).

The weight and style of the line selected in the preview window are displayed on the line menu, but not in the preview window.

7. Repeat Steps 4 through 6 to create as many lines as required.

8. Click OK and then OK again to close the dialog boxes.

To add a filled cavity:

1. Follow steps 1 through 6 above to create a line in the Cavity Setup dialog box.

2. Select the Double Line tool from the 2D Tools palette.

3. Click on the Double Line Preferences icon in the Mode bar.

The Double Line Preferences dialog box opens.

4. Click Cavity Lines in the Double Line Preferences dialog box to open the Cavity Setup dialog box, and then click New Cavity.

A new line is displayed on the centerline in the preview window.

5. Check the Filled Cavity box.

The Width and Fill options are activated (**Figure 2.46**).

6. In the Offset field, enter the distance you want to offset the edge of the fill from the centerline of the double lines.

A positive value puts the line above center; a negative value puts it below.

7. In the Width field, enter the width of the filled cavity.

A positive value puts the fill above the line; a negative value puts it below it.

continues on next page

CAVITY LINES AND FILLED CAVITIES

8. Click the Pattern radio button and select a pattern from the Pattern pop-up menu (**Figure 2.47**)

or

Click the Hatch radio button and select a hatch from the Hatch pop-up menu (**Figure 2.48**).

9. Repeat to add additional filled cavities and click OK.

The Cavity Setup dialog box closes.

10. In the Double Lines Preferences dialog box, select either Create Polygons or Create Lines and Polygons to create the filled areas as you use the Double Lines tool.

Click OK and create the double lines as above.

To edit cavity lines and filled cavities:

1. On the Mode bar, click the Double Lines Preferences button.

The Double Line Preferences dialog box opens.

2. Click the Cavity Lines button.

The Cavity Setup dialog box opens.

3. Click the cavity line or filled cavity you want to edit.

Handles are displayed on the selected cavity line or filled cavity.

4. Change the settings for the selected cavity line or filled cavity.

5. Click OK to close the Cavity Setup dialog box, and Click OK again to close the Double Lines Preferences dialog box.

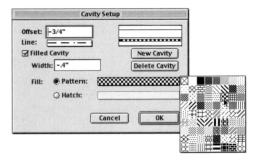

Figure 2.47 The drop-down menu for patterns has the same set of 71 patterns (including solid foreground and background colors) as the Attributes palette.

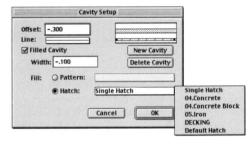

Figure 2.48 The menu for hatches includes the names of all the hatches that are part of the drawing resources.

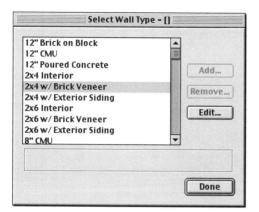

Figure 2.49 Choose Menu > Select Wall Type to open the Select Wall Type dialog box, and choose a preset wall type with its line and fill settings.

Changing Your Mind Midstream

In the middle of creating an object, you may want to either remove a point you have placed (especially if you're in the middle of drawing a complicated polyline) or abandon the process completely.

◆ To delete the last point placed, press the Delete/Backspace key.

◆ To undo all the points placed while leaving the same tool selected, press Esc.

◆ To undo all the points and change to a different tool, press the key for the shortcut to the new tool.

✔ Tips

■ In the Double Lines Preferences dialog box, click Create Lines and Polygons to draw all the cavity lines, the filled cavities with their assigned patterns and hatches, and an additional polygon the full width of the double lines (with its fill set by the active attributes that also control the double lines themselves).

■ In the Double Lines Preferences dialog box, click Create Polygons to draw only the filled cavities and the polygon defined by the full width of the principal lines.

■ Click Create Lines to draw the principal lines, the cavity lines, and a line on each side of each filled cavity.

■ The Select Wall Type command on the Model menu controls the Double Line tool as well as the Wall tool (see Chapter 9, "Architectural Applications"). You can choose one of the preset wall types from the list (**Figure 2.49**). You need to have Architect installed to add to the list, however.

■ To delete the last point placed, press the Delete / Backspace key.

■ To undo all the points placed while leaving the same tool selected, press Esc.

■ To undo all the points and change to a different tool, press the key for the shortcut to the new tool.

Rectangles

Rectangles are one of the basic 2D building blocks for drawing almost anything. You use them to create not only rectangular things, but all kinds of more complex shapes as well as using VectorWorks's range of tools and commands for manipulating objects.

There are three rectangle tools stacked up as flyout alternatives on the 2D Tools palette. By default, the one visible at start up is the Rectangle tool, which draws rectangles along the axes (**Figure 2.50**).

The other two tools are the Rounded Rectangle tool, which draws rectangles with either circular or ellipsoid fillets in the corners, and the Rotated Rectangle tool, which creates rectangles at angles to the axes of the grid (**Figure 2.51**).

To draw a rectangle:

1. Click the Rectangle tool on the 2D Tools palette.

2. In the drawing area, click where you want one of the corners of the rectangle.

3. Click again where you want to place the diagonal corner.
   The rectangle is created.

Figure 2.50 The flyout for the Rectangle tools has three tools.

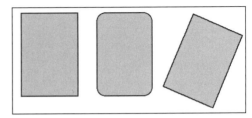

Figure 2.51 Variations on a rectangle: Normal, Rounded, and Rotated.

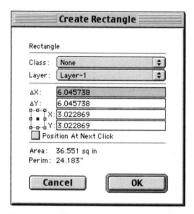

Figure 2.52 The Create Rectangle dialog box–for those who like to do it that way.

To draw a rectangle using the dialog box:

1. On the 2D Tools palette, double-click the Rectangle tool.

   The Create Rectangle dialog box opens (**Figure 2.52**).

2. Select the class and layer in which the rectangle is to be created from the pop-up menus.

3. Set the width and height of the rectangle by typing values for ΔX/±X and ΔY/±Y in the fields.

4. Click one of the small squares on the Box Position diagram to select which point on the rectangle will be placed at the insertion point chosen in the next step.

5. Position the rectangle in the drawing area by doing one of the following:

   Click the Next Mouse Click checkbox

   or

   Type X and Y values into the fields to set the coordinates at which the selected point on the rectangle will be located.

6. Click OK. The dialog box closes and the rectangle is placed in the drawing area if you chose to enter its location in step 5. Otherwise, click in the drawing area to register the insertion point and complete the rectangle.

RECTANGLES

To draw a rounded rectangle:

1. Click the Rounded Rectangle tool on the 2D Tools palette.

2. Click the Rounded Rectangle Preferences button on the Mode bar.

   The Rounded Rectangle Preferences dialog box opens (**Figure 2.53**).

3. Click the Proportional Corners checkbox to have the curvature of the corners set automatically relative to the size of the rectangle

   or

   Enter the X Diameter and Y Diameter of the corner ellipses. If you check Symmetrical Corners, the corners will be circular and that dimension will be the same for both X and Y.

4. Click the Symmetrical Corners checkbox to create corners with circular arcs.

   If you click the Proportional Corners checkbox, the radius of the corners will be controlled by the short side of the rectangle.

5. Click OK.

   The Rounded Rectangle Preferences dialog box closes.

6. Click the mouse in the drawing area to locate one corner of the rectangle that defines the rounded rectangle you're creating.

7. Click the mouse at the corner diagonally opposite.

   The rounded rectangle is completed.

Figure 2.53 In the Rounded Rectangle Preferences box (Round Rect Prefs), offers the choice of proportional or symmetrical corners. Deselecting the proportional option opens fields for presetting what the corner configurations will actually be.

RECTANGLES

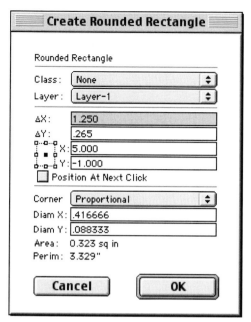

Figure 2.54 The Create Rounded Rectangle dialog box sets the class and layer as well as the shape and position of the shape before it is placed.

To create a rounded rectangle using the dialog box:

1. Double-click the Rounded Rectangle tool on the 2D Tools palette.

   The Create Rounded Rectangle dialog box opens (**Figure 2.54**).

2. Select the class and layer in which the rectangle is to be created.

3. Set the width and height of the rectangle by typing values for ΔX and ΔY (Mac) or ±X and ±Y (Windows) in the fields.

4. Click one of the squares on the Box Position diagram to select which point on the rectangle will be placed at the insertion point chosen in the next step

5. From the Corner pop-up menu, do one of the following:

   Choose Proportional; the values for Diam X and Diam Y will be set automatically according to the lengths of the sides

   or

   Choose Symmetrical; type a value into either Diam X or Diam Y and it will automatically be entered in the other field

   or

   Type values of your own devising into the Diam X and Diam Y fields, and the Corner menu will change to Unconstrained.

6. Position the rectangle in the drawing area by doing one of the following:

   Click the Next Mouse Click checkbox

   or

   Type X and Y values into the fields to set the coordinates at which the selected point on the rectangle will be located.

7. Click OK. The rectangle is placed in the drawing area if you chose to enter its location in step 6. Otherwise, click in the drawing area to register the insertion point and complete the rectangle.

RECTANGLES

To draw a rotated rectangle:

1. On the 2D Tools palette, click the Rotated Rectangle tool.

2. In the drawing area, click where you want the first corner.

3. Move the mouse to a second corner and click again.

   The edge is drawn and the rectangle is sketched as you move the mouse perpendicular to it (**Figure 2.55**).

4. Move the mouse perpendicular to the edge created by the first two clicks to define the size of the rectangle.

5. Click to complete the rotated rectangle.

✔ Tips

■ The Rectangle tool draws objects VectorWorks considers members of the "rectangle" category only if they are created on the *x*- and *y*-axes and not rotated off axis. Otherwise, they are considered polygons.

■ Using the rectangle tool when the grid is rotated creates a polygon. Using the rotated rectangle to draw a rectangle aligned to the *x-y* grid still creates a polygon.

■ A rounded rectangle becomes a polyline when you rotate it.

■ There is no dialog box for creating rotated rectangles. Double-click the Rotated Rectangle tool button and the Create Rectangle dialog box opens.

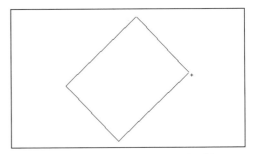

Figure 2.55 After establishing the first side of the rectangle, move the mouse away from it to create the rectangle.

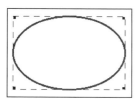

Figure 2.56 The ellipse is defined by the rectangle into which it fits.

Figure 2.57 The Mode bar has four choices of tool, but three of them are circles.

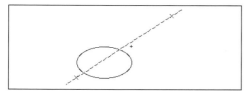

Figure 2.58 The ellipse is started by clicking at the lower-left corner of the bounding box. (The *x*'s and the dotted diagonal are shown for illustration only; they aren't a part of the actual drawing process.)

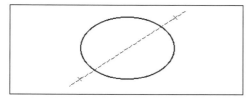

Figure 2.59 Move the mouse diagonally to the upper right corner and click again to complete the ellipse.

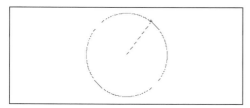

Figure 2.60 To draw a circle by radius, click once to set the center point and again on the circumference to complete the circle.

Circles and Ellipses

If you think back to high school geometry, you may remember that circles are only a special class of ellipses. VectorWorks groups them together on the 2D Tools palette. You may also remember that a circle can be defined by its center and its radius, by two points on a diameter, or by three points on the circumference. VectorWorks creates an ellipse by defining the rectangular bounding box to which it is tangent on all four sides (**Figure 2.56**). You select among the three modes for circle creation and the Ellipse (or oval) mode on the Mode bar (**Figure 2.57**).

To create an ellipse:

1. On the 2D Tools palette, click the Ellipse tool.

2. On the Mode bar, click the Ellipse mode button.

3. Click in the drawing area to set one corner of the bounding box (**Figure 2.58**).

4. Click again to set the diagonally opposite corner.

   The ellipse is created (**Figure 2.59**).

To create a circle by center and radius:

1. On the 2D Tools palette, click the Ellipse tool.

2. On the Mode bar, click the Circle by Radius mode button.

3. Click in the drawing area to set the center of the circle.

4. Click again to set the radius of the circle (**Figure 2.60**).

To create a circle by diameter:

1. On the 2D Tools palette, click the Ellipse tool.

2. On the Mode bar, click the Circle by Diameter mode button.

3. Click in the drawing area to set one end of the diameter.

4. Click again to set the opposite end of the diameter and complete the circle (**Figure 2.61**).

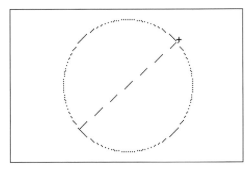

Figure 2.61 When you're drawing a circle by diameter, the first click sets one end of the diameter; the second sets the other.

To create a circle by 3 points:

1. On the 2D Tools palette, click the Ellipse tool.

2. On the Mode bar, click the Circle 3 Points mode button.

3. Click in the drawing area to set the first point on the circle.

4. Click again to set the second point on the circle.

5. Click again to complete the circle with the third point on the circle (**Figure 2.62**).

✔ Tip

- Unlike the Rectangle tool, ellipses aren't aligned to a rotated grid. They are always drawn relative to the x- and y-axes.

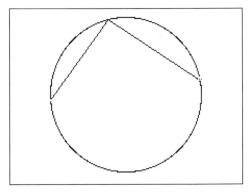

Figure 2.62 Three points uniquely define a circle.

CIRCLES AND ELLIPSES

Figure 2.63 Drawing an arc is pretty much like drawing a circle — and you have two more modes to work with.

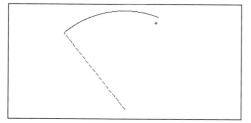

Figure 2.64 The first click sets the center of the arc, the second sets one end of the arc, and the third sets the other end of the arc, completing the operation.

Drawing Arcs

VectorWorks has two distinct tools for drawing arcs on the 2D Tools palette. The Arc tool draws circular arcs of any sweep; the Quarter Arc tool draws elliptical arcs of 90 degrees.

Elliptical arcs drawn by the Quarter Arc tool are polylines. As far as VectorWorks is concerned, circles and arcs are the same kind of object; an arc of 360 degrees is a circle, and changing the sweep setting in a circle's Object Information palette turns it into an arc.

The Arc tool has five modes from which to choose (**Figure 2.63**). Three of these are the same modes that the Circle tool offers; in addition, you can draw the arc to a user-defined tangent, or you can click two points and then specify the arc's radius in a dialog box.

To draw a circular arc by radius:

1. Click the Arc tool in the 2D Tools palette. The Mode bar displays buttons for the five modes.

2. On the Mode bar, click the Arc by Radius button.

3. Click in the drawing area where you want the arc centered.

   As you move the mouse, the radius is sketched as a dotted line (**Figure 2.64**).

4. Click to set the starting point of the arc.

   As you move the mouse, the arc is sketched and the sweep is displayed in the Data Display bar. You can type a value and press Enter to set it.

5. Click again at the end point of the arc. The arc is completed.

To draw a circular arc by 3 points:

1. Click the Arc tool in the 2D Tools palette. The Mode bar displays buttons for the five modes.

2. On the Mode bar, click the Arc by 3 Points button.

3. Click in the drawing area to set the starting point of the curve.

   As you move the mouse, the chord between the first and second points is sketched as a dotted line.

4. Click to set a second point on the arc.

   As you move the mouse, the arc is sketched (**Figure 2.65**).

5. Click again at the end point of the arc.

   The arc is completed.

To draw a circular arc by tangent:

1. Click the Arc tool in the 2D Tools palette. The Mode bar displays buttons for the five modes.

2. On the Mode bar, click the Arc by Tangent button.

3. Click in the drawing area where you want to place both the arc starting point and the point of tangency.

   As you move the mouse, the tangent is sketched as a dotted line (**Figure 2.66**).

4. Click to define the tangent.

   The sketched tangent disappears, and the arc is sketched as you move the mouse (**Figure 2.67**).

5. Click again at the end point of the arc.

   The arc is completed tangent to the line defined by the first two clicks.

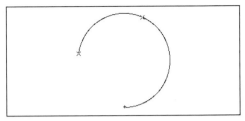

Figure 2.65 After clicking the first two points on the curve, the curve is sketched as you move the mouse in the drawing area.

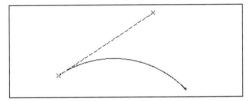

Figure 2.66 Drawing a curve by tangent, your first click sets both the start of the curve and one point on the tangent, the second click defines the tangent, and the third sets the endpoint of the curve.

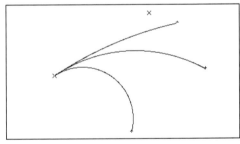

Figure 2.67 After establishing the tangent, the mouse sets the sweep of the curve and its radius as well.

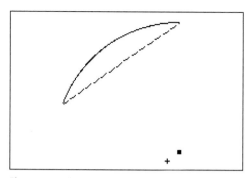

Figure 2.68 After defining a chord with the first two mouse clicks, set the center (and the curvature) with the third.

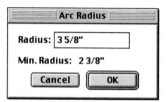

Figure 2.69 When you use the last mode on the Mode bar, you set the radius in a dialog box rather than graphically.

To draw a circular arc by two points and center:

1. Click the Arc tool in the 2D Tools palette.
   The Mode bar displays buttons for the five modes.

2. On the Mode bar, click the Arc by Two Points and Center button.

3. Click in the drawing area where you want to place the arc starting point.
   As you move the mouse, the chord between the two end points is sketched as a dotted line (**Figure 2.68**).

4. Click to define the chord.
   The sketched chord disappears, and the arc is sketched as you move the mouse.

5. Click again to set the center point of the arc.
   The arc is completed.

To draw a circular arc by two points and the radial dimension:

1. Click the Arc tool in the 2D Tools palette.
   The Mode bar displays buttons for the five modes.

2. On the Mode bar, click the Arc by Two Points and Radius button.

3. Click in the drawing area where you want to place the arc starting point.
   As you move the mouse, the chord between the two end points is sketched as a dotted line.

4. Click to define the chord.
   The sketched chord disappears and the Arc Radius dialog box opens (**Figure 2.69**).

5. Type the radius in the Radius field.
   The Min. Radius number in the dialog box (and the default figure in the field) would result in a 180-degree sweep. Larger radiuses mean smaller angular sweeps.

DRAWING ARCS

To draw a quarter arc:

1. On the 2D Tools palette, click the Quarter Arc tool. (It may be hiding under the Arc tool.)

2. Click in the drawing area to set one end of the arc.

   As you move the mouse, the arc and the bounding box are sketched (**Figure 2.70**). Until you click the mouse button to finish a line, it remains unfixed as you move your mouse around.

3. Click again to finish.

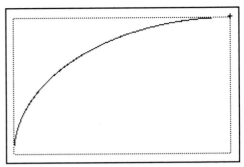

Figure 2.70 As you draw using the Quarter Arc tool, the bounding box is shown.

✔ Tip

■ Hold down the Shift key as you draw a Quarter Arc to create a circular arc of 90 degrees.

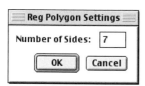

Figure 2.71 Set the number of sides in the Regular Polygon Settings dialog box.

Regular Polygons

The Regular Polygon tool can draw polygons with equal sides and equal angles numbering anywhere from 3 to 4000, although the lower numbers are generally more useful. The tool operates in three drawing modes.

To create a regular polygon:

1. On the 2D Tools palette, click the Regular Polygon tool.

   The Mode bar displays buttons for the three drawing modes and for the Polygon Preferences.

2. Click the Polygon Preferences button on the Mode bar.

   The Regular Polygon Settings dialog box opens (**Figure 2.71**).

3. In the Number of Sides field on the Regular Polygon Settings dialog box, type the number of sides you want the polygon to have. Click OK.

4. On the Mode bar, choose one of drawing modes as follows:

   Choose Inscribed Polygon to draw the polygon by defining its center and one of its vertices

   or

   Choose Circumscribed Polygon to draw the polygon by defining its center and the center of one of its sides

   or

   Choose Edge-Drawn Polygon to draw the polygon by defining one of its sides.

5. Click the mouse in the drawing area to start the polygon by defining either the center of the object or (for edge-drawn polygons) one vertex.

   As you move the mouse, the polygon will be sketched.

6. Complete the polygon with another click of the mouse.

✔ Tips

■ You can toggle between the Inscribed and Circumscribed Polygons modes by holding down the Option key as you draw.

■ By default, polygons drawn in the Edge-Drawn mode continue the object clockwise from the side you draw. Hold down the Option key to flip the polygon.

■ If, in the middle of creating a polygon, you decide to change the number of sides it should have, fear not. Use the I key to cue the Polygon Preferences button in the Mode bar. When the Regular Polygon Settings dialog box opens, type a new number into the Number of Sides field, press Enter, and continue the construction.

Irregular Polygons

Regular polygons are a small subset of polygons in general: objects consisting of at least two connected straight segments. Irregular polygons have to be drawn vertex by vertex. Polygons can be either open or closed (**Figure 2.72**).

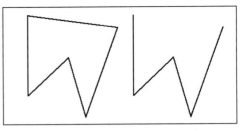

Figure 2.72 Polygons can be open or closed (and you can close an open one in the Object Information palette).

To draw a single line polygon:

1. From the 2D Tools palette, click the Single-Line Polygon tool.

2. Click the mouse in the drawing area to place the first vertex.

   The side of the polygon is sketched in a thin black line.

3. Click again for each vertex you want to place.

   As you draw, the entire polygon is sketched (**Figure 2.73**).

4. Close the polygon by clicking again on the starting point

   or

   Double-click in the drawing area to complete an open polygon.

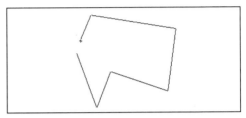

Figure 2.73 Drawing a polygon is as easy as connecting the virtual dots.

✔ Tip

- VectorWorks also has a Double Line Polygon tool, but unfortunately it doesn't create a double-line polygon. It only lets you draw a series of double lines that you can then manually turn into concentric polygons by joining the lines one by one. If you want to create a double-line polygon, you are better advised to create a single-line polygon and then use the offset tool to double it (see Chapter 3, "Modifying 2D Objects").

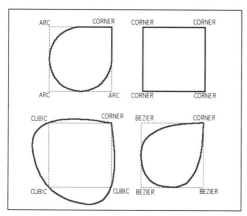

Figure 2.74 Changing the vertex of a polyline to another mode has a profound effect on the curve.

Figure 2.75 The Polyline Mode bar has buttons for each of the four types of vertices and one more to set the radius for the Arc vertex mode.

Using Polylines

Many drawing applications create curved lines using Bézier control points on the line with handles extending outward. VectorWorks uses four vertex modes to create a wide variety of polylines. Corner and Cubic vertices lie on the line; Arc and Bézier vertices are off the line. A single polyline in VectorWorks can use all four types of vertex, with the character of the curve depending on which of the modes are used.

For example, putting four Corner points in a square array produces a square; four Arc points make a circle. Four Bézier or Cubics make something between a squishy square and a lumpy circle.

To understand the effects of the different vertex modes, look at the squares on which three of the control points have been converted to other modes (**Figure 2.74**). In each case, all the vertices remain at the corners of the dotted square.

To draw with the Polyline tool:

1. On the 2D Tools palette, click the Polyline tool.

   The Mode bar displays the four vertex modes and a Polyline Preferences button linked to the Fillet Settings dialog box (**Figure 2.75**).

2. On the Mode bar, click the Polyline Preferences button.

   The Fillet Settings Preferences dialog box opens.

3. In the Fillet Preferences dialog box, type the maximum fillet radius to be used when you are in the Arc vertex mode. Click OK.

   The radius actually used is determined by the lengths of the adjoining segments. The default value is 0, which does not place any limit on the radius.

   continues on next page

4. On the Mode bar, choose a vertex type for the initial vertex.

The cursor will display an icon indicating the vertex mode (**Figure 2.76**).

5. Click to place the first vertex.

6. Select the mode for the next vertex by doing one of the following:

Click one of the buttons on the Mode bar to select the control point mode

or

Press U to toggle among the four modes.

7. Click in the drawing area to place the vertex.

As you draw, the polyline will be sketched. Because each curve point interacts with those on either side of it, the curve will be somewhat fluid until you complete it.

8. Continue adding vertices, changing the mode as required.

9. Complete the polyline either by clicking again on its starting point to close it or by double-clicking somewhere else in the drawing area to end it as an open object.

✔ Tip

■ Press I at any time to open the Fillet Settings dialog box and change the default radius for Arc points on the fly.

■ Keep in mind that you can use the Data Display bar to place any or all of the vertices in a polyline or other figure.

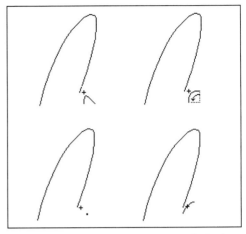

Figure 2.76 Each vertex mode has its own distinctive cursor.

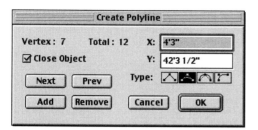

Figure 2.77 The Create Polyline dialog box is not the most straightforward way of creating an object, but it's an option.

You can create a polyline using the Create Polyline dialog box, entering each vertex and its mode in turn. It is a rather tedious procedure and, at least as far as I'm concerned, not worth the effort, since the same level of control is available by way of the Data Display bar. But for those of you who care to know, here it is.

To create a polyline using the dialog box:

1. On the 2D Tools palette, click the Polyline tool.

2. In the Fillet Preferences dialog box, type the maximum fillet radius to be used when you are in the Arc vertex mode. Click OK.

   The radius actually used is determined by the lengths of the adjoining segments. The default value is 0, which does not place any limit on the radius.

3. Double-click the Polyline tool on the tool palette. The Create Polyline dialog box opens (**Figure 2.77**).

4. Click Add as many times as necessary to set the Total vertices to the desired number.

5. Check or uncheck the Close Object box as required.

   Checking the Close Object box adds a segment from the last vertex to the first one, creating a closed path.

6. Click Next or Previous to select the vertex for which you need to enter data.

7. Enter X and Y values, select a mode for the vertex, and click Next to move to the next one or Previous to step back.

8. When all the vertices have been defined, click OK to create the polyline.

USING POLYLINES

The Freehand tool

The Freehand tool is like a pencil, except that drawing with a mouse is notoriously difficult and thus of limited use in the CAD environment. The tool's button is a flyout behind the Polyline and Spiral tools on the 2D Tools palette; you select it by click-dragging on the Polyline tool (**Figure 2.78**).

The Freehand tool overrides all the constraints and creates an open or closed polygon with lots of corner vertices created as much by the unsteadiness of your hand as by the corners you meant to draw (**Figure 2.79**). Fortunately, VectorWorks offers a smoothing function under the Edit menu that can convert the polygon to a polyline, removing most of the vertex points and converting the corner points to another of the control points if desired (**Figure 2.80**).

To draw a freehand line:

1. On the 2D Tools palette, click the Freehand tool.

2. Click in the drawing area to start the line.

3. Move the mouse to create the line.

4. Click again to end the line.

Figure 2.78 Drag the Freehand tool out from its hiding place behind the Polyline tool.

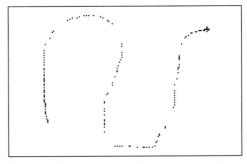

Figure 2.79 The Freehand tool is as easy as drawing with a pencil, but it's very imprecise. Click once to start and again to stop.

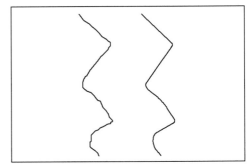

Figure 2.80 Smoothing a polygon drawn with the Freehand tool takes out all the little jaggies.

To smooth a freehand line:

1. With the 2D Selection tool, select the freehand line you want to smooth.

2. Choose Edit > Smoothing, and then select one of the following:

No Smoothing to reduce the number of vertices (though the vertices remain corner points).

Bézier Spline Smoothing to reduce the number of vertices and change them all to Bézier control points.

Cubic Spline Smoothing to reduce the number of vertices and change them all to Cubic Spline control points.

Arc Smoothing to reduce the number of vertices and change them all to Arc control points.

✔ Tips

■ The speed with which you move the mouse as you draw with the Freehand tool has a lot to do with how many points the polygon contains. Unfortunately, there is no way to set the sensitivity of the tool to slight movements; the slower you move the mouse, the more little jiggles you add to the path.

■ The Smoothing commands also work on other polygons and polylines to change all the vertices (except the ends of open figures) to the single type selected from the menu. The number of vertices is not, however, reduced.

The Spiral tool

The Spiral tool creates a plug-in object (see Chapter 6, "2D Symbols and PIOs") that you edit in the Object Information palette rather than directly. You can create the spiral and then reset its dimensions from the Object Information palette. With the Spiral tool (unlike most other plug-in objects), you can set the dimensions in the dialog box before you create the spiral.

To create a spiral:

1. On the 2D Tools palette, click the Spiral tool.

   The Mode bar displays the buttons for insertion into a wall; ignore them.

2. On the Mode bar, click the Preferences button.

   The Spiral Preferences dialog box opens (**Figure 2.81**).

3. Type values into the fields as follows:

   Distance per Turn sets the space between the coils of the spiral.

   Number of Turns is the number of coils the spiral makes from the inside to the outside.

   Start Radius is the distance from the center of the spiral to its starting point.

   Increment sets the angular distance between the vertices of the polyline that the plug-in object generates. A higher increment means a smaller file, but (at values above 30 degrees) a lumpy spiral.

   Thickness, when set to a value other than 0, converts the spiral line to a spiral surface of that width.

Figure 2.81
The Spiral Preferences dialog box has all the settings for the plug-in object the tool draws.

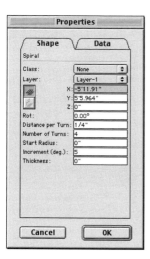

Figure 2.82 You can open the Properties dialog box for any object by holding down the Control key and clicking the object in the drawing area.

4. Click in the drawing area to place the spiral at its center point.

The original settings in the Spiral Preferences dialog box (as well as its position) can be modified in the Object Information palette when the spiral is selected.

✔ Tips

■ A spiral is actually a polyline. If you convert it to a group (see Chapter 8, "Editing 3D Objects"), you can edit it point by point. But once you destroy its identity as a spiral plug-in object, you lose the ability to edit it as a unit in the Object Information palette.

■ Hold down the Control key and click an object then and choose Properties on the pop-up menu to open a Properties dialog box very much like the Object Information palette (see Chapter 1, "Getting Started") (**Figure 2.82**). You can edit the object by changing the information displayed.

USING POLYLINES

Text

One more component of a drawing that we can't overlook is text. Text objects (which is what VectorWorks calls individual blocks of text) can be put anywhere in a drawing and formatted by font, size, color, alignment, and so forth. VectorWorks even offers a spell check.

Text blocks include an insertion point, which is a locus to which the text is aligned according to the settings

To create a text object:

1. Choose Text > Format Text or press Command+T (Mac) or Ctrl+T (Windows). The Format Text dialog box opens (**Figure 2.83**).

2. On the Attributes palette, choose a solid pen color for the type and a solid color or a pattern for the fill of the text box behind the text. Choose None for the fill if you want the text box to be transparent.

3. Format the text block by doing the following:

   From the Font menu, choose the font you want to use.

   In the Size pane, select the units for sizing type from the drop-down menu and then set the size by entering the number of those units in the edit box.

   In the Spacing pane, click one of the radio buttons to set the line spacing. If you pick Other, choose units from the drop-down menu and enter a number in the edit box.

   In the Style pane (it doesn't have a label) click either the Plain radio button or the one marked Styled. If the latter, check as many of the style checkboxes as you need to.

4. In the Alignment pane, set the relationship between the insertion point and the text itself using the H (horizontal) and V (vertical) drop-down menus (**Figure 2.84**).

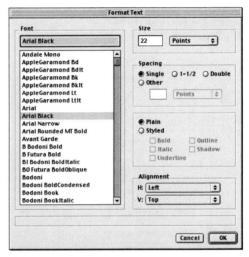

Figure 2.83 The Format Text dialog box contains most of the options on the Text menu in one convenient package.

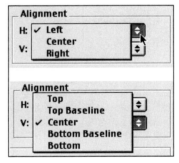

Figure 2.84 Text is laid down relative to a locus called the insertion point. You need to set both the horizontal and vertical alignments.

Figure 2.85 The Text tool on the 2D Tools palette.

Left align

Center align

Right align

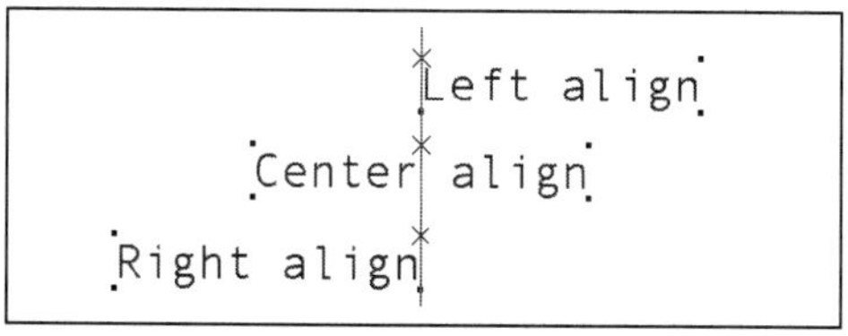

Figure 2.86 Left-aligned type starts at the insertion point and advances to the right. Right-aligned type advances to the left as you type. Centered type expands both ways to remain centered.

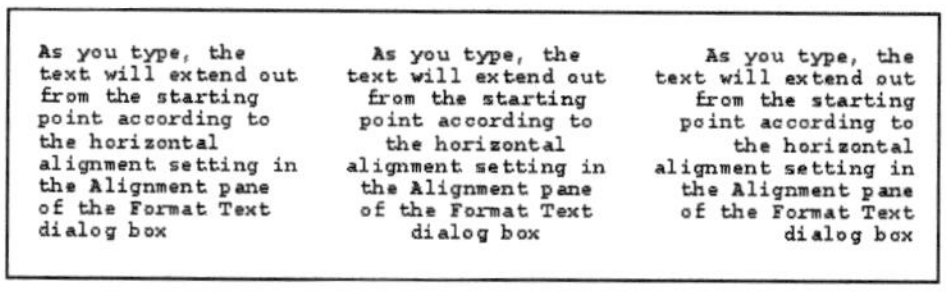

| As you type, the text will extend out from the starting point according to the horizontal alignment setting in the Alignment pane of the Format Text dialog box | As you type, the text will extend out from the starting point according to the horizontal alignment setting in the Alignment pane of the Format Text dialog box | As you type, the text will extend out from the starting point according to the horizontal alignment setting in the Alignment pane of the Format Text dialog box |

Figure 2.87 The three horizontal alignment options always leave ragged edges; there is no justified type option.

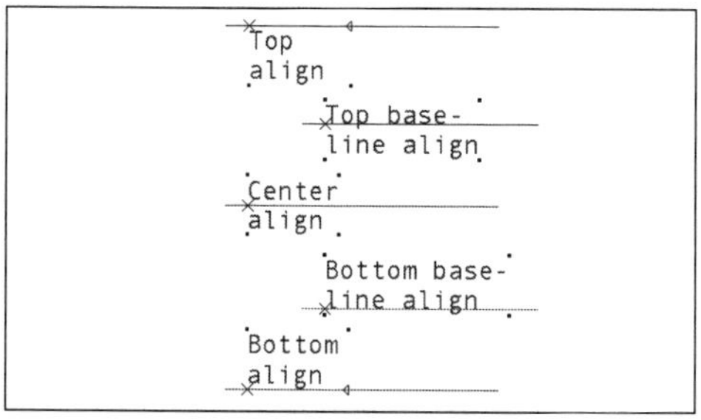

Top align

Top base-
line align

Center align

Bottom base-
line align

Bottom align

Figure 2.88 There are five options for vertical alignment. Top, Center, and Bottom alignments relate the insertion point to the text block as a whole. Top and Bottom Baseline alignments relate the point to the baselines of the text itself.

This text has been wrapped to fit the text box.

Figure 2.89 A text object has four corner handles and an insertion point. When text has been wrapped to fit the box, there is an arrow showing which side (or sides) is unaligned.

5. Click OK.

The dialog box closes.

6. Click the Text tool on the 2D Tools palette (**Figure 2.85**).

7. Click in the drawing area to place a flashing cursor on the screen and begin typing in your text.

As you type, the text will extend out from the starting point according to the horizontal alignment setting in the Alignment pane of the Format Text dialog box (**Figure 2.86**). When you create a multiple-line text object, the text will be either aligned to one edge or centered (**Figure 2.87**).

Its vertical position is controlled by the vertical alignment setting (**Figure 2.88**).

8. Press Return to start a new line of text. Press Enter or Esc to finish the text box.

The text object is placed with its attributes. The text box is defined by four corner points and the insertion point (**Figure 2.89**).

TEXT

65

✔ Tips

- The No Fill Behind Text checkbox on the Display tab of the VectorWorks Preferences panel controls whether or not there will be fill behind the text when you create it (**Figure 2.90**). You can edit that attribute after the text block is in place.

- You can also set the font, size, spacing, style, and alignment from individual menus under the Text menu.

- Instead of just clicking a starting point, which allows the text to run horizontally as long as you keep typing, use the Text tool to drag a rectangle that defines the width (but not the height) of the text box (**Figure 2.91**).

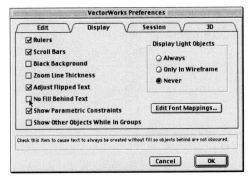

Figure 2.90 If you want the text block filled when it is created, uncheck the No Fill Behind Text checkbox in the VectorWorks Preferences.

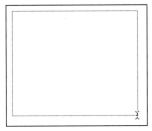

Figure 2.91 Drag the Text tool to set the width of the text object. The text will wrap as you type to fit its width.

TEXT

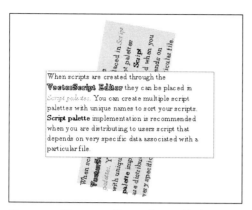

Figure 2.92 When you edit text, the text block temporarily returns to its primeval state.

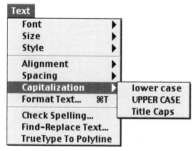

Figure 2.93 You can set whole text blocks — or a selection within one — to lowercase, all capitals, or title caps (initial capitals) using the Capitalization commands on the Text menu.

Within a single text block, you can vary the font, style, size, and so on by editing the text after you've created it. Editing the text in a text block is much like editing text in a word processing application.

To edit the text within a text block:

1. Click the Text tool on the 2D Tools palette.

2. In the drawing area, click to select the text block you want to edit.

   The text is shown unrotated without any background color and surrounded by a dotted boundary. The pointer becomes a flashing vertical bar (**Figure 2.92**).

3. Click where you want to insert text and type in the new text.

4. Drag the pointer to highlight a selection to make a change, or do any of the following:

   Press Delete or Backspace to remove the text.

   Go to the Text menu and choose among the formatting options offered.

   Use the Attributes palette to change the pen color of the selected text.

5. Press Enter or Esc to exit the editing mode.

✔ Tips

- Select a text block with the 2D Selection, and you can change its attributes and the styling of the text as a whole.

- Select several text blocks, and you can modify their attributes and formatting. Text editing, however, can be done only one block at a time unless you resort to the Find-Replace Text command. Spell checking can be done globally or block by block.

- Double-click a word in a text object with the Text tool to select it.

- Once you have created a text object, you can choose Text > Capitalization to set all the words in the block to lowercase, uppercase, or title caps (**Figure 2.93**).

TEXT

While a text object looks like a rectangle with text in it, you can't reshape it as you would a rectangular object. Dragging the corners with the 2D Selection tool changes its width, but its height changes automatically to contain the text.

To reshape a text object:

1. On the 2D Tools palette, click the 2D Reshape tool.

2. Select the text object you want to reshape. It will display handles at its four corners (even if it's rotated) and an enlarged locus at its insertion point (**Figure 2.94**).

3. Click on one of the handles and drag it to change the width of the box (the height will adjust automatically to accommodate the text) (**Figure 2.95**)

   or

   On the Object Info palette, change the value in the Width field to adjust the box width. Unchecking the Wrap Text checkbox puts the text onto a single line.

4. On the 2D Tools palette, click the 2D Rotate tool and rotate the text block (see Chapter 3)

   or

   On the Object Info palette, change the value in the Rot (short for Rotation) field to rotate the text block (**Figure 2.96**).

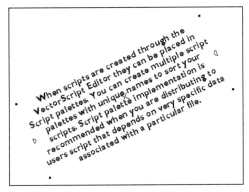

Figure 2.94 Unlike other objects, the text object's corner points rotate with it.

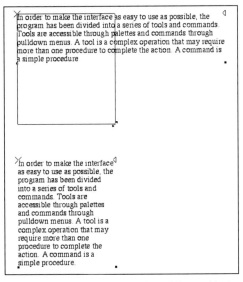

Figure 2.95 As you drag the handles of the text block so that the width changes, the height adjusts to fit the text.

Figure 2.96 The Object Info palette has fields only for the width and the rotation of a text object.

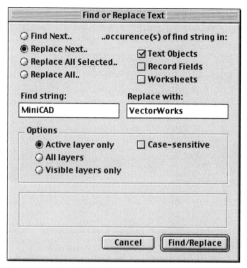

Figure 2.97 The Find or Replace Text dialog box.

To replace one text string with another:

1. Choose Text > Find-Replace Text.

   The Find or Replace Text dialog box opens (**Figure 2.97**).

2. At the top left of the Find or Replace Text dialog box, click the radio button for the function you want.

   Replace Next begins with the object furthest back in the stack.

3. At the top right of the dialog box, click all the areas in which you want the action to take place; for present purposes, click only Text Objects.

4. In the middle of the dialog box, enter the text you want to change on the left and what you want to change it to on the right.

   Leave the right field blank if you want to simply remove the text entered in the left field.

5. At the bottom of the dialog box, choose among the available options.

6. Click Find/Replace to close the dialog box and make the changes.

TEXT

To run a spell check:

1. Do one of the following:

    Select the objects for which you want the spelling of the text blocks, symbols, records, and worksheets

    or

    Don't select anything, which will run a spell check on the entire drawing file.

2. Choose Text > Check Spelling.

    If there are any misspelled (or unrecognized) words in the selection or the records associated with it, the Selection Spelling Check dialog box opens (**Figure 2.98**)

    or

    If no objects are selected, the Spelling Check Filter dialog box opens. Check the boxes for the areas you want checked. Then click OK and the Document Spelling Check dialog box opens for any questionable words.

3. In the Document or Selection Spelling Check dialog box, click Options to specify what kinds of special combinations VectorWorks should overlook.

    The Spelling Check Options dialog box opens (**Figure 2.99**).

4. In the Spelling Check Options dialog box, uncheck the types of combinations you want to skip when the spelling is checked.

    Click OK to close the dialog box and return to the Spelling Check dialog box.

    In the Spelling Check (the Document and Selection dialog boxes are the same, but the titles change depending on whether you selected objects or not), the questioned word appears in the Not In Dictionary field at the top, below the text fragment indicating the context in the drawing file in which the word appears.

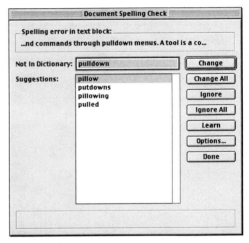

Figure 2.98 The Selection Spelling Check and the Document Spelling Check dialog boxes differ only in their title bars.

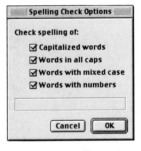

Figure 2.99 The Spelling Check Options dialog box lets you limit your checks to skip certain kinds of terms.

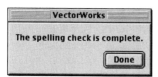

Figure 2.100
When the spell check is finished, this alert is presented.

5. *Do one of the following:*

   ▲ Choose the correct word on the Suggestions list and click Change to substitute it for that instance of the word in the drawing file.

   ▲ Choose the correct word on the Suggestions list and click Change All to substitute that word for the suspect word everywhere it appears in the drawing file.

   ▲ Type the correct word in the Not In Dictionary field and click either Change or Change All.

   ▲ Click Ignore to leave the word unchanged.

   ▲ Click Ignore to leave the suspect word unchanged everywhere.

   ▲ Click Learn to add a word not recognized by the standard dictionary to the custom dictionary so it will no longer be considered suspect.

6. Continue as above until either you are finished and the "spelling check is complete alert" is presented. Click Done to return to the drawing (**Figure 2.100**)
   or
   Click Done on the Spelling Check dialog box to terminate the check.

✔ Tips

   ■ If there are no suspect words in the selection, the "spelling check is complete" alert is posted right away.

   ■ To edit the custom dictionary, open the User Dictionary.txt file in the Dictionaries folder in VectorWorks's Plug-Ins folder and make the necessary changes.

TEXT

When you really want to mess with the type, you need to turn it into a regular object that can be manipulated with all the tools in the Editing palette. The transformed type object is no longer recognized as text, so make sure the spelling is right and the font is the one you want before you begin. This command works only with TrueType fonts, and all the text is rendered as Normal (all the style options are discarded).

To convert TrueType text objects to polylines:

1. Select the type object you want to convert.

2. Choose Text > TrueType to Polyline.

   The type object is converted to a group of polylines, taking its attributes from the current settings in the Attributes palette. (**Figure 2.101**).

3. Use the standard editing tools (see Chapter 3) to reshape the text as necessary.

✔ Tip

■ The Shear and Fixed Point Resize tools produce dramatic results on converted text with minimal effort. The 2D Reshape tool can do more but requires more care on your part (**Figure 2.102**).

Figure 2.101 Changing text to polylines lets you manipulate it like any other object.

Figure 2.102 Shearing the group that used to be a text object lets you mimic various perspective effects.

MODIFYING 2D OBJECTS

The last chapter laid out the basics of 2D object creation. This chapter deals with changing those objects you have already put onto the page. Sometimes you'll need to move them around a little; other times they'll need some reshaping. The VectorWorks Editing palette contains a reasonably ample set of tools for modifying objects; other operations are handled by tools in the Menu and Data Display bars and by various dialog boxes.

While it's a good thing to be able to draw such design building blocks as lines, rectangles, and circles, most of what you'll want to depict will be a little more complicated. In this chapter, we will explore some of the techniques for putting objects together into more complex units.

In the real world of design, it is rare indeed to put things initially exactly where they are ultimately going to end up. One of the great strengths of CAD in general is the ease with which you can manipulate objects. It may sometimes be quicker to sketch something with a pencil and paper, but making changes is much more tedious—not to mention messy.

Selecting Objects

In general, before you can edit objects, you have to select them. There are a number of ways to do this.

To select objects directly:

1. On the 2D Tools palette, click the 2D Selection tool.

   The cursor changes to an arrow. The cursor will change to an open arrow head without a stem when it has found the object

   or

   If you have the Snap to Object, Snap to Intersection, or Snap to Distance constraint selected (see Chapter 4, "Drawing With Constraints") the arrow changes to a cross instead when it approaches a designated snap point. (**Figure 3.1**).

2. Click on the object you want to select.

   The object will display handles to show that it has been selected (**Figure 3.2**). The Object Info palette will show the object's properties.

3. Hold down the Shift key and click additional objects to select them.

   Shift-clicking an object that's already selected deselects it.

To select objects with the Marquee or Lasso:

1. On the 2D Tools palette, click the 2D Selection tool.

2. Do one of the following (**Figure 3.3**):

   Choose the Marquee mode on the Mode bar and hold down the mouse as you drag diagonally to create a marquee around the objects you want to select. (**Figure 3.4**)

   or

   Choose the Lasso mode and draw an outline around the objects you want to select (**Figure 3.5**).

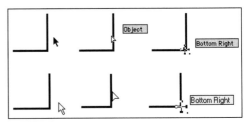

Figure 3.1 Selecting objects with the 2D Selection tool is made easier by the cursor cues it displays.

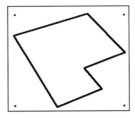

Figure 3.2 When it's selected, an object displays handles that you can use to modify it.

Figure 3.3 Choose either the Marquee (bottom) or the Lasso (top) mode on the Mode bar.

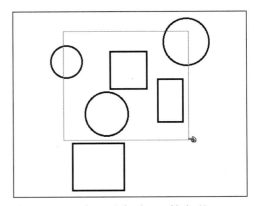

Figure 3.4 Drag the 2D Selection tool in its Marquee mode to define the rectangular box that selects only the objects that lie entirely within it.

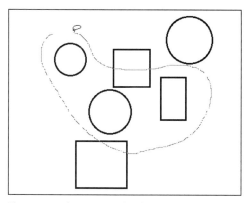

Figure 3.5 In the Lasso mode, the 2D Selection tool selects everything that lies completely within its irregular boundary.

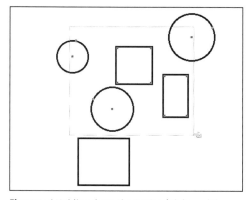

Figure 3.6 Holding down the Option/Alt key while you draw a marquee or a lasso selects all the objects it encloses or touches.

The objects completely within the boundary drawn are selected.

✔ Tips

- To select both objects that lie within the marquee or lasso boundary and those that overlap the line, hold down the Option (Mac) or Alt (Windows) as you draw (**Figure 3.6**).

- Sometimes the easiest way to select only some of the objects in a crowded area is to use the marquee or lasso and then Shift-click the ones you want to deselect.

Sometimes, after you've put a certain amount of effort into selecting a set of objects, you inadvertently deselect them. Don't worry—all is not lost!

To recover a lost selection:

- ◆ Choose Edit > Previous Selection.
  The last selection is again selected.

Every object in a VectorWorks drawing file has an identity, including its kind (line, rectangle, polyline, and so on), attributes, layer, and class, that you can use to select it. You might, for example, want to select all the walls on the first floor that are members of the class Demolition so that you can change their attributes.

To select objects by criteria:

1. Choose Organize > Custom Selection.

   The Custom Selection dialog box opens (**Figure 3.7**).

2. In the Command pane of the Custom Selection dialog box, click one of the following:

   Select to select all the objects that meet the requirements set up in the Criteria dialog box (see below).

   Select Only to select the objects as above and to deselect all others.

   Deselect to deselect objects that meet the criteria.

3. In the Option pane of the Custom Selection dialog box, click Execute Immediately to have the selection occur as soon as you close the Criteria dialog box

   or

   Click Create Script to add a command to the drawing file that selects objects according to the defined criteria. You can use this custom command over and over, and export it to other drawing files as needed.

4. Click the Criteria button.

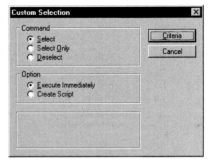

Figure 3.7 The Custom Selection dialog box allows you to select objects according to clearly defined criteria. You can create a script for multiple uses or just find them this time.

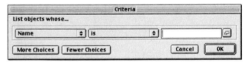

Figure 3.8 The Criteria dialog box can find objects by a single criterion or a whole set.

Figure 3.9 Add criteria as required by clicking the More Choices button.

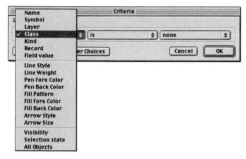

Figure 3.10 Choose the first criterion you want to select (or deselect) for.

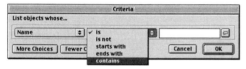

Figure 3.11 The other drop-down menus are context-sensitive and change with the category you select.

5. Click More Choices to add another row of fields with additional criteria for your selection process. You can add as many lines as you need to pinpoint just those objects you want to select (**Figure 3.9**).

Click Fewer Choices to eliminate the bottom row of fields.

6. From the left-hand drop-down menu, choose the type of entity you want to search for (**Figure 3.10**).

The other drop-down menus then change to set up the search criteria.

7. Choose options from the remaining drop-down menus to complete a set of criteria for the selection (**Figure 3.11**).

8. Click OK.

The defined objects are selected (or deselected).

✔ **Tip**

■ In general, you can edit a selection of objects as a single object. The center of the invisible rectangle that encloses the objects serves as the default center of the set.

Locking Objects

VectorWorks lets you lock objects to protect them against any changes you might make. Locking an object also lets you align others to it rather than to the center of the group, as it would by default.

To lock and unlock objects:

1. Select the objects you want to lock using one of the methods above.

2. Choose Edit > Lock.

   The object is locked. You can still select it, but its selection handles are gray instead of black and its Object Info palette is grayed out (**Figure 3.12**).

3. Select the object and choose Edit > Unlock to return the object to active duty.

✔ Tip

■ When you try to modify a locked object, an alert box appears (**Figure 3.13**). Trying to delete a locked object or change its attributes won't produce the alert, but the object will remain unaffected by the attempted change.

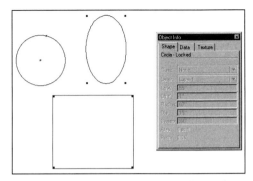

Figure 3.12 A locked object has gray handles, and its Object Info palette is grayed out.

Figure 3.13 An alert pops up when you try to modify a locked object.

Figure 3.14 Deselect the Enable Interactive Scaling function to prevent inadvertent reshaping of objects you want to move. When deselected, the button will appear flush with the bar in Windows (top) and raised in the Mac environment (bottom).

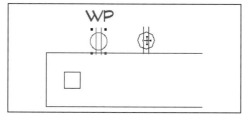

Figure 3.15 Drag the object you want to move; the object's position is previewed as you move it.

Moving Objects

One thing computers do well is move objects around on the page, whether they are words, lines, or pixels. VectorWorks lets you drag things around the page, move them by specifying x and y distances to a new location, or move them by specifying new coordinates.

To move objects by dragging them:

1. On the 2D Tools palette, click the 2D Selection tool.

2. Deselect the Enable Interactive Scaling button on the Mode bar.

   This setting prevents the 2D Selection tool from reshaping the objects you're trying to move. (**Figure 3.14**).

3. Select the objects you want to move.

4. Click on the object (or one of the selected objects) and hold down the mouse while you drag to the new location.

   An image of the object (and the rectangle or lasso enclosing all the selected objects if there are any) will preview the movement (**Figure 3.15**).

   Release the mouse to complete the operation.

✔ Tips

- You don't *really* have to deselect the Enable Interactive Scaling button, but if you don't, you have to be more careful how you grab the objects you move. Be sure the pointer doesn't turn into the double-headed arrow and reshape the object instead of moving it.

- You can make your modifications more exact by entering distances, angles, and/or new coordinates in the Data Display bar (see Chapter 2, "Creating 2D Shapes").

To move objects with the Move command:

1. Select the objects you want to move.

2. Choose Tool > Move > Move, or press Command-M (Mac) or Ctrl-M (Windows). The Move Selection dialog box opens (**Figure 3.16**).

3. Do one of the following:

   Click the Cartesian radio button and set the X and Y distances you want to move the objects

   or

   Click the Polar radio button and set the distance and angle to move the selected objects (**Figure 3.17**).

4. Click OK. The movement is completed

   or

   Click Cancel to close the dialog box without changing anything.

The Object Info palette is a flexible tool that not only provides information, but also allows you to move and reshape objects. (It has a number of other functions on the Data and Texture tabs, but those will be covered in later chapters.)

The Object Info palette moves only one object at time (groups count as single objects).

Figure 3.16 The Move Selection dialog box is a way to move objects precisely by distance.

Figure 3.17 You can use either X and Y distances or polar coordinates (distance and angle) to move objects.

Figure 3.18 The Object Info palette includes the location of the object.

Figure 3.19 Use the Box Position to set the reference point for the object's position .

✔ Tips

- You can accomplish the same thing by snapping to the vertex with the 2D Selection tool and using the Data Display Bar to set the new *x* and *y* coordinates.

- Rectangles have their vertices the corners of the bounding box, so locating the bounding box is the same as locating the shape itself.

To move an object using its bounding box:

1. Select the object you want to move.

2. Choose Palettes > Object Info to open the Object Info palette (**Figure 3.18**).

3. Click one of the points on the position on the Box Position indicator to set the point on the object's bounding box you want to use as the reference point (**Figure 3.19**).

   The X and Y edit boxes will show the current coordinates of that point.

4. On the Object Info palette, click on the X edit box next to the Box Position and enter the *x* coordinate to which the selected point on the bounding box is to go.

   Click on the Y edit box and enter the *y* coordinate.

   Press Enter to complete the move.

To position a polygon or polyline by one of its vertices:

1. Select the object you want to move.

2. Choose Palettes > Object Info to open the Object Info palette.

3. On the Move drop-down menu, choose Entire Object.

4. Use the Vertex buttons to select the vertex you want to position at a specific point.

   The center button highlights the active vertex; the arrow buttons let you move forward or backward along the line to get to a specific vertex.

5. In the X and Y fields below the Vertex buttons, type the new coordinates for the selected vertex and press Enter to complete the move.

MOVING OBJECTS

To move an object relative to its present position using the Object Info palette:

1. Select the object you want to move.

2. Choose Palettes > Object Info to open the Object Info palette.

3. In the X and Y fields to the right of the Box Position, leave the current values in place and add or subtract the distance you want to move the object using standard arithmetic expressions.

   Add a plus or minus symbol followed by the distance you want to move, and press Enter; VectorWorks calculates the new coordinates and moves the object. You can use any mixture of decimals and fractions and units of measurement (**Figure 3.20**).

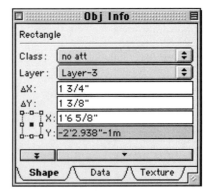

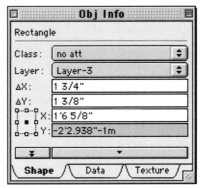

Figure 3.20 Moving objects is easy if you enter the new position as an arithmetic expression on the Object Info palette. You can mix units with impunity. Shaded fields on the top are resolved into the values on the bottom.

Guides

In VectorWorks, guides are created by granting normal objects a special status. Any object—even a 3D object—can be made into a guide. This is unlike most other applications, which have guide lines that you drag from the rulers. Guides can be anything from lines parallel to the grid to a detailed drawing of a complex machine into which the part you are designing has to fit.

To create guides:

1. Select the objects you want to convert into guides.

2. Choose Edit > Guides > Make Guide.

    The objects are moved into the class Guides and locked. They have the default attributes of the class, for example a 5 mm line patterned in two shades of mauve and no fill.

Once created, guides are by design immutable. Unless, of course, you first unlock them; then you can make changes to them.

To modify guides:

1. Select the guides you want to adjust.

    They will have selection handles, but the handles will be gray instead of black.

2. Choose Edit > Unlock.

    The handles will turn black to indicate that the objects are no longer locked.

3. Make whatever changes you like.

4. With the objects selected, choose Edit > Lock.

To hide (or show) guides:

◆ Choose Edit > Guides > Hide Guides.

The class is set to Invisible in the Classes dialog box. Unless Guides is the active class, the guides will be rendered invisible.

◆ To show the guides again, choose Edit > Guides > Show Guides. The class is set to Visible in the Classes dialog box.

Other guide commands:

◆ Choose Edit > Guides > Select Guides to select all the members of the Guides class. This is essentially a preset way of using the "selection by criteria" command (see above).

◆ Choose Edit > Guides > Delete All Guides to delete all members of the class from the drawing file.

✔ Tips

■ You can copy a guide; the copy is a member of the Guide class but is not locked.

■ If you make a guide out of a symbol or a plug-in object, the settings that created the original object override those of the class setting. Thus, the object won't look like other guides, even though it is locked and assigned to the Guides class.

GUIDES

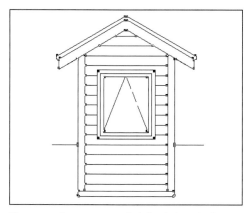

Figure 3.21 Groups are created simply by selecting objects and choosing the Group command.

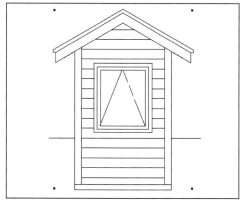

Figure 3.22 After you group objects, their individual handles are replaced by the four for their bounding box.

Working with Groups

When you select multiple objects, they are transformed as a unit when you scale or rotate them or change their attributes, layer, or class.

If you think you are going to use this same collection over again, you may want to give it official status as a group so that when you select any of its members, the entire group is selected. Groups in VectorWorks are much like groups in other graphics programs. They are easy to create and easy to dissolve, and members can be individually edited. Groups themselves can be members of higher-order groups.

In VectorWorks, a group is essentially a sublayer that behaves as a unit until you enter it. Then you can modify individual objects or add and delete objects. When you leave the confines of the group, it once again functions as a single unit.

To create a group:

1. Select the objects you want to group (**Figure 3.21**).

2. Choose Organize > Group, or press Command-G (Mac) or Ctrl-G (Windows).

   The group is created on the active layer and assigned to the class None.

   The objects lose their individual handles, and new handles are displayed for the rectangle enclosing them (**Figure 3.22**).

To break up a group:

◆ Select the group you want to ungroup and choose Organize > Ungroup, or press Command-U (Mac) or Ctrl-U (Windows).

✔ Tip

■ When you break up a group you originally created with objects from different layers and classes, the objects return to their original classes but remain in the layer on which the group was formed.

Editing a group means temporarily entering it so you can make modifications to individual objects (or subgroups) without ungrouping. When you exit the group, it still has its identity, but the objects within it may have been changed.

To edit a group:

1. Select the group you want to edit.

2. Choose Organize > Edit Group, or press Command-[(Mac) or Ctrl-[(Windows).

   The Level drop-down menu now shows the name of the group instead of the name of the layer. The objects and subgroups that make up the group are now individually selectable (**Figure 3.23**).

3. Modify the individual objects (or subgroups) by selecting them and modifying them as you normally would.

   When you have groups within groups, you may have to use the Edit Group command repeatedly to get to the level of the individual objects.

4. When you have finished working within the group, choose Organize > Exit Group to move up one level toward the layer in which the group resides (**Figure 3.24**).

   If you have tunneled way down into a nested group, you may need to do this several times or choose Organize > Top Level to return to the active layer in a single step.

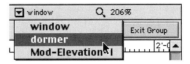

Figure 3.23 Once you have chosen to edit a group, the levels menu on the Data Display bar changes to reflect only the structure of the group.

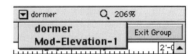

Figure 3.24 Click Exit Group to move up one level toward the layer in which the group resides.

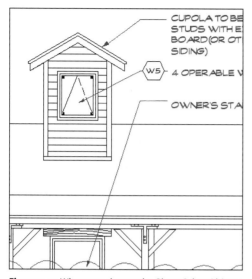

CUPOLA TO BE
STUDS WITH E
BOARD(OR OT
SIDING)

W5   4 OPERABLE V

OWNER'S STA

Figure 3.25 When you choose the Show Other Objects While In Groups option on the Display tab of the VectorWorks Preferences, the group is not isolated when you edit it.

✔ Tips

■ By default, a group is named Group #1 when you enter it. The next level down, if there is one, is called Group #2, and so on. Alternatively, you can identify each group with a name (see Chapter 3, "Modifying 2D Objects").

■ If you don't want the group isolated (as is the default) while you edit it (**Figure 3.25**), Click the Show Other Objects While In Groups checkbox in the VectorWorks Preferences dialog box.

■ While you are inside a group, the Layer menu on the Data Display bar changes to display the level at which you are operating inside the group. If you have gone down to a sub-subgroup, the drop-down menu will display the all the levels you have gone through. You can use this menu to move to up to a higher level in a nested group or back to the active layer.

■ The Convert to Group command for symbols and plug-in objects can't be undone. Once a symbol or PIO is converted to a group, ex-symbols can no longer be changed by editing the symbol and ex-PIOs can no longer be changed by entering new values in the Object Info palette (See Chapter 6, "2D Symbols and PIOs").

Changing Object Attributes

In Chapter 2 we showed how to control the attributes of an object by selecting its options from the Attributes palette. Sometimes you'll want to change the attributes to help you distinguish different functional units in the design. Think, for example, about how much clearer a plumbing detail would be if you could code cold water lines blue, hot water lines red, and waste lines black. With Vector-Works, that's easy to do.

To change the attributes of an object from the Object Info palette:

1. With the Selection tool from the 2D Tools palette, select the objects whose attributes you want to change.

2. On the Attributes palette, choose a new setting for the attribute you want to change.

   That attribute on all selected objects will be changed to the new settings. The other attributes will remain as they were.

To copy the attributes of one object onto another:

1. On the Editing palette, click the Eyedropper tool (**Figure 3.26**).

2. On the Mode bar, click the Eyedropper tool's Preferences button.

   The Pick Up/Put Down Filter dialog box opens (**Figure 3.27**).

3. In the Pick Up/Put Down Filter dialog box, click the checkboxes for the attributes you want to affect. (For more about layers, see Chapter 5, "Using Layers and Classes." For more about records, see Chapter 10, "Worksheets, Reports, and Presentations.")

   Click the Pen, Line, or Fill box to select all the attributes for that element.

Figure 3.26 The Eyedropper tool on the Editing palette.

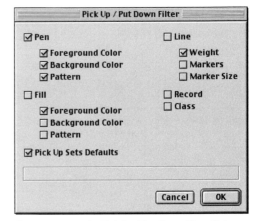

Figure 3.27 Use the Pick Up / Put Down Filter dialog box to set what the eyedropper picks up and what it leaves alone.

Figure 3.28 The Eyedropper has an Apply Attributes mode and a Pick Up Attributes mode. Toggle between them with the Option key (Alt key for Windows).

Click the Pick Up Sets Defaults checkbox if you want the Eyedropper tool to change the settings in the Attributes palette so that newly created objects take their attributes from the object selected in the drawing.

Click OK to close the dialog box.

4. Pick up the attributes (the ones you checked in the dialog box) by doing one of the following:

Click the Eyedropper button in the Mode bar and then click on the object from which you want to copy attributes

or

Click the Paint Bucket button and hold down the Option (Mac) or Alt (Windows) key to toggle the function of the tool to its pickup (Eyedropper) mode (**Figure 3.28**). The bulb of the dropper will turn white when it has snapped to the object.

5. Change to the Apply Attributes mode by clicking the Paint Bucket button on the Mode bar

or

(if the Eyedropper mode is active) holding down the Option (Mac) or Alt (Windows) key.

6. Click on the objects you want to give the picked-up attributes.

The Paint Bucket will tip over when it has snapped to the object, and the object will take on its new attributes.

✔ Tips

- The relationship between the Attributes palette and plug-in objects is managed by the scripts that generate them; generally you can change some attributes but not others. For example: In Plan view of a column, you can change the pen color for the whole object, pen weight for the shaft (not for the base, however), but you cannot change pen styles for any of it.

- You can't change the attributes of a symbol without either converting it to a group or editing it so as to change all its instances in the drawing (see Chapter 6, "2D Symbols and PIOs").

- The Eyedropper tool picks up only attached Records from groups (see Chapter 10, "Worksheets, Reports, and Presentations").

CHANGING OBJECT ATTRIBUTES

Copying and Pasting

If you are familiar with even basic word processing software, you know most of what there is to know about copying and pasting. It is one of the great time-savers that computers offer.

In CAD, before you can paste an object into a drawing, you have to get it to the clipboard either by cutting it or copying it from the same or another file.

To copy an object:

1. Select the object you want to copy.

2. Choose Edit > Copy, or press Command-C (Mac) or Ctrl-C (Windows).

   The object is copied to the clipboard for later use. The original is left in place.

✔ Tip

■ You can copy objects from other VectorWorks drawing files and from many other applications with good results. Use each application's method of copying. In some cases, it will be necessary to use a special Copy As command to create a copy that can be pasted into VectorWorks.

To paste an object into a drawing file:

◆ With an object copied onto the clipboard of your computer, choose Edit > Paste or press Command-V (Mac) or Ctrl-V (Windows).

The object is pasted into the drawing, centered at the site of the last mouse click

or

◆ Choose Edit > Paste In Place, or press Command-Option-V (Mac) or Ctrl-Alt-V (Windows).

An object copied from a VectorWorks file is pasted at the coordinates it was copied from

or

◆ Choose Edit > Paste As Picture.

The object is converted to a bitmap object and pasted at the last mouse click.

✔ Tips

■ You can copy text from almost any other application, and it will be pasted into a drawing file as editable text, but its size will vary with the zoom factor of the drawing at the time it is pasted in.

■ Objects copied from other applications are pasted into your VectorWorks files at "paper scale" (1:1), regardless of the scale of the active layer.

■ Some illustration applications allow you to bring a vector illustration into VectorWorks as a polygon or other editable shape, and not just as a bitmap object.

COPYING AND PASTING

Duplicating Objects

Duplicating objects is almost like cutting and pasting in one step except that the new objects will be in the original layer rather than the active layer. VectorWorks also offers a few enhanced forms of the process.

To duplicate objects:

1. Select the object(s) you want to duplicate.

2. Choose Edit > Duplicate, or press Command-D (Mac) or Ctrl-D (Windows).

    Copies of the selected objects are placed in the same layer as the original.

    If you have selected Offset Duplications on the Edit tab of the VectorWorks Preferences dialog box, the copy will be above and to the right of the original. Otherwise, the duplicate will sit right on top of it.

To duplicate objects by dragging:

1. Select the object(s) you want to duplicate.

2. Click on the object (or one of the objects), hold down the mouse while you also hold down the Option (Mac) or Alt (Windows) key, and drag the object to another place on the drawing.

    You will see a little plus sign next to the pointer (**Figure 3.29**).

3. Release the mouse before you release the Option (or Alt) key.

    The new objects are placed.

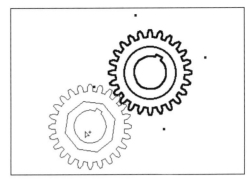

Figure 3.29 Duplicating by dragging is as easy as holding down the Option key (Alt key for Windows).

Figure 3.30 The Duplicate Along Path tool on the Editing palette.

Figure 3.31 The Duplicate Along Path tool has two modes and a Preferences button.

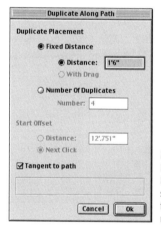

Figure 3.32 The Duplicate Along Path dialog box sets preferences for both the tool's modes.

To duplicate objects as you draw a polygon path:

1. Select the object(s) you want to duplicate.

2. Choose the Duplicate Along Path tool on the Editing palette (**Figure 3.30**).

3. On the Mode bar, click the Create Path Mode button (**Figure 3.31**).

4. Click the Duplicate Along Path Preferences button on the mode bar.

   The Duplicate Along Path Preferences dialog box opens (**Figure 3.32**).

5. Do one of the following:

   Click the Fixed Distance radio button and enter the distance between objects in the Distance field

   or

   Click the Number Of Duplicates radio button and enter the number of objects in the Number field.

6. Click the "Tangent to path" check box if you want the objects to rotate so that their *x*-axis is always parallel to the path (**Figure 3.33**).

   Click OK to close the dialog box.

   continues on next page

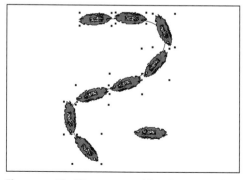

Figure 3.33 The "Tangent to path" option rotates the duplicated object along the path.

DUPLICATING OBJECTS

7. Click in the drawing area to define the starting point of the polygon path. Click at each vertex.

   The objects are previewed as you draw (**Figure 3.34**).

8. Double-click to end the polygon. The objects are placed, but no path object is created (**Figure 3.35**).

✔ Tip

- When you choose the Create Path mode, the Distance setting in the edit box still controls the operation of the tool even though the Start Offset control is grayed out. You may need to switch modes temporarily and reset that value.

The Duplicate Along Path tool is useful for lots of things. For example, you could use it to distribute trees along curved roadways or bolts around a flange (**Figure 3.36**).

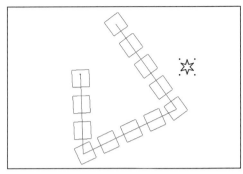

Figure 3.34 As you draw the polygon, the objects appear along it according to the settings in the Duplicate Along Path dialog box.

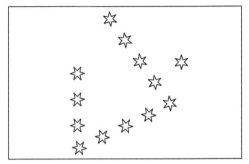

Figure 3.35 The objects are placed, but there is no sign of the polygon along which they were distributed.

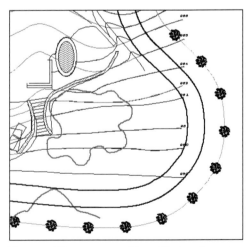

Figure 3.36 You can space objects (like trees) evenly along irregular contours (like roads) with the Duplicate Along Path tool.

To place duplicate objects along an existing path:

1. Select the object(s) you want to duplicate along a path already drawn.

2. Click the Duplicate Along Path tool on the Editing palette.

3. On the Mode bar, click the Click on a Path Object Mode button.

4. On the Mode bar, click the Duplicate Along Path Preferences button.

   The Duplicate Along Path dialog box opens.

5. In the Duplicate Placement section, click the Fixed Distance or the Number Of Duplicates radio button.

   If you choose Fixed Distance, as many duplicate objects as can fit are placed along the selected path. If you choose Number of Duplicates, the specified number of copies of the object will be spaced evenly between the offset point and the end of the path.

6. If you chose Fixed Distance in Step 5, click either the Distance radio button and enter the distance along the path between objects or click With Drag and set it with the mouse

   or

   If you chose Number of Duplicates, enter the number in the Number field.

7. In the Start Offset area, do one of the following:

   Select Distance and enter the distance from the starting point of the path to the first object

   or

   Click the Next Click radio button so that the point on the path at which you click the mouse will be the offset.

   continues on next page

DUPLICATING OBJECTS

8. Click the "Tangent to path" checkbox if you want the objects to rotate so their original *y*-axes are perpendicular to the path.

9. Click OK to close the dialog box, then click on the path you want the objects duplicated along in one of the following ways:

If you have clicked the Number of Duplicates radio button, the next mouse click tells the objects in which direction to propagate the copies.

If you have opted to set the offset using Next Click, the point on the path at which you click will be the site of the first object. But it only works with the Number Of Duplicates option if you drag in the direction in which the path was created. (**Figure 3.37**).

If you have chosen the Fixed Distance and With Drag combination, move the mouse in the direction tangent to the path at the first click to set the distance between subsequent objects and click to set the distance. The position of the objects will be previewed along the path (**Figure 3.38**).

The objects will be placed along the path.

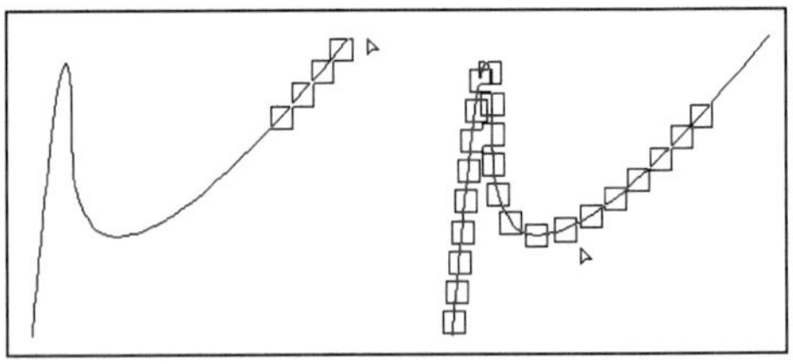

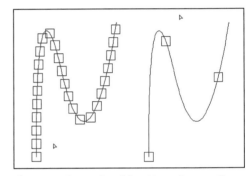

Figure 3.37 It makes a big difference which direction you drag when you are duplicating objects along a path using the Number Of Duplicates and Offset by Next Click options. The polyline was drawn left to right; dragging to the right gives the desired six objects, but dragging against the grain gives too many.

Figure 3.38 The spacing of the objects along a path depends on how far you move the cursor along the axis defined by the tangent to the curve at the first click.

✔ Tips

■ At this writing, VectorWorks has a bug that prevents you from using the Duplicate Along Path tool to space objects neatly around a circle. The work-around is either to convert the circle to a polygon by choosing Tool > Convert to Polygons or to go to the Object Info palette and change the sweep to something less than 360 degrees (359.99 will work) and then, in the Duplicate Along Path dialog box's Number edit field, increase by one the number of duplicates you really want. You should also be sure to click the Distance radio button under Start Offset, and specify an offset of 0. This bug is on the list and should be fixed in some future release.

■ Remember that you can hold down the spacebar and the X key to temporarily call the 2D Selection tool. When you release the keys, you return to the active tool.

■ With Click-Drag Drawing chosen in the VectorWorks Edit Preferences, spacing between objects along the path is controlled by the release of the mouse after the first click rather than by a second click.

■ If you choose to draw using the Number of Duplicates option, you have to drag in the direction in which the path was created.

■ Duplicate Along Path operations place objects in the same layer as the original object.

To create a linear array of duplicate objects:

1. Select the object(s) you want to duplicate.

2. Choose Edit > Duplicate Array.

   The Duplicate dialog box opens (**Figure 3.39**).

3. In the Duplication Shape pane of the Duplicate dialog box, click the Linear Array radio button and enter the number of additional objects you want to place.

4. In the Offset pane of the dialog box, choose either Next Mouse Click or Manual (**Figure 3.40**).

   If you choose Manual, enter the X and Y distance between each object in the line and the one after it.

   If you select Next Mouse Click, after you close the dialog box the pointer will become crosshairs and your next click will define the X and Y distances for the offset of the linear array (**Figure 3.41**).

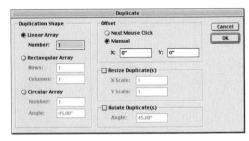

Figure 3.39 The Duplicate dialog box. Here you set up Linear, Rectangular, and Circular arrays.

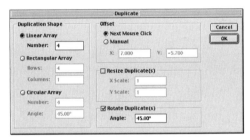

Figure 3.40 Choose Next Mouse Click to set the angle and spacing of the linear array with a click of the mouse in the drawing area.

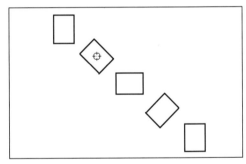

Figure 3.41 Click the mouse (crosshairs) and the array is placed accordingly.

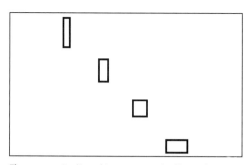

Figure 3.42 Scaling objects as you duplicate them offers you yet another design possibility.

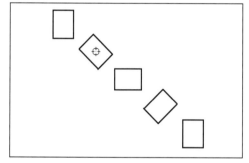

Figure 3.43 Rotating the objects you duplicate creates another kind of effect.

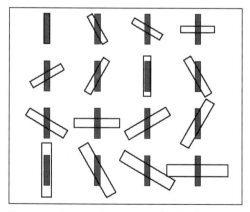

Figure 3.44 Rectangular arrays can be simple or you can progressively rotate and scale the objects.

5. If you want to resize the objects in the array, click the Resize Duplicate(s) check-box and enter values for the X and Y scales.

Each successive copy will bye scaled by the factors you enter (**Figure 3.42**).

6. If you want to rotate the duplicates successively, check the Rotate Duplicate(s) box and enter an angle in the edit box.

Each copy will be rotated by that angle relative to the one before it (**Figure 3.43**).

7. Click OK. If you entered the offset manually, the array is created. Otherwise, click the mouse to set the offset relative to the original object and create the array.

✔ Tip

■ You can rotate symbols, but you can't resize them when you duplicate them in an array.

To create a rectangular array of objects:

1. Select the object(s) you want to duplicate.

2. Choose Edit > Duplicate Array.
The Duplicate dialog box opens.

3. In the Duplication Shape pane of the Duplicate dialog box, click the Rectangular Array radio button and enter the number of rows and columns for your array in the edit boxes.

4. Set the Offset, Resize, and Rotate options as above.

Resize and Rotate functions are applied to duplicated objects successively as they go across each row and then to the following rows in the direction defined by the Offset setting (**Figure 3.44**).

5. Click OK. If you entered the offset manually, the array is created. Otherwise, click the mouse to set the offset relative to the original object and create the array.

To create a circular array of duplicate objects:

1. Select the object(s) you want to duplicate.

2. Choose Edit > Duplicate Array.
   The Duplicate dialog box opens.

3. In the Duplication Shape pane of the Duplicate dialog box, click the Circular Array radio button.

   In the Center pane—where the Offset settings used to be—click the Next Mouse Click radio button (**Figure 3.45**)

   or

   Click the Manual radio button and enter the *x* and *y* coordinates for the center around which the array will be formed.

4. Enter the number of copies and the angle between them in the corresponding edit boxes.

5. Set the Resize and Rotate fields as above.

6. Click OK. If you entered the center manually, the array is created. Otherwise, click the mouse to set the center relative to the original object and create the array.
   The array is created (**Figure 3.46**).

✔ Tip

- Unlike the linear and circular arrays, the rectangular array command gives you an array to total the numbers in the Rows and Columns boxes rather than creating that many additional objects. In other words, if you set up a linear or circular array of four objects, you wind up with that number plus the original object, making five; but if you set up a 2x3 array, you get five objects in addition to the original.

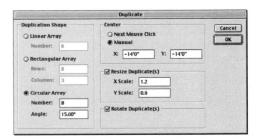

Figure 3.45 The Duplicate Array dialog box changes slightly when you select Circular Array so that you can set the center of the array.

Figure 3.46 The square on the left is rotated 15 degrees and scaled in both the *x* and *y* dimensions as it is duplicated along a circle.

DUPLICATING OBJECTS

Removing Objects from the Drawing

When you want to remove an object from a drawing, you can either *cut* it and store it temporarily on the clipboard for later use, or you can *clear* it, in which case it will vanish without leaving a trace (except in the VectorWorks Undo buffer).

To cut an object from a drawing:

1. Select the object you want to eliminate.

2. Choose Edit > Cut or press Command-X (Mac) or Ctrl-X (Windows).

   The object is removed from the drawing file and resides on the clipboard until replaced by the next object copied or cut from one of your applications.

To clear an object from the drawing:

1. Select the objects you want to clear.

2. Choose Edit > Clear, or press Delete (Mac) or Backspace (Windows).

   The object is removed, but not put on the clipboard.

Rotating Objects

To rotate an object 90 or 180 degrees:

1. Select the object (or objects) you want to rotate.

2. Choose Tool > Rotate, then select one of the following options from the drop-down menu that appears (**Figure 3.47**):

    ◆ Rotate Left 90° (Command-L for Mac; Ctrl-L for Windows) to rotate the object around its own center 90 degrees counter-clockwise (**Figure 3.48**).

    ◆ Rotate Right 90° to rotate the object 90 degrees clockwise around its own center (**Figure 3.49**).

    ◆ Flip Horizontal to mirror the object across its vertical center line (**Figure 3.50**).

    ◆ Flip Vertical to mirror the object across its horizontal center line (**Figure 3.51**).

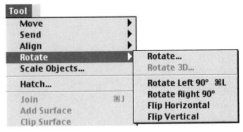

Figure 3.47 The Tool > Rotate submenu.

Figure 3.48 You can press Command/Ctrl-L to rotate an object 90 degrees counter-clockwise.

Figure 3.49 Choose Tool > Rotate > Rotate Right 90° to rotate an object clockwise.

Figure 3.50 Flip Horizontal mirrors the object left and right.

Figure 3.51 Flip Vertical turns the object on its head. It is not, however, the same as rotating it 180 degrees.

Figure 3.52 The 2D Rotate tool on the Editing palette.

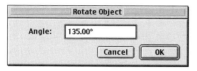

Figure 3.53 Double-click the 2D Rotate tool or choose Tool > Rotate > Rotate to open the Rotate Object dialog box.

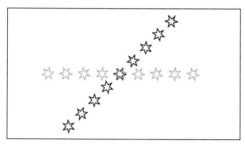

Figure 3.54 Typing 135° in the Rotate Object dialog box pivots the group around its center point.

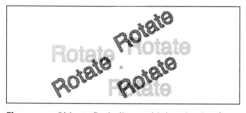

Figure 3.55 Objects (including multiple selections) rotated by way of the dialog box use their own centers as the center of rotation.

Figure 3.56 Rotate walls and lines by changing the A field in the Object Info palette.

To rotate an object by any designated angle:

1. Select the object you want to rotate.

2. Choose Tool > Rotate > Rotate

   or

   Double-click the 2D Rotate tool on the Editing palette (**Figure 3.52**).

   The Rotate Object dialog box opens (**Figure 3.53**).

3. Type in the angle at which you want to rotate the object around its own center.

   Positive values signify counter-clockwise rotations; negative values rotate the object clockwise.

   Click OK to complete the action (**Figure 3.54**).

✔ Tips

- When you rotate objects by means of a command or dialog box, the center of rotation is the center of the object or the set of objects you have selected.

- Text, wall objects, and 2D symbols can be rotated by changing the angle setting in the Object Info palette. Plug-in objects can be rotated around the *z*-axis the same way (**Figure 3.55**).

- Lines and wall objects can be rotated in the Object Info palette by changing the angle component of their polar coordinates (**Figure 3.56**).

- By default, the Adjust Flipped Text box is checked in the VectorWorks Display Preferences text—regardless of its rotation—will always be right-reading with this setting.

ROTATING OBJECTS

103

To rotate objects manually:

1. Select the objects you want to rotate.

2. Click the 2D Rotate tool on the Edit palette. The pointer becomes a small cross.

3. Click the mouse at the center of rotation and define the angle of the handle that you use to turn the object (**Figure 3.57**).

   Once the angle is set, you can drag the handle out to whatever length you want.

   If you are using click-drag drawing, the default handle will be horizontal; otherwise hold down the mouse and drag it along the angle you want before releasing it.

4. Move the mouse around the center to rotate the object and click again to set the rotation.

   As you move the mouse, the object's position is previewed (**Figure 3.58**).

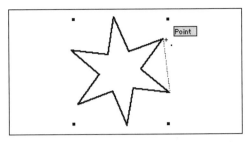

Figure 3.57 Rotating objects with the 2D Rotate tool begins with creating an anchor and a handle for the selected objects.

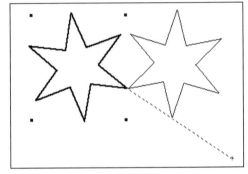

Figure 3.58 Just drag the handle around until you get the rotation you want.

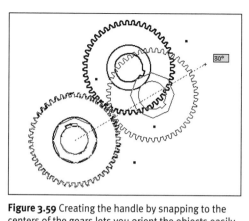

Figure 3.59 Creating the handle by snapping to the centers of the gears lets you orient the objects easily.

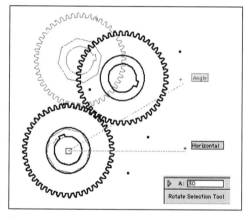

Figure 3.60 Both Snap to Angle and the Data Display bar help set rotation angles accurately.

✔ Tips

- You can Snap to Object to align the handle to one of the sides of a shape or to some other key point in the design. Or, you can use the Snap to Angle constraint to orient the handle along one of the main angles (see Chapter 4, "Drawing with Constraints").

- Create the handle along the axis you want to set to a specific angle, and then use either the Snap to Angle constraint or the Data Display bar to accomplish the deed (**Figure 3.59**).

- After you have created a handle to rotate an object, the Data Display bar shows the angle of the handle. You can lock the angle as you would any other field in the Data Display bar (see Chapter 2, "Creating 2D Shapes"). If you create the handle at 0 degrees, the Data Display bar will display how far you've rotated the object (**Figure 3.60**).

Mirroring Objects

Call it narcissism if you will, but bilateral symmetry is a feature of both the human body and a great deal of our designed environment as well. (Circular arrays—another favorite arrangement—is discussed above.) The ability of CAD applications to select a set of objects and then create their mirror image on the other side of a user-defined centerline is a major time-saver for designers. You can use if for everything from architectural detailing to bolts on a cylinder head. You can even use to create left-right symmetry and then mirror and copy that set of objects to develop top-bottom symmetry.

To mirror objects:

1. Select the objects to mirror.

2. On the Edit palette, click the Mirror tool button (**Figure 3.61**).

3. On the Mode bar, click either:

   The Mirror button to flip the objects across the control line

   or

   The Mirror and Duplicate button to flip a copy of the selected objects over the line (**Figure 3.62**).

4. Define the control line over which the object will be mirrored by clicking at its starting point and then at its end point (**Figure 3.63**).

   The mirror image is placed on the opposite side of the line. If you are operating in Mirror and Duplicate mode, the original object is left in place as well (**Figure 3.64**).

✔ Tips

■ Using the Mirror tool with a text object will result in the text being displaced but not mirrored if you have checked the Adjust Flipped Text box in the VectorWorks Display Preferences (**Figure 3.65**).

Figure 3.61 The 2D Mirror tool button on the Editing palette.

Figure 3.62 Both the Mirror and the Mirror and Duplicate buttons on the Mode bar.

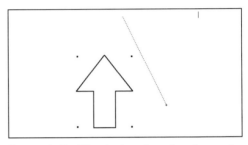

Figure 3.63 The Mirror tool requires a line of symmetry that you draw with the mouse.

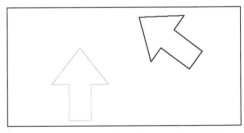

Figure 3.64 The result of the Mirror tool's work; if you choose Mirror and Duplicate on the Mode bar, both copies remain. Otherwise, there is only one.

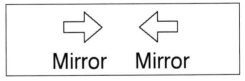

Figure 3.65 Both the arrow and the text have been mirrored and duplicated. This shot shows how VectorWorks corrects flipped text if that option has been selected in the Preferences dialog box.

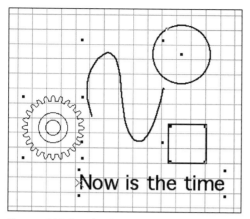

Figure 3.66 Select the objects you want to align to the grid.

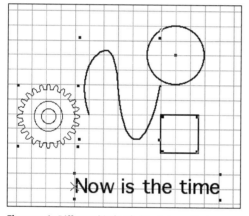

Figure 3.67 Different kinds of objects have their own ways of aligning to the grid.

Alignment and Distribution

Esthetically and functionally, designs rely heavily on objects being laid out, aligned, and distributed evenly. Aligning the objects to the grid can help, but what if the grid doesn't happen to coincide with the layout you want to create? In that case, you can align and distribute the objects relative to one another along both the horizontal and vertical axes.

To align objects to the grid:

1. Select the objects you want to align to the grid (**Figure 3.66**).

2. Choose Tool > Align > Align to Grid, or press Command-hyphen (Mac) or Ctrl-hyphen (Windows)

   Each individual object moves to align with the closest grid point as follows:

   Most objects, including groups, move so that the upper-left corner of the rectangle that encloses them is on a grid point.

   Symbols and plug-in objects are placed as if they had been converted to groups; their bounding boxes may not fit tightly around the object as it is drawn.

   A line, polygon, or polyline moves so that its starting point falls on a grid point.

   A text object places its locus on a grid point (**Figure 3.67**).

   Loci do not move.

To align objects to one another:

1. Select the objects you want to align (**Figure 3.68**).

2. Choose Tool > Align > Align/Distribute, or press Command-= (Mac) or Ctrl-= (Windows).

   The Align/Distribute Objects dialog box opens (**Figure 3.69**).

3. Click either the Align or the Distribute checkbox for the horizontal and vertical positioning of the selected objects.

   Leave both boxes unchecked if you don't want to affect the placement of the objects along that axis.

4. For each axis, click one of the radio buttons to select which point on each object is to be used for alignment or distribution.

   When you are distributing objects along an axis, you can choose to put equal spacing between them as well as to equalize the distances between their left or right edges or their centers.

   As you set the controls in the dialog box, the preview window changes to reflect the alignment and distribution options you have selected (**Figure 3.70**).

5. Click OK to move the objects into their new positions (**Figure 3.71**).

Figure 3.68 Aligning objects to one another also begins with selecting the objects you want to affect; unselected objects are not moved.

Figure 3.69 The Align/Distribute Objects dialog box opens when you choose the command from the menu or press Command/Ctrl-=.

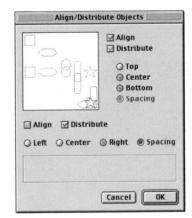

Figure 3.70 The preview window on the Align/Distribute Objects dialog box gives you an indication as to what will actually happen on the drawing.

ALIGNMENT AND DISTRIBUTION

Figure 3.71 Aligning the objects vertically and distributing them horizontally gives this result.

Figure 3.72 Locking the gear object and choosing the same horizontal distribution and vertical alignment aligns all the other objects to it and prevents it from being distributed.

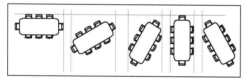

Figure 3.73 Trying to align these tables by their tops and distribute them with even spacing leads to problems.

✔ Tips

■ You can lock some of the objects in the selection you are aligning and distributing to control where the new array is created. When some of the selected objects are locked, the effective center for alignment is their centers and they won't be distributed. Otherwise, it will default to the center of the selection (**Figure 3.72**).

■ Because of the way symbols and plug-in objects are constructed, you may not get exactly the results you had hoped for when you use the Align/Distribute command with them. This is especially true when they are rotated (**Figure 3.73**).

Resizing Objects

Now that we have covered how to move objects around the screen, it's time to come to grips with modifying them in more substantial ways. The first of these is resizing, which can be either symmetrical or asymmetrical.

To scale objects:

1. Select the objects you want to resize.

   If you select multiple objects, they will be scaled as if they were a group (**Figure 3.74**).

2. Choose Tool > Scale Objects.

   The Scale Objects dialog box opens (**Figure 3.75**).

3. Click the Symmetric radio button and type the factor by which you want to multiply the size of the selected objects into the X,Y, Z Factor edit box (**Figure 3.76**)

   or

   Click the Asymmetric radio button and enter values for the X and Y scaling factors in their fields (**Figure 3.77**).

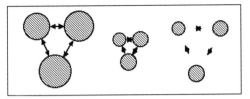

Figure 3.74 Scaling a selection of objects (center) is not the same as scaling them one at a time (right); on the left is the original group.

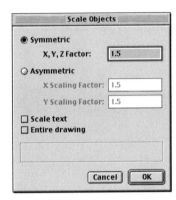

Figure 3.75 The Scale Objects dialog box.

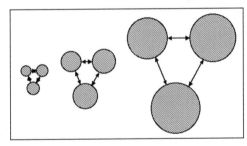

Figure 3.76 Symmetric scaling increases or decreases the size of the selected objects; but it does not affect line thicknesses or terminators.

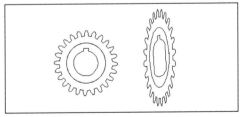

Figure 3.77 Asymmetric scaling distorts the object. The gear is scaled .5 in the X dimension and 1.5 in the Y.

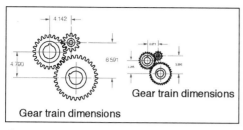

Gear train dimensions

Gear train dimensions

Figure 3.78 Leaving the "Scale Text" checkbox unchecked moves text objects but does not change the point size of the type.

4. Click the "Scale text" checkbox if you want the point size of selected text to be scaled.

If the box is not checked, text that is part of a selection will be moved as the selection is scaled up or down, but the point size of the type won't be affected (**Figure 3.78**).

5. Click the "Entire drawing" checkbox to scale everything in the drawing (except type, if that box is unchecked).

6. Click OK to close the dialog box and effect the change.

✔ Tips

■ Even if "Scale text" has not been selected, the Scale command scales the text size of any dimensions you have selected. You may want to take care to deselect them when you scale objects in the drawing.

■ Associated dimensions change to reflect the new dimensions of the scaled objects (see Chapter 10, "Worksheets, Reports, and Presentations").

The Scale Objects command operates symmetrically from the center of the selection along the X and/or Y dimensions. The Resize tool on the Editing palette, on the other hand, lets you choose the center and the X and Y scaling factors on screen. However, this tool is difficult to use precisely. To quote the VectorWorks Reference, "It is best used for visual effects."

RESIZING OBJECTS

Using the Resize tool:

1. Select the objects you want to modify.

2. On the Editing palette, click the Resize tool (**Figure 3.79**).

   The pointer turns into a bombsight.

3. Click in the drawing area to locate the fulcrum (reference point) around which the scaling will be performed (**Figure 3.80**).

   The pointer changes to a double-headed arrow.

4. Click again to create a handle to stretch the object around the fulcrum and then drag it around to reshape the object.

   As you move the mouse, the modified shape is previewed (**Figure 3.81**).

5. Click again to complete the resizing operation (**Figure 3.82**).

   If you are using click-drag drawing, steps 4 and 5 will involve a click and release of the mouse rather than two clicks.

Figure 3.79 The Resize tool button on the Editing palette.

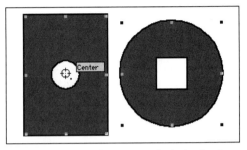

Figure 3.80 You can choose any point in the drawing area as the anchor point, or fulcrum, around which the distortion of the object will occur.

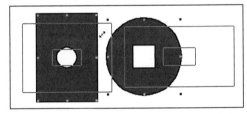

Figure 3.81 An outline previews the new shape of the selected objects.

Figure 3.82 Click the mouse again to complete the modification.

Figure 3.83 Make sure the Enable Interactive Scaling button is depressed or the object will just move rather than reshape.

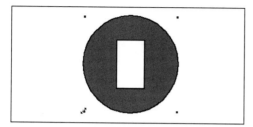

Figure 3.84 The cursor becomes a double-headed arrow cursor when it snaps to the handle of the selected object.

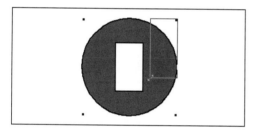

Figure 3.85 The preview of the new shape is only the outline of its bounding box.

Figure 3.86 You scale the object in both X and Y dimensions by dragging the mouse relative to the first snap location.

Resizing with the Selection tool:

1. Select the objects to resize.

2. Click the 2D Selection tool on the 2D Tools palette.

3. On the Mode bar, select the Enable Interactive Scaling button (**Figure 3.83**).

4. Click one of the handles of one of the objects.

   The pointer becomes a double-headed arrow when it snaps to the handle (**Figure 3.84**).

5. Drag the handle to scale the selected objects.

   As you drag, the bounding box of the objects is previewed (**Figure 3.85**). Circles and curves are displayed directly.

   Click again (or release the mouse if you're click-dragging) to finish the process (**Figure 3.86**).

RESIZING OBJECTS

To resize an object on the Object Info palette:

1. Select the object you want to modify (**Figure 3.87**).

   Handles will be displayed at the corners of the bounding box.

2. Choose Palette > Object Info, or press Command-I (Mac) or Ctrl-I (Windows) to open the Object Info palette .

3. On the Object Info palette, change the ΔX and ΔY (Mac) or ±X and ±Y (Windows) fields to change the shape of the object (**Figure 3.88**).

   The Box Position setting determines which point remains fixed as the object changes its other coordinates.

✔ Tips

- When modifying a line (or a wall) in the Object Info palette, you have the option of switching to polar coordinates and changing the L or A value (**Figure 3.89**).

- Rounded rectangles have a pop-up menu for corner configuration and edit boxes for the corner radiuses (**Figure 3.90**).

Figure 3.87 Simple objects can be rescaled in the Object Info palette by entering new values in the ΔX and ΔY (Mac) or ±X and ±Y (Windows) fields.

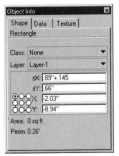

Figure 3.88 You can change the shape of an object by changing the dimensions of its bounding box on the Object Info palette. Don't underestimate the convenience of using arithmetic expressions to do so.

Figure 3.89 Polar coordinates are a handy option for lines and walls; they give you direct control of length and direction.

Figure 3.90 Set the corner style and the corner diameters of rounded rectangles in the Object Info palette.

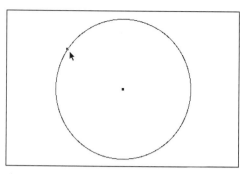

Figure 3.91 A circle has one handle on the circumference (for resizing) and another at the middle (for dragging it around).

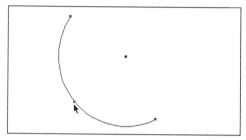

Figure 3.92 Arcs have the same handles as circles, plus one more on each end of the arc for changing the sweep.

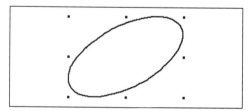

Figure 3.93 When you put eight handles on an object, the corner ones rescale the object in two directions; the non-corner ones rescale in only one dimension.

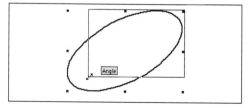

Figure 3.94 You can rescale an object symmetrically by holding down the Shift key as you drag a corner.

- Circles have one handle on the circumference that you can grab and drag to resize the object (**Figure 3.91**).

- Arcs have a handle at the midpoint of the segment to change the radius and handles at the ends of the segment that can be dragged to change their start and end points (**Figure 3.92**).

- Choose Eight Selection Handles on the Edit tab of the VectorWorks Display Edit Preferences dialog box and the four non-corner handles on each side of an object scale objects in only one dimension (**Figure 3.93**).

- Grab a corner handle and hold down the Shift key while you drag it to scale the objects symmetrically on both axes (**Figure 3.94**).

Offsets

Creating an offset from an object lies some-where on the boundary between resizing and reshaping, which we will address in the next section. An offset can be either larger or smaller than the original, but it is created by drawing a shape equidistant from it at all points rather than as a proportional transformation.

Offsets are useful for drawing walls (intricate or simple), for creating clearance distances between mating parts, for drawing thin shells, fancy patterns of parallel lines, and so on (**Figure 3.95**).

To create an offset from an object:

1. Select the object you want to offset

2. Click the Offset tool on the Editing palette (**Figure 3.96**).

   The pointer becomes a small cross.

3. On the Mode bar, click the Offset by Distance button to create the offset at a preset distance (on either side) from the original

   or

   Click the Offset by Point button to set the distance between the original and the copy with a mouse click (**Figure 3.97**).

4. On the Mode Bar, click the Offset Tool Preferences button

   The Offset Tool Preferences dialog box opens (**Figure 3.98**).

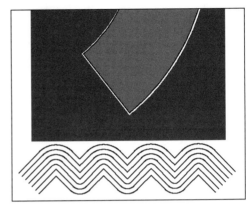

Figure 3.95 Decorative friezes and close-fitting parts are good applications for the Offset tool.

Figure 3.96 The Offset tool on the Editing palette.

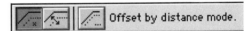

Figure 3.97 There are two modes for the Offset tool: Distance and Point.

Figure 3.98 The Offset Tool Preferences dialog box has only one field and one checkbox.

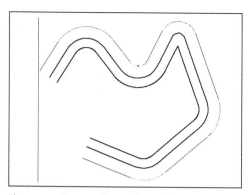

Figure 3.99 Once you have selected the object you want to offset, click to show on which side you want the offset and (if you are in Offset by Distance mode) how far away it should be.

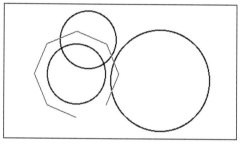

Figure 3.100 Even though all three circles are selected for multiple offset, only the furthest back (the lower left) is previewed.

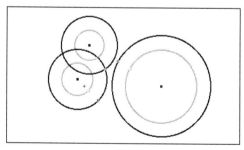

Figure 3.101 The lower-left circle controls the offsets of all the objects. Clicking inside it (but outside the others) puts the offsets inside all of them.

5. In the Offset field of the Offset Tool Preferences dialog box, enter the distance you want to place between the original and the offset shape (when the Offset by Distance mode is used).

If you want to copy several objects at once, check the Multiple Objects checkbox. The position of the offset will be controlled by the rearmost object selected.

Click OK.

6. If you are operating in Offset by Distance mode, click on one side or the other of the selected object to set the direction of the offset and create the new object. (**Figure 3.99**)

or

If you are operating in the Offset by Point mode, click in the drawing area and drag the mouse as the offset is previewed to set the direction and the distance between the original and the offset. Then, click again to complete the procedure.

✔ Tips

■ When you are creating offsets from multiple objects, only the object controlling the offset is previewed (**Figure 3.100**).

■ Because the back object controls how the offset objects relate to the originals, you will find that although you clicked outside one of the other objects, its offset is nonetheless drawn inside (**Figure 3.101**).

■ Offset objects are placed in the active layer, regardless of the layer inhabited by the originals, but they have the originals' classes and attributes.

OFFSETS

Reshaping Objects

The tools on the 2D Tools palette—which include the Split, Trim, and Shear tools—are great for creating relatively simple objects and even relatively complex polygons and poly-lines. But you will generally find that cutting up and stretching objects and putting various pieces together to build more complex shapes is the most efficient way to do things.

To split an object:

1. On the Editing palette, click the Split tool (**Figure 3.102**).

   The pointer becomes a small cross.

2. On the Mode bar, click either the Split by Point mode button, or the Split by Line button (**Figure 3.103**).

   Splitting by point breaks one path at one point; splitting with a line can divide many in one action.

3. With Split by Point selected, click on an object where you want to divide it in two (**Figure 3.104**)

   or

   Choose the Split by Line mode and draw the line that will divide all the objects it crosses (**Figure 3.105**).

Trimming objects to one another:

1. On the Editing palette, click the Trim tool (**Figure 3.106**).

2. In the drawing area, click on the part of an object you want to delete.

   The pointer turns to a pointing finger when it snaps to the object, and the part of the object between two intersecting lines disappears (**Figure 3.107**). If the object is not bounded, the whole thing is removed.

Figure 3.102 The Split tool.

Figure 3.103 The Mode bar has the Split by Point and Split by Line mode buttons.

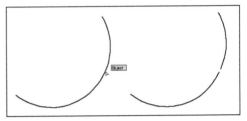
Figure 3.104 With the Split by Point mode selected, just click on the object at the point at which you want to cut it.

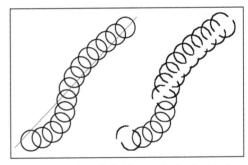
Figure 3.105 In its Split by Line mode, the Split tool cuts everything through which the line passes (parts separated for illustration).

Figure 3.106 The Trim tool on the Editing palette.

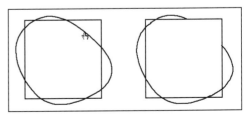
Figure 3.107 The Trim tool removes part the object you touch that is bounded by other objects.

Figure 3.108 The Shear tool on the Editing palette.

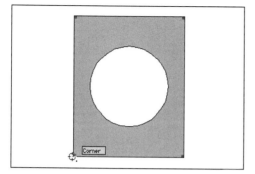

Figure 3.109 Click to set an anchor, or fulcrum point.

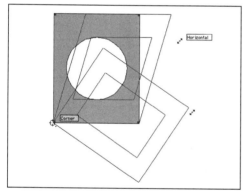

Figure 3.110 As you move the mouse, the object will be deformed along both the *x* and *y* axes while the fulcrum remains fixed.

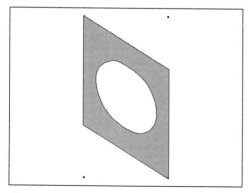

Figure 3.111 The final sheared (a.k.a., skewed) object.

Like the Resize tool, the Shear tool is hard to use with any precision, but it is useful for creating illustrative distortions of objects. Some folks use it as a quick and dirty way of getting perspective effects. (In some other CAD applications, it is called the Skew tool.)

To shear an object:

1. Select the objects you want to shear.

2. Click the Shear tool on the Editing palette (**Figure 3.108**).

   The pointer becomes the bombsight.

3. In the drawing area, click the point you want to anchor as the fixed point of the shear (**Figure 3.109**).

4. Click again in the drawing area to set a handle to shear the objects.

   Drag the mouse to get the effect you want (**Figure 3.110**). Click again to complete the action (**Figure 3.111**).

The 2D Selection tool is often the easiest way to modify an object, but it doesn't let you reshape polygons or polylines except to adjust the size of their bounding boxes. For this purpose, the 2D Reshape tool is easy to use and versatile. Actually, it's a whole collection of tools, and is managed from the Mode bar (**Figure 3.112**).

To reshape a polygon or polyline by moving its control points:

1. On the Editing palette, click the 2D Reshape tool (**Figure 3.113**).

   The pointer becomes a center mark.

2. Click the object you want to modify.

   Handles are displayed for vertices and center points according to the geometry of the object (**Figure 3.114**).

3. On the Mode bar, click the Move Polygon Handles button.

   The pointer will change to the double-headed arrow when it snaps to a vertex and will display a cue naming the type of point.

4. Click the mouse on the handle you want to move and drag it to a new location (**Figure 3.115**).

   The polygon or polyline is reshaped (**Figure 3.116**).

✔ Tips

■ The pointer cues that the 2D Reshape tool displays are as follows (**Figure 3.117**):

   A center point's cue is "Center."

   A corner point reads "Corner" ("Point," for a polygon).

   A Bézier point reads "Bézier."

   A cubic spline point reads "Fit."

   A circular fillet point reads "Arc."

Figure 3.112 The Mode bar for the 2D Reshape tool has five subtools, four vertex modes, and a preferences button.

Figure 3.113 The 2D Reshape tool on the Editing palette.

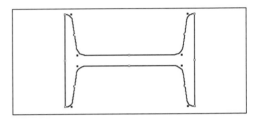

Figure 3.114 Instead of the normal handles, the object displays its vertex and center point handles when you select it with the 2D Reshape tool.

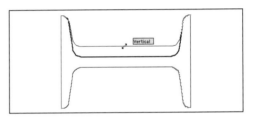

Figure 3.115 You can drag any handle to a new location to reshape the object.

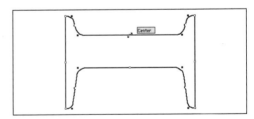

Figure 3.116 Once you have the vertices where you want them, click again to complete the operation.

Figure 3.117 The different modes that make up the 2D Reshape tool all use the same cursor cues to identify the points to which they have snapped.

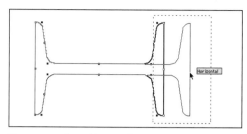

Figure 3.118 Stretching an I-beam is easy when you draw a marquee around one end of it and gently pull.

Figure 3.119 The rotating arrows cursor shows that you are about to change the vertex to the type selected on the Mode bar. The cursor label indicates the existing vertex type.

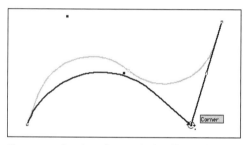

Figure 3.120 Set the radius to 0 in the Fillet Preferences dialog box to let the geometry of the object figure the maximum possible radius. Too bad you can't do that with the Fillet tool.

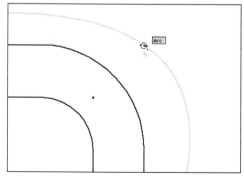

Figure 3.121 Changing an existing fillet (arc) point to a cubic vertex point reshapes the polyline.

- You can select multiple points to move by dragging a marquee around the points and dragging them as a group. Hold down the Option (Mac) or Alt (Windows) key, and the pointer changes to a lasso that lets you drag an irregular selection set (**Figure 3.118**).

To reshape a polyline by converting its vertex points:

1. On the Editing palette, click the 2D Reshape tool.

   The pointer becomes a center mark.

2. On the Mode bar, click the Change Vertex Mode button.

   When the pointer snaps to a vertex, it becomes a pair of rotating arrows, and a tag displays the vertex type (**Figure 3.119**).

3. On the Mode bar, click the type to which you want to convert the selected vertex.

   Set the radius to be used in the circular arc mode by clicking the Fillet Preferences button and entering the value in the Fillet Radius edit box of the Fillet Settings dialog box.

   A setting of 0 will give you the maximum radius possible given the lengths of the adjacent segments (**Figure 3.120**).

4. Click the vertex you want to transform.

   The vertex changes to the selected type and the object changes accordingly (**Figure 3.121**).

RESHAPING OBJECTS

The 2D Reshape tool also gives you a way to add or remove vertices on polygons and polylines.

To add a vertex to a polyline or polygon:

1. On the Editing palette, click the 2D Reshape tool.

2. On the Mode bar, click the Add Vertex mode button.

   When the pointer snaps to a vertex or segment center, it becomes an arrow with solid boxes on either side and a tag displays the type of the existing point.

3. On the Mode bar, click the type of vertex you wish to insert. Set the radius of the arc point, if that's your choice.

4. Click on one of the points adjacent to where you want to place the new vertex, and drag to the new location (**Figure 3.122**).

   The point is placed and the object modified (**Figure 3.123**).

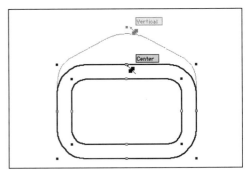

Figure 3.122 Adding a vertex requires selecting the type you want to insert and then starting at a vertex or center point and dragging it where you want it to go.

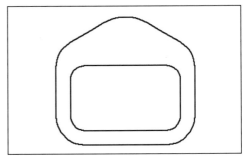

Figure 3.123 You can set the radius of the inserted arc point before you start or, midstream, press "O" to open the Fillet Settings dialog box to change the radius. Then complete the operation with the new radius set.

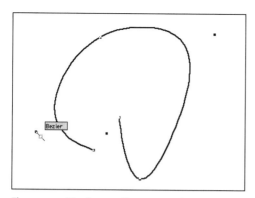

Figure 3.124 The Remove Vertex cursor becomes an arrow with a single open box when it finds a vertex it can remove.

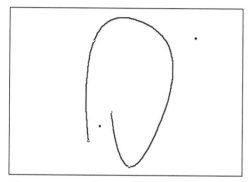

Figure 3.125 Removing the Bézier vertex reshapes the polyline.

To remove a vertex from a polyline or polygon:

1. On the Editing palette, click the 2D Reshape tool.

2. On the Mode bar, click the Delete Vertex mode button.

    When the pointer snaps to a vertex or segment center, it becomes an arrow with a single open box; a tag displays the point type (**Figure 3.124**).

3. Click on the vertex you want to remove.

    The vertex is removed and the object reshaped (**Figure 3.125**).

✔ Tip

■ Changing one of the corner points of a polygon to a curve vertex converts the object to a polyline. A polyline becomes a polygon when all its vertices are corner points.

Reshaping Objects on the Object Info Palette

Most of 2D editing operations are managed using the Editing palette and the commands on the menu bar, but you also have the option of using the Object Info palette as an object editing tool.

Figure 3.126 The Move menu lets you choose between moving just a vertex and moving the whole object using the selected vertex as the control point.

To reshape a polyline or polygon from the Object Info palette:

1. Select the object you want to modify.

2. Choose Palette > Object Info, or press Command-I (Mac) or Ctrl-I (Windows) to open the Object Info palette.

3. On the Object Info palette, click the Move pop-up menu and select Vertex Only (**Figure 3.126**).

4. On the Object Info palette, use the Vertex navigation buttons to select the vertex you want to modify.

   The arrow buttons sequentially select the vertexes in either direction; the center button highlights the currently selected vertex (**Figure 3.127**).

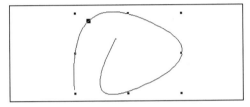

Figure 3.127 As you click the arrow buttons, the vertexes on the object are highlighted successively so you can select the one you want to work with.

5. Enter a new *x* or *y* coordinate in the X or Y field, and press Enter to move the selected vertex on that axis (**Figure 3.128**).

6. Click Add Vertex to place a new corner vertex midway between the selected vertex and the next one (**Figure 3.129**).

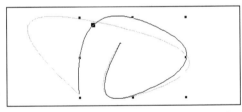

Figure 3.128 Entering a new *x* value for the selected vertex moves it to the new location and reshapes the polyline.

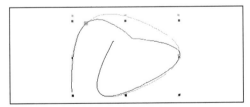

Figure 3.129 When you use the Object Info palette to insert a new vertex, it's always a corner and always midway between the active vertex and the next one.

OBJECT INFO PALETTE RESHAPING

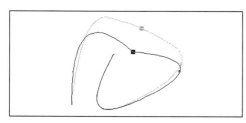

Figure 3.130 By changing the new corner point to an arc point, setting its fillet radius to 0 (for maximum), and moving it up to −10.000, you get this polyline.

Figure 3.131 If, instead of adding a vertex when we did, we had clicked Delete Vertex, this is what we would see.

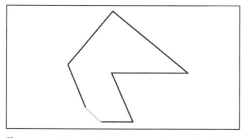

Figure 3.132 We can close an open polygon by clicking the Closed checkbox on the Object Info palette.

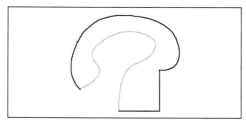

Figure 3.133 Clicking the Hide Next Edge or Show Next Edge button toggles the visibility of the part of the polyline bounded by corner points.

7. Use the controls in the Object Info palette to change the vertex type and to reposition it as required (**Figure 3.130**).

8. On the Object Info palette, use the Vertex arrow buttons to select a vertex you want to remove and click Delete Vertex.

   The vertex is removed and the object reshaped (**Figure 3.131**).

9. Click the Closed checkbox (for polygons only) to automatically draw the line between the first and last vertexes and close the figure (**Figure 3.132**).

   Uncheck the Closed box to remove the last segment of a closed polygon.

10. Click Hide Next Edge or Show Next Edge to toggle the visibility of the line segment that lies between corner points (polylines only) (**Figure 3.133**).

11. Click Set Arc Radius (when an arc vertex is selected) to open the Fillet Settings dialog box, and change the radius of the arc.

    Enter 0 to set the arc to the maximum possible for the adjacent segment lengths.

To reshape a circle or arc on the Object Info palette:

1. Select the circle or arc you want to modify.

2. On the Object Info palette, change the values in the Radius or Diameter field to change the size of the object (**Figure 3.134**).

3. Type a new value into the Sweep, Start, or End field to change the length and orientation of the arc.

   Pressing Tab or Enter or clicking in another field effects the change.

✔ Tip

- The Sweep and End values are interdependent, so changing one changes the other; the Start value remains fixed. Changing the Start value changes the Sweep but leaves the End value unchanged.

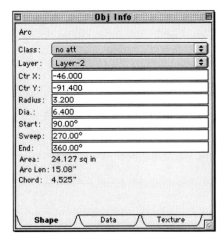

Figure 3.134 The Object Info palette for circles has fields for Radius, Diameter, and Sweep; the version for arcs also has edit boxes for Start and End.

Figure 3.135 The top line was drawn with the Freehand tool and has 118 vertices; the lower line has been smoothed with Bézier curves and has only 21 well-placed control points.

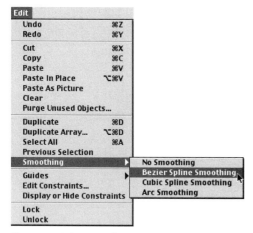

Figure 3.136 The Smoothing menu is under the Edit heading on the menu bar.

Figure 3.137 You can use the Smoothing command for any polygon or polyline, and it will make all the vertexes the same type. It does not reduce the number, however. Vertex types give varying results on different shapes.

Smoothing

The Smoothing commands convert all the vertex points to one type. Applied to a line drawn with the Freehand tool, the commands also eliminate many of the vertices on the line thanks to a clever algorithm that calculates which ones are superfluous (**Figure 3.135**).

To smooth an object:

1. Select the object you want to smooth.

2. Choose Edit > Smoothing and select one of the options from the menu as follows (**Figure 3.136**):

   Choose "No Smoothing" to make all the vertices corner points.

   Choose "Bézier Spline Smoothing" or "Cubic Spline Smoothing" to set all vertices to those types.

   Choose "Arc Smoothing" to make all the vertices circular arcs using the radius in the Fillet Settings dialog box (**Figure 3.137**).

SMOOTHING

Joining Lines

Despite its name, the Join command doesn't exactly join lines; it just extends or trims them to a nice neat intersection. You can also join the lines with a fillet or chamfer (see below).

To join lines by command:

1. Select the lines you want to intersect. Choose either a pair of nonparallel lines or a pair of nonparallel double lines.

2. Choose Tool > Join > Join, or press Command-J (Mac) or Ctrl-J (Windows). The lines are extended or trimmed at their intersections

   or

   Choose Tool > Join > Join (no trim), or press Command-Option-J (Mac) or Ctrl-Alt-J (Windows), to extend lines to their intersection without trimming any overlap. (**Figure 3.138**)

   or

   Choose Tool > Join > Join and Fillet, or press Command-Shift-J (Mac) or Ctrl-Shift-J (Windows), to join a pair of double lines with fillets. The fillet joining the outer pair of lines is controlled by the current value in the Fillet Settings dialog box; the inner pair of lines is joined by a parallel arc (**Figure 3.139**).

✔ Tips

■ To set the fillet radius for this tool, you have to open the Fillet Settings dialog box from another tool. Try choosing the Fillet, Polyline, or 2D Reshape tool and opening the dialog box from the Mode bar.

■ Actually, the double-line functions of the Join command work with any four lines as long as two of them are parallel. But the results may look a little screwy.

Figure 3.138 A pair of single lines (left) can be brought together and trimmed (center) or intersected without trimming by the Join Command.

Figure 3.139 Double lines can be brought to their intersection and trimmed or filleted together with the Join command.

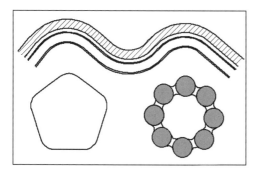

Figure 3.140 The Fillet tool is good for many things besides placing fillets at the intersections of lines.

Figure 3.141 The Fillet tool and the Chamfer tool are related in function and share a location on the default palette.

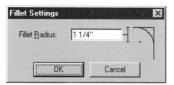

Figure 3.142 The Fillet Preferences dialog box is the same one used by the Polyline tool and the Object Info palette for setting arc radiuses.

Fillets and Chamfers

A *fillet* is nothing more than an arc object automatically placed between two objects according to the settings in the dialog box. Fillets can be drawn between curves and polylines as well as between straight lines. The Fillet tool is an excellent way to create wavy walls and, in general, soft-edged forms (**Figure 3.140**).

A *chamfer* cuts a vertex into two vertices, and spreads them apart evenly. If the vertex is on a shape's corner, the chamfer nips the corner at a 45-degree angle. It's like creating a beveled edge in carpentry or cabinet making.

In detail drawings (kitchen cabinets, for instance) and mechanical drawings (extrusions, weldments, castings, and so on), you'll probably want to be able to add fillets at the intersections and to chamfer some of the sharp corners, to make them a little more user-friendly.

The Fillet and Chamfer tools share a berth as flyout options on the default 2D Tools palette.

To draw a fillet between two objects:

1. On the 2D Tools palette, click the Fillet tool (**Figure 3.141**).

   If it's hidden under the Chamfer tool, click the Chamfer tool and hold down the mouse while you drag to the Fillet tool.

2. On the Mode bar, click on the Fillet Preferences button to open the Fillet Settings dialog box (**Figure 3.142**).

3. In the Fillet Settings dialog box, type the radius for the fillet in the edit box.

continues on next page

4. On the Mode bar, click one of the three modes in which the fillet can be applied:

Choose Fillet mode to place a fillet on the lines without affecting them.

Choose Fillet and Split mode to place the fillet and break the lines where it intersects them. VectorWorks automatically extends the lines.

Choose the Fillet and Trim mode to extend or trim the lines to their intersection with the fillet (**Figure 3.143**).

5. Click on one of the lines to start the fillet.

The pointer changes to a small cross when it snaps to the object, and it sketches a thin line as you move to the second object (**Figure 3.144**).

6. Click on the second line.

The fillet is drawn and the lines extended and/or trimmed according to the mode selection.

Figure 3.143 The three options on the Mode bar (left to right): add a fillet but change nothing else; add the fillet, extend lines where necessary, and trim the excess, leaving the pieces in place, and extend and trim to fit.

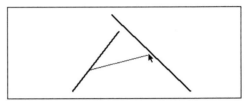

Figure 3.144 To create the fillet, just click on the first object, drag to the second, and click again.

✔ Tips

- The Fillet tool is also part of the default Wall palette, and fillets (but not chamfers) can be applied to walls to create a round wall object (see Chapter 9, "Architectural Applications").

- If a fillet is drawn between two lines that are not the same style, the fillet will be the same style as the first line clicked. But fillets involving other kinds of objects will take their attributes from the Attributes palette (or the class attributes, if they are assigned on creation).

- While you are drawing a fillet, press I to open the Fillet Settings dialog box and change the radius without interrupting the operation.

FILLETS AND CHAMFERS

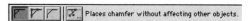

Figure 3.145 The Chamfer tool mode bar is pretty much like the one for fillets.

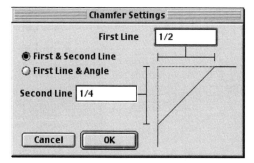

Figure 3.146 In the Chamfer Settings dialog box, there are two ways of configuring the chamfer.

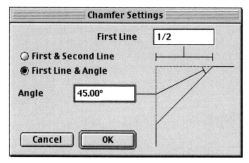

Figure 3.147 The First Line & Angle approach to defining the chamfer allows you to configure chamfers the way they will probably be cut in the shop.

Figure 3.148 Chamfer modes are much like those of their rounded cousins, the fillets.

The Chamfer tool is a little more limited than the Fillet tool; chamfers can be placed only on straight lines (including those that comprise a polygon), and they can't be used with walls. But when you're looking for a way to cut corners, the Chamfer tool is the way to go.

To place a chamfer:

1. On the 2D Tools palette, click the Chamfer tool.

2. On the Mode bar, click on the Chamfer Preferences button to open the Chamfer Settings dialog box (**Figure 3.145**).

3. In the Chamfer Settings dialog box, do one of the following:

   Click the First & Second Line radio button and enter values for the distance that the chamfer line should be offset from the intersection (or the projected intersection) on each of the affected lines (**Figure 3.146**).

   Click the First Line & Angle radio button and enter the offset from the intersection along the first line selected and the angle between it and the chamfer line (**Figure 3.147**).

4. On the Mode bar, click one of the three modes in which the chamfer can be applied:

   Choose Chamfer mode to place a chamfer on the lines without affecting them.

   Choose Chamfer and Split mode to place the chamfer and break the lines where it intersects them. VectorWorks automatically extends the lines.

   Choose the Chamfer and Trim mode to extend or trim the lines to their intersection with the chamfer (**Figure 3.148**).

continues on next page

FILLETS AND CHAMFERS

5. Click on one of the lines to start the chamfer.

The pointer changes to a small cross when it snaps to the line, and it sketches a dotted line as you move to the second line.

6. Click on the second line.

The chamfer is drawn and the lines are extended and/or trimmed according to the mode selection.

The order in which you click the objects to chamfer is important when the chamfer is asymmetrical (**Figure 3.149** and **Figure 3.150**).

✔ Tip

■ The First Line & Angle method may correspond better to the actual capabilities of a cabinet shop than the First & Second Line approach, even though the latter may give better results for a variety of angled joints.

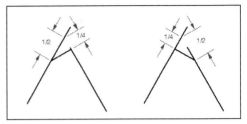

Figure 3.149 Cutting a chamfer 1/2 inch by 1/4 inch and clicking on the left line and then the right has a different effect than reversing the order.

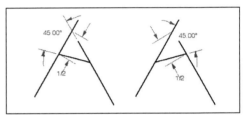

Figure 3.150 Setting the chamfer tool for 1/2 inch by 45 degrees and clicking first on the left line and then on the right gives you the figure on the left. Reverse the process and you get the opposite result.

Figure 3.151 The Connect/Combine tool on the Editing palette.

Figure 3.152 The first two modes on the Mode bar are connection modes. The third is the combination mode discussed below.

Combining Objects

The objects the VectorWorks tools create can be used as "primitives" from which you build more complex forms—not to mention 3D objects (see Chapter 7, "Creating 3D Objects")—by combining them in a variety of ways. The most obvious operation is simply adding shapes, but the other Boolean operations that use one object to clip others or that find the intersections among objects are also very useful.

The Connect/Combine tool is new with Version 9 and is a fine addition to the application. It has three modes (controlled as usual from the Mode bar) and does everything the Join command does and much more. (The exception is that it doesn't handle double lines.) The tool also works with curves, polygons, and polylines and with NURBS (for these wonderfully named "Non-Uniform Rational B-Spline curves," see Chapter 7, "Creating 3D Objects").

For clarity, we will separately discuss the connect and combine functions of the Connect/Combine tool.

To connect lines using the Connect/Combine tool:

1. On the Editing palette, click the Connect/Combine tool (**Figure 3.151**).

2. On the Mode bar, choose one of the two connection modes:

Choose Single Object Connect to extend the first line clicked to its point of intersection with another object.

Choose the Dual Object Connect mode to extend both lines to the point of intersection and trim them there (this is also what the Join command does) (**Figure 3.152**).

continues on next page

3. In the drawing area, click on the first object you want to connect or combine (**Figure 3.153**).

A dotted line is drawn from where you click to the pointer.

4. Click on the second object.

The objects are extended and trimmed according to the mode setting of the tool (**Figure 3.154**).

To combine lines using the Connect/Combine tool:

1. On the Editing palette, click the Connect/Combine tool.

2. Choose the Dual Object Combine mode.

3. Click on the first object you want to combine.

A dotted line is drawn from the point at which you clicked to the pointer.

4. Click on the second object.

If you click the end points of the polylines and NURBS curves, the Connect/Combine Options dialog box opens and you can click either the Mid-Point or the Blend radio button (**Figure 3.155**).

The Mid-Point option moves the end points of both lines to the midpoint between them. The Blend Option creates a third curve to smoothly connect the two (**Figure 3.156**).

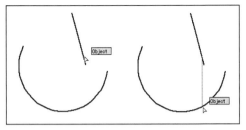

Figure 3.153 Click on the first object and then on the second. A dotted line is drawn while you drag to help you see what you're doing.

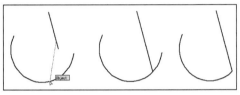

Figure 3.154 Clicking on the line and then on the arc extends the line to the arc, but it trims the arc only if the Dual Object Connect mode is selected (right).

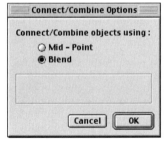

Figure 3.155 When you are connecting or combining curves, VectorWorks needs to know how you want to tie up the loose ends.

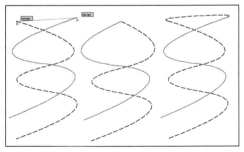

Figure 3.156 When you click the ends as shown, the two options are MidPoint (center) and Blend (right).

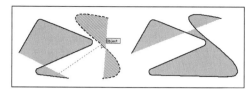

Figure 3.157 When you combine (as opposed to merely connect) two objects, the resulting polyline take on the attributes of the first one clicked.

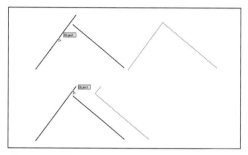

Figure 3.158 The side of the projected intersection on which you click decides how the lines are extended and clipped.

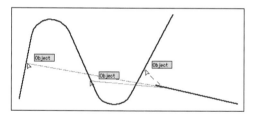

Figure 3.159 The segment of the polyline on which you click is the one to which the line will be extended.

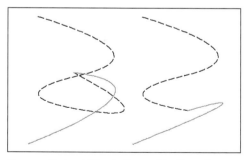

Figure 3.160 In addition to the combinations shown in Figure 3.156, depending on where you click your mouse, there are many other possible combinations of complex curves.

If the combination is possible, it will be made and the new single object will be a polygon or polyline (or a NURBS curve) with the attributes of the first object (**Figure 3.157**).

✔ Tips

- Where you click on a line will determine which way an intersection is made if the situation is ambiguous. (**Figure 3.158**).

- Where on the second object you click will determine the intersection point if there are more than one possible points (**Figure 3.159**).

- Complex figures may require you to click at a particular part of the object to get the result you're after, and you may have to try several times to get the tool to perform the way you want (**Figure 3.160**).

- Dual Object Combine doesn't work across layers; the other modes do.

- The Dual Object Combine mode won't extend a line to an object if it can't in fact combine them; choose one of the other modes for this purpose.

COMBINING OBJECTS

Boolean Operations

The standard Boolean operators are used for developing complex surfaces. You can add surfaces, intersect them, and clip them.

The simplest way to combine 2D surfaces is to add them together. Any overlapping (or contiguous) surfaces can be combined into a single surface. Surfaces need not be closed shapes; included are arcs and open and closed polygons and polylines, as well as rectangles, ovals, and circles. But objects that are parts of groups cannot be combined; text, symbols, and plug-in objects are also exempt.

To add surfaces:

1. Select the surfaces you want to add (**Figure 3.161**).

2. Choose Tool > Add Surface.

   The selected surfaces are added to the one farthest back on the uppermost layer, and the new object takes its attributes from that surface (**Figure 3.162**).

Two other commands on the Tool menu create new surfaces more or less subtractively. The Intersect command uses the front-most object (both by layer and within the layer) to create a new object where it overlaps another selected object. The Clip command uses the same front object to modify the underlying objects by cutting away the parts of them that it overlaps.

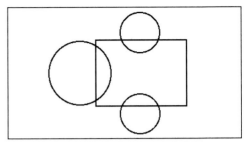

Figure 3.161 Adding surfaces begins with selecting a number of overlapping or adjacent surfaces.

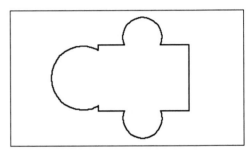

Figure 3.162 When you add surfaces, they are combined into a single polygon or polyline.

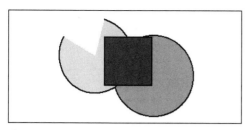

Figure 3.163 Intersection creates new surface wherever the front object overlaps other selected objects.

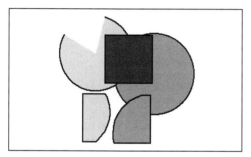

Figure 3.164 The square at the front of the stack creates new objects (moved for clarity) wherever it overlaps the others.

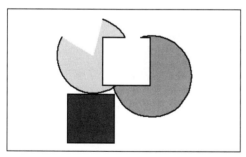

Figure 3.165 The square (moved to display results) cuts away the objects below wherever it overlaps them.

To create new surfaces by intersection:

1. Select the surfaces from which you want to generate new shapes (**Figure 3.163**).

2. Use the Send (Forward/Backward) commands on the Tool menu (see Chapter 5, "Using Layers and Classes") to get the desired "cutter" to the front of the stack. You have to move it into the top layer if it is not already there.

3. Choose Tool > Intersect Surface.

   New surfaces are created in the layer of the object that did the cutting; however, they have the attributes (including the class) of the surface from which they were cut (**Figure 3.164**).

To clip selected objects with a surface:

1. Select the objects you want to modify.

2. Use the Send (Forward/Backward) commands on the Tool menu to get the desired "cutter" to the front of the stack. You have to move it into the top layer if it is not already there.

3. Choose Tool > Clip Surface.

   The front surface remains unchanged, but the selected objects behind it are all cut away (as if punched by the front one). No new surfaces are created (**Figure 3.165**).

✔ Tip

■ The Intersect command trims off selected line objects extending beyond the boundary of the cutting object. The Clip object deletes the parts within the boundary.

BOOLEAN OPERATIONS

The Clipping tool uses a rectangular marquee instead of an existing object as a punch and operates in three modes (**Figure 3.166**). You can choose to keep the part left behind when the area within the marquee is punched out, the part within the marquee, or both parts (**Figure 3.167**).

The Clipping tool is a good choice when you want to quickly clear a space for text or separate a piece of an object so you can move it or give it different attributes. (**Figure 3.168**).

To modify surfaces with the Clipping tool:

1. Select the surfaces you want to modify.

   Leave the object you do not want to clip unselected.

2. On the Editing palette, click the Clipping tool.

3. Click in the drawing area to mark the first corner of the marquee.

   As you draw the marquee, it appears as a dotted rectangle (**Figure 3.169**).

Figure 3.166 The Clipping tool on the Editing palette.

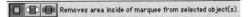

Figure 3.167 The Clipping tool offers three modes of operation: Remove inside marquee, remove outside marquee, split at marquee boundary.

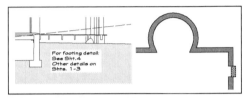

Figure 3.168 Selecting the patterned polygon and clipping away an area opens up some space for the text box (left). Using the Clipping tool in its Splits at Boundaries mode defines a detail (right).

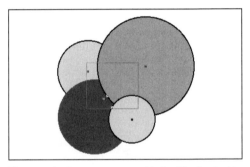

Figure 3.169 Draw a marquee with the Clipping tool to demarcate the area to be clipped according to the setting on the Mode bar. Unselected objects (here, the darkest circle) will not be clipped.

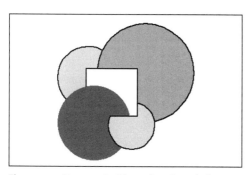

Figure 3.170 Removes Inside mode cuts a window through the selected objects.

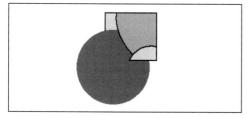

Figure 3.171 Removes Outside mode cuts away everything on the selected objects except what's inside the marquee.

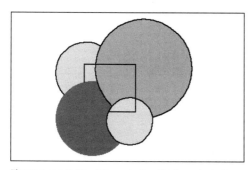

Figure 3.172 Splits at Boundaries divides selected objects at the boundaries of the marquee you drew.

4. On the Mode bar, click the mode you want to use as follows:

   Choose Removes Inside mode to leave what lies outside the marquee (**Figure 3.170**).

   Choose Removes Outside mode to discard all of the selected surfaces except what lies within the marquee (**Figure 3.171**).

   Choose Splits at Boundaries mode to cut out the parts within the marquee and leave it in place (**Figure 3.172**).

5. Click again to complete the marquee and cut the selected objects.

Creating Surfaces by Boundary

The Boolean tools above add, intersect, and clip objects to create new ones. You can also choose any region defined in the drawing area by an assortment of lines and the edges of other objects and turn that region into an object in its own right.

To create a new surface from an enclosed region:

1. In the drawing area, select the objects that define an enclosed region.

2. Choose Tool > Combine Into Surface.

   The pointer becomes a paint bucket (**Figure 3.173**).

3. Click the pointer in the region that defines the new surface.

   The new surface is created with the active attributes in the active layer and class (**Figure 3.174**).

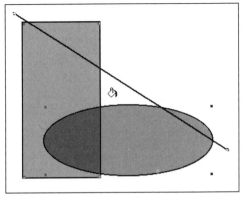

Figure 3.173 After selecting the objects that enclose a region, choose the Combine Into Surface command from the Tool palette. The cursor becomes a paint bucket.

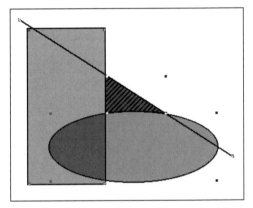

Figure 3.174 Pour the paint bucket into the area you want to define as a new surface and voilà! A new surface is created.

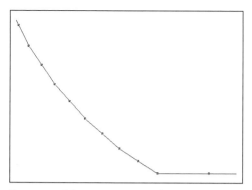

Figure 3.175 When you convert an object to a polygon, it usually has enough segments on the curves that the difference is not too apparent. Here's what you see when you zoom in with the corner points displayed.

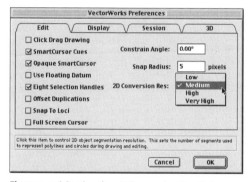

Figure 3.176 Setting the 2D Conversion Resolution up or down controls the number of segments used to convert a curve to a polygon.

The Disintegration of Objects

As important as it is to learn to put things together, the ability to take things apart—or at least to convert them to simpler components—is not to be underrated.

There are several reasons you might want to do this. In general, curves are harder for your computer to model so breaking them down into lots of straight segments can speed up processing considerably. In most cases, the segments will be short enough that you won't even notice the difference.

The Create Wall from Polygon and Create Roof from Polygon commands VectorWorks provides for architectural work just don't work with curves. If you want to create curvaceous structures, you will need to convert the curves to polygons before you can use them to draw curved walls and roofs.

To convert objects to polygons:

1. In the drawing area, select the objects to be modified.

2. Choose Tool > Convert to Polygons

   The object is converted to a polygon (**Figure 3.175**).

   If it has curved edges, the number of straight segments used to draw that curve is determined by the 2D Conversion Res setting on the Edit tab of the VectorWorks Preferences dialog box (**Figure 3.176**).

   The Low setting will usually give a rough approximation of the original; the higher settings will give a better rendition, but at the cost of increasing the file size.

✔ Tip

■ Choose Convert Copy to Polygons to preserve the original figure and convert a copy to polygons.

THE DISINTEGRATION OF OBJECTS

Converting objects to lines works the same way as converting them to polygons except that each segment is an individual object. It's the same as converting to polygons and then choosing Decompose Curve (see below).

To convert objects to lines:

1. In the drawing area, select the objects to be modified.

2. Choose Tool > Convert to lines.

   The object is converted to line objects.

   If it has curved edges, the number of lines used to draw that curve is determined by the 2D Conversion Res setting on the Edit tab of the VectorWorks Preferences dialog box.

Another approach to breaking down an object is to choose the Decompose Curve command. Instead of turning polyline objects into collections of straight segments, this command breaks them into lines, arcs, and elementary polyline particles made up of one Bézier vertex between two corner vertices. The command can also be used to break down rectangles (including rounded rectangles), polygons, and ovals.

To decompose an object:

1. Select the objects to be broken down.

2. Choose Tool > Decompose Curve.

   The objects splits into simple parts (**Figure 3.177**).

Figure 3.177 Decomposing one of the clipped shapes from above yields 4 arc objects and 5 lines–including two with zero length at the top and bottom of the figure.

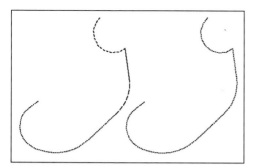

Figure 3.178 Select the objects you want to assemble and choose the Compose Curve command from the Tool menu. If the objects are in the same layer and have their end points touching, a new polygon or polyline is created.

You can use the Compose Curve command to connect a chain of straight and curved segments that have their end points touching to get a single polyline or polygon.

A decomposed object can be resurrected by the Compose Curve command, except that the corner points added when the curve was broken down are still there and the Cubic vertex points that were converted to Bézier vertexes are not returned to their previous status. A deconstructed rectangle or oval doesn't regain its previous identity.

To assemble an object from pieces:

1. Select the objects with contiguous end points that you want to integrate into a single object

2. Choose Tool > Compose Curve.

   The objects are joined as a single object with the attributes of the object furthest back in the stack. If the selection included curved objects, the new object is a polyline; if it was all straight-edged objects, the result is a new polygon (**Figure 3.178**).

✔ Tip

■ Objects have to be in the same layer (though not necessarily the active one) to be composed into a single object.

The Drafting Tools

Finally, two more commands fall into the category of taking things apart: Line into Segments and Arc into Segments. They are found on the Drafting Aids submenu under the Tool menu.

To divide a line into segments:

1. Select a line object you want to divide into segments of equal length.

2. Choose Tool > Drafting Aids > Line into Segments.

   The Line into Segments dialog box opens (**Figure 3.179**).

3. In the Options pane on the Line into Segments dialog box, you can do the following:

   Check "Place loci" to place a locus at each division.

   Check "Break line into segments" to cut the line into pieces at the divisions.

   Check "Leave original line intact" to leave a copy of the line in place if you have chosen the "Break line into segments" option. Otherwise, it will have no effect.

4. In the "Number of segments" edit box, type the number of divisions you want to create.

5. Click OK.

   The dialog box closes; the loci are placed (if that option is chosen), and the line is divided into equal segments (if that option is chosen) (**Figure 3.180**).

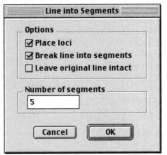

Figure 3.179
The Line into Segments dialog box has three option checkboxes and an edit box for the number of divisions.

Figure 3.180 Starting with the line on the left, you can replace it with loci at the division points, break the line into segments, or do both. You can leave the original line intact or remove it.

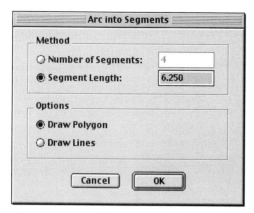

Figure 3.181 The Arc into Segments dialog box has a pane dedicated to method and another in which you choose a polygon or individual lines.

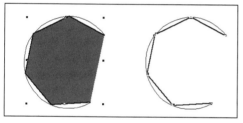

Figure 3.182 Choosing Draw Polygon in the dialog box yields a polygon with whatever settings are current in the Attributes palette. Draw Lines reduces that to a series of joined line objects (right).

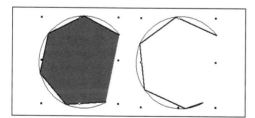

Figure 3.183 Choosing the number of segments into which you want the arc divided always produces segments of even length; if, on the other hand, you set the length of the segment, there may be a short one at one end or the other.

A similar function is provided for circles and arcs. This tool always creates a new object or objects.

To divide an arc into segments:

1. Select the arc or circle you want to segment.

2. Choose Tool > Drafting Aids > Arc into Segments.

   The Arc into Segments dialog box opens (**Figure 3.181**).

3. In the Method pane of the Arc into Segments dialog box, click the Number of Segments radio button and type the number into the edit box

   or

   Click the Segment Length radio button and enter a value in its edit box.

4. In the Options pane, choose Draw Polygon to create a single object

   or

   Click Draw Lines to create the same polygon as contiguous line objects (**Figure 3.182**).

5. Click OK.

   The dialog box closes and the objects are drawn.

If you have chosen the Segment Length method, any remainder will be drawn as a short segment (**Figure 3.183**).

DRAWING

WITH CONSTRAINTS

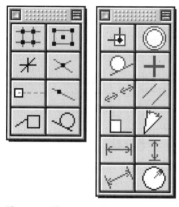

Figure 4.1 The constraints are managed with two palettes: one for the SmartPointer constraints (left) and one for the Parametrics (right).

In the last chapter, we drew some lines and shapes with the mouse, and tried out the more precise modes of creating objects using dialog boxes and using the Data Display bar to enter data points.

But if we used only those methods, we would be drawing with one hand tied behind our backs. In the real-life working environment, the points that define your objects will either be on a regular grid or they will be positioned relative to other objects in the drawing, or both.

To this end, VectorWorks provides two independent sets of helpful drawing tools: Smart-Pointer constraints and Parametric constraints (**Figure 4.1**).

SmartPointer Constraints

When you are creating new objects, Smart-Pointer constraints help you accurately place points without slowing down to type values into dialog boxes or the Data Display bar. As you draw, the SmartPointer automatically jumps to key points in the drawing area (key points you designate when you set up the preferences for the individual constraints). To avoid the chaos of the pointer jumping around uncontrollably, you can choose which constraints are active at any time. And you can control which classes and layers will be available to the SmartPointer, because you can limit the pointer's search to only the relevant objects.

The SmartPointer Constraints palette has eight buttons that can be used in any combination, from a single function through all eight applied at once. (When you're operating in three dimensions, the last two constraints change to adapt to the 3D drawing environment. We will deal with that in Chapter 7, "Creating 3D Objects.")

To set up the preferences for the SmartCursor:

1. Choose File > Preferences > VectorWorks. The VectorWorks Preferences dialog box opens (**Figure 4.2**).

2. On the Edit tab of the VectorWorks Preferences dialog box, click the Smart-Pointer Cues checkbox so that a screen hint will show up when your pointer has found a snap point (**Figure 4.3**). With the box unchecked, the pointer will have a little dot next to it, but no text. (Snap to Grid doesn't present any hints.)

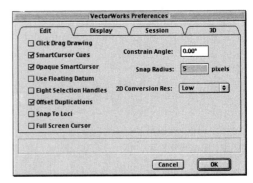

Figure 4.2 The VectorWorks Preferences dialog box controls a lot of preferences; among them are the SmartPointer cues.

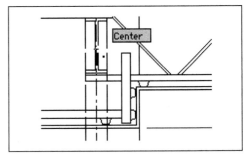

Figure 4.3 The SmartPointer cues tell you which of the many constraints has seized control of your pointer.

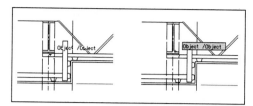

Figure 4.4 Giving your pointer cues an opaque background makes them easier to read.

3. On the Edit tab of the VectorWorks Preferences dialog box, click the Opaque SmartPointer if you want the pointer cues to appear in a little box with a colored background that makes them easier to read—a useful option (**Figure 4.4**).

4. On the Edit tab of the VectorWorks Preferences dialog box, you can also change the Snap Radius for the Smart-Pointer by typing a different value into the edit box.

   The snap radius is the minimum distance (in pixels and therefore not related to the scale of the drawing) the pointer will jump to a nearby snap point.

✔ Tip

■ While setting SmartPointer preferences you are in the VectorWorks Preferences dialog box, you might want to go to the Session tab and uncheck the Use Sound option. This shuts off the little clicking noises the computer makes as your mouse goes past all the potential snap points.

SMARTPOINTER CONSTRAINTS

Snapping to the Grid

The Snap to Grid constraint allows you to place points only at the points on a grid you set up in the Set Grid dialog box unless another active constraint overrides it. This overriding constraint can be either one you create ad hoc using the Data Display bar, or one imposed by the relationship of the pointer position to other objects in the drawing when one of the other constraints on the palette is active.

To set up the dimensions of the snap grid:

1. Choose Page > Set Grid; press Command-8 (Mac) or Ctrl-8 (Windows); or double-click the Snap to Grid button on the Constraints palette.

   The Set Grid dialog box opens (**Figure 4.5**).

2. In the Snap Grid pane of the Set Grid dialog box, set the distance between the points to which the pointer will snap by typing it into the X box.

   If you want the grid to be symmetrical, click the Symmetrical checkbox so that the same value is automatically placed in the Y box. Otherwise, type a value in the Y field to set the distance along that axis.

3. Click OK to close the Set Grid dialog box and accept the settings you have made.

The reference grid is that lattice of light blue lines you see on the screen when you check the Show Grid Lines box in the Grid Options pane of the Set Grid dialog box (**Figure 4.6**). It's there to help you find your snap grid points or to let you quickly add a visible grid to a drawing.

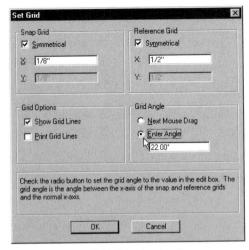

Figure 4.5 The Set Grid dialog box has four panes; together they set the options for the snap grid.

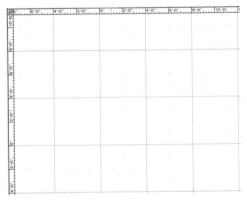

Figure 4.6 The reference grid helps you see what you are doing. You can also use it as a background grid when you print out your work.

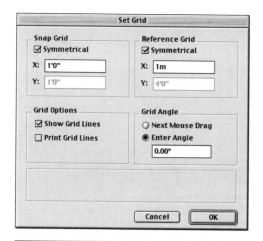

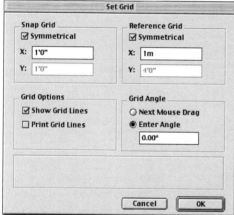

Figure 4.7 VectorWorks automatically converts units you type in with a suffix (top) into the drawing's default units (bottom).

The reference grid has the same angle as the snap grid, and they both originate at the 0,0 point of the drawing, but the reference grid can be set to any dimension you choose. Most often, it refers to the snap grid by being either the same dimension or some multiple of it.

To set up the Reference grid:

1. Choose Page > Set Grid; or press Command-8 (Mac) or Ctrl-8 (Windows); or double-click the Snap to Grid button on the Constraints palette.

    The Set Grid dialog box opens.

2. In the Reference Grid pane of the Set Grid dialog box, set the distance between the lines of the reference grid by typing it into the X box.

    If you want the grid to be symmetrical, click the Symmetrical checkbox so that the same value is automatically placed in the Y box. Otherwise, type a value in the Y field to set the distance along the *y* axis.

3. Click OK.

✔ Tips

■ You can set the reference grid to another system of measurement by following the number you type in the field with the abbreviation for the units you want to use. VectorWorks will make the conversion into the drawing's default units.

    For example, in a drawing that has feet as its primary unit, you can set up a 1-meter reference grid by typing 1m into the X field in the Reference Grid pane. When you click in another field or close the dialog box, that will be converted to 3' 3.37" (**Figure 4.7**).

■ You can't make the reference grid smaller than the snap grid.

SNAPPING TO THE GRID

151

To control the visibility of the reference grid:

1. Choose Page > Set Grid; or press Command-8 (Mac) or Ctrl-8 (Windows); or double-click the Snap to Grid button on the Constraints palette.

   The Set Grid dialog box opens.

2. In the Grid Options pane of the Set Grid dialog box, click the Show Grid Lines checkbox if you want light blue grid lines to be displayed on the screen.

3. Also in the Grid Options pane, click Print Grid Lines if you want the reference grid to print (or plot) with the drawing.

4. Click OK.

You can set the snap grid at an angle, and the reference grid will follow suit. This is easy and useful; many projects have objects oriented to axes other than the basic x and y of the page, and rotating the grid lets you use the Snap to Grid constraint to draw complex designs efficiently (**Figure 4.8**).

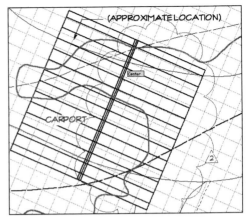

Figure 4.8 Rotate the grid to align it with a feature you're working on.

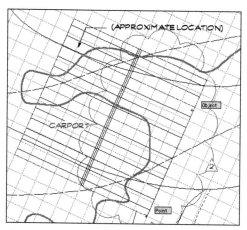

Figure 4.9 Click on a corner of the object and then again along one side to align the grid.

Figure 4.10 The Data Display bar for a rotated grid situation gives dimensions in terms of I and J rather than X and Y.

To rotate the grids:

1. Choose Page > Set Grid; or press Command-8 (Mac) or Ctrl-8 (Windows); or double-click the Snap to Grid button on the Constraints palette.

   The Set Grid dialog box opens.

2. In the Grid Angle pane of the Snap to Grid dialog box:

   Click the Next Mouse Drag radio button

   or

   Click the Enter Angle radio button and type the angle to which you want the grid rotated into the field.

3. Click OK to close the Set Grid dialog box.

   If you chose the Enter Angle option, the grid will now be rotated.

   If you clicked the Next Mouse Drag radio button, click once in the drawing area to set the origin of the grid and again to set its angle. While you are setting the angle, you will see the reference grid, whether or not you have chosen to make it visible (**Figure 4.9**).

✔ Tips

- Use the Snap to Object constraint (see below) to align the grid to some important feature of your drawing by snapping the points of that Next Mouse Drag to two points that define the rotated grid axis.

- The Snap grid portion of the Set Grid dialog box refers to the X and Y spacing of the grid points, but when you rotate the grid (see below), the grid axes are called *i* and *j*. The X and Y fields of the Data Display bar also change to I and J (**Figure 4.10**).

To draw a line between points on the snap grid:

1. On the Constraints palette, click the Snap to Grid button.

   The button will look as if it has been pressed down when it has been selected (**Figure 4.11**).

2. On the 2D Tools palette, click the Line tool.

3. In the drawing area, click near the point at which you want to start your line.

   The pointer will jump to the nearest point on the snap grid and place the starting point of the line.

4. As you move the mouse to place the second point, the pointer will jump from grid point to grid point (**Figure 4.12**). Click to complete the line.

✔ Tips

- The example above will serve as a guide for the other tools on the 2D Tools palette as well.

- Toggle the Snap to Grid constraint on and off by pressing the A key.

- Double-click the A key (i. e., press it twice in quick succession) to open the Set Grid dialog box and change any of its settings. You can do this in the middle of an operation; when you close the dialog box, you will be returned to the point at which you left.

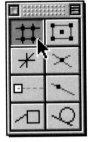

Figure 4.11 Click the Snap to Grid button on the Constraints palette to activate the grid as a set of snap points.

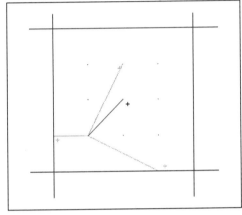

Figure 4.12 The pointer jumps from point to point on the grid as you move it around the drawing area.

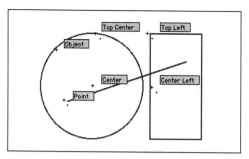

Figure 4.13 Each point the Snap to Object constraint finds is identified by a SmartPointer cue—if you have that option selected in the VectorWorks Preferences.

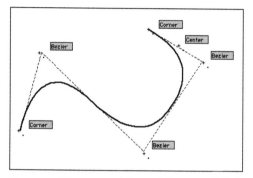

Figure 4.14 When you snap to a polyline, you will find that some of your points are quite a distance from the curve itself.

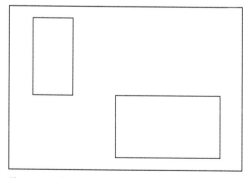

Figure 4.15 Draw two rectangles to start this exercise.

Snapping to Objects

Once you have some objects on the page, the Snap to Object constraint becomes a key player in the drawing environment. With the Snap to Object constraint active, the pointer will seek objects in the drawing, showing a particular preference for certain key points on the objects. When it finds one, the pointer will get a little dot and display a cue for the kind of point found (Center, Arc End, Point, and so on) (**Figure 4.13**).

On straight segments, whether individual lines or parts of polygons or polylines, the pointer will cue their centers and end points. The tops, bottoms, center-left, and center-right sides of circles and rectangles are tagged. When you work with a polyline, the pointer will snap to the vertices and the points midway between them, effectively treating the polyline as a polygon defined by the vertex points (**Figure 4.14**).

To draw a rectangle using the Snap to Object constraint:

1. On the Constraints palette, click the Snap to Object button.

   The button will look depressed. For this example, make sure the Snap to Object button is the only one selected.

2. On the 2D Tools palette, click the Rectangle tool.

3. Draw two random rectangles (**Figure 4.15**).

   continues on next page

4. Bring the pointer to the one of the corners of one of the rectangles.

The SmartPointer will have a little dot and the cue will read the name of the corner (**Figure 4.16**).

5. Click to place the first point.

6. Move the pointer to the center of one of the sides of the other rectangle.

The SmartPointer will again show a little dot and the cue will read the name of the point it has found (**Figure 4.17**).

7. Click to complete the rectangle (**Figure 4.18**).

✔ Tips

- Snap to Object takes precedence over Snap to Grid. If you're trying to snap to a grid point and the pointer keeps jumping onto a point on a nearby object, press Q to toggle off the Snap to Object constraint.

- The Object cue (without the little dot by the pointer) is presented when you bring the pointer near an object somewhere other than at one of its snap points. It doesn't work reliably on polylines.

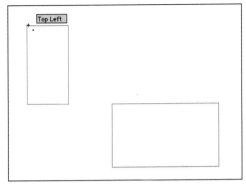

Figure 4.16 Click on one of corners when the pointer snaps to it.

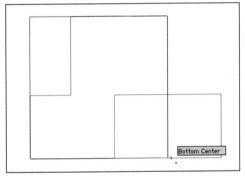

Figure 4.17 Click the center of one of the sides when the SmartPointer cue reads (for example) Bottom Center.

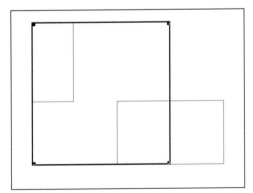

Figure 4.18 The completed rectangle extends from the first corner to the snap point at the center of the edge of the other.

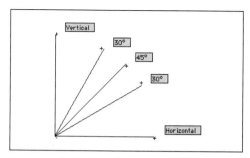

Figure 4.19 On the Mac, the standard angle snaps are vertical and horizontal as well as 30° and 45° each side of each axis if you make that selection in the Snap Angle dialog box.

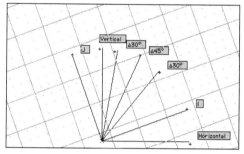

Figure 4.20 When you rotate the grid, you get a different set of angle snaps.

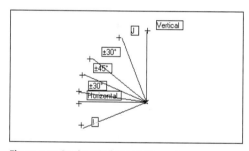

Figure 4.21 On the Windows platform, the SmartPointer cues are slightly different, but not in any important way.

Constraining Angles

The Snap to Grid and Snap to Object constraints discussed above make the pointer jump to particular points in the drawing area. In doing so, they obviously can also have an impact on the angle of a line. Constrain Angle does this directly.

When you click the Constrain Angle button on the Constraints palette and you place a first point to start a line (including the mouse movement that creates a shape), the pointer will jump to the angles you have selected in the Angle Snaps dialog box when the end point of the line is within the minimum pixel radius (set in the VectorWorks Preferences) of the angle (**Figure 4.19**). When you hold down the Shift key, you draw lines only at the ordained angles.

The Constrain Angle constraint is affected by the grid angle. When you rotate the grid, you will get SmartPointer cues both for Horizontal and Vertical and for I and J—the new grid axes (**Figure 4.20**). The optional angle snaps, 30,60 degrees and 45 degrees, will shift to align with the grid and will be displayed as Δ30 and Δ45 (Mac) and ±30 and ±45 (Windows) (**Figure 4.21**).

To select the optional angles for the Constrain Angle constraint:

1. On the Constraints palette, double-click the Constrain Angle button.

   The Angle Snaps dialog box opens (**Figure 4.22**).

2. In the Angles pane, click the 30, 60 check-box to activate the constraint for angles 30 degrees on either side of the grid axes.

   Click the 45 checkbox to activate the constraint for angles 45 degrees from the grid axes.

3. Click OK to close the Angle Snaps dialog box and accept the settings.

If you set up an Alternate Coordinate System, you will see two additional labels, Alt and Alt 90°, that signal when you are aligned with the axes of that system (**Figure 4.23**).

To set up an Alternate Coordinate System:

1. On the Constraints palette, double-click the Constrain Angle button.

   The Angle Snaps dialog box opens (**Figure 4.24**).

2. In the Alternate Coordinate System pane, click the Next Mouse Drag radio button

   or

   Click the Enter Angle radio button and type the angle to which you want the grid rotated into the field.

3. In the Alternate Coordinate System pane, click the Extensions Lines checkbox to display extension lines at the alternate angle (analogous to the lines projected horizontally and vertically from snap points) when the Smart Points constraint is active.

   Extensions will also be projected at 90 degrees to the alternate angle.

Figure 4.22 The Angle Snaps dialog box.

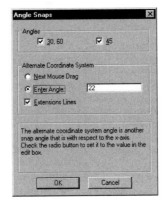

Figure 4.23 The Alternate Coordinate System gives you two more axes to which you can snap.

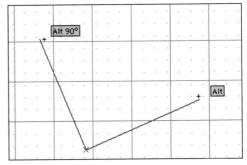

Figure 4.24 Type an angle into the edit field in the Angle Snaps dialog box to create another pair of axes to which you can snap.

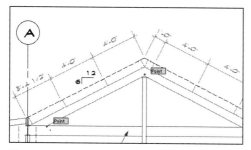

Figure 4.25 Another way to set the angle of the Alternate Coordinate System is to drag the mouse — or, better yet, snap it to two points on an object such as a rafter.

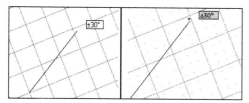

Figure 4.26 Constrained angles are set relative to the snap grid and rotate from the *x-y* axes when you rotate the grid. In Windows, they have a ±; on the Mac, they have a Δ.

4. Click OK.

If you chose the Enter Angle option, the new coordinate system will now be active.

If you clicked the Next Mouse Drag radio button, click once in the drawing area to set the origin of the line that defines the angle and click again to set its angle (**Figure 4.25**).

The angle will be rounded to the nearest degree.

✔ Tips

- The constrained angles are read relative to the grid axes, rotated or otherwise. They are indicated by Δ (Mac) or ± (Windows) in front of the SmartPointer cue (**Figure 4.26**).

- You can enter angles as degrees, radians, or gradians by typing *d, r,* or *g* after the number to designate a unit that is not the default setting in the Units dialog box. VectorWorks makes the conversion to the default unit of angular measurement.

- The angle of an Alternate Coordinate System is always an integer value in degrees; VectorWorks adjusts the setting in any units to equal an integer value in degrees.

- When you have both an Alternate Coordinate System and a rotated grid, you lose the snaps to the drawing area's vertical and horizontal axes.

- The Alternate Coordinate System doesn't influence snaps to the optional angles (30 degrees, 60 degrees, and 45 degrees) the way rotating the grid does.

CONSTRAINING ANGLES

To draw a polygon using the Angle Constraint (a mini-tutorial):

1. On the Constraints palette, click the Constrain Angle button.

   The button will look depressed. For this example, make sure the Constrain Angle button is the only one selected.

   For the purposes of this example, open the Angle Snaps dialog box (see above) and select both the 30, 60 and the 45 checkboxes in the Angles pane. Set the Alternate Coordinate System to 15 degrees (**Figure 4.27**).

2. On the 2D Tools palette, click the Polygon tool.

3. Click in the drawing area to start the polygon.

4. Move the pointer horizontally so that the cue reads Horizontal, and click (**Figure 4.28**).

5. Move the pointer at about 30 degrees so that the cue 30° is displayed, and click again to set the vertex (**Figure 4.29**).

6. Hold down the Shift key so that the next segment is constrained to the predetermined angles, and draw another segment at 15 degrees, using the Alternate Coordinate System.

   The pointer will read Alt (**Figure 4.30**).

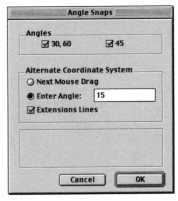

Figure 4.27 Set the Alternate Coordinate System to 15 degrees and check both the 30, 60 and the 45 checkboxes.

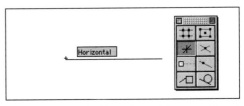

Figure 4.28 Place the first point and then move the pointer across so the SmartPointer cue reads Horizontal.

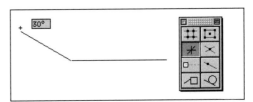

Figure 4.29 Then move the pointer up until the cue reads 30°.

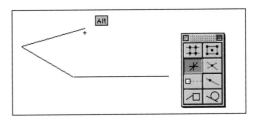

Figure 4.30 Holding down the Shift key locks the line to one of the preset angles. In this case, it is the Alternate Coordinate System axis we set to 15°.

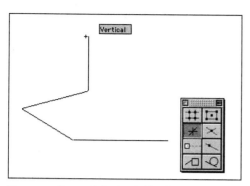

Figure 4.31 The *y* axis is signaled by the SmartPointer cue Vertical.

7. Draw a segment upward as the cue reads Vertical (**Figure 4.31**).

8. Draw a segment down at 75 degrees as the cue reads Alt 90° and click (**Figure 4.32**).

9. From that vertex, hold down the Shift key and draw upward again at 45 degrees as the SmartPointer cue reads 45° (**Figure 4.33**). Double-click to complete the polygon.

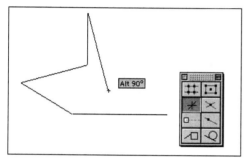

Figure 4.32 At 75 degrees, the pointer cue tells you that your line is perpendicular to the main axis of the Alternate Coordinate System.

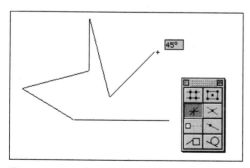

Figure 4.33 Complete the polygon by drawing the final segment at 45 degrees and double-clicking to end the line.

To draw a line parallel or perpendicular to an object:

1. On the Constraints palette, click the Snap to Angle and Snap to Object buttons (**Figure 4.34**).

2. Start the line by clicking on the object (it can be a line, a rectangle, a polygon, a circle, an arc, or an oval) once the pointer snaps to it and displays a cue signifying it has found the object (**Figure 4.35**).

3. Move the pointer away and click again once the cue reads Perpendicular or Parallel (**Figure 4.36**).

   The line is drawn either parallel or at 90 degrees to the object.

Figure 4.34 To snap to an object at any of the preset angles, you have to use the Snap to Angle and Snap to Object constraints together.

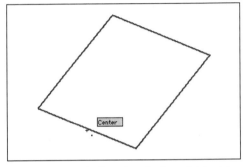

Figure 4.35 Start the line when the SmartPointer lets you know you have found a point on the object.

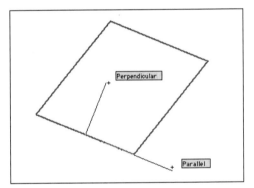

Figure 4.36 As you move the pointer, the cue will tell you when you have snapped to either perpendicular or parallel from the starting line.

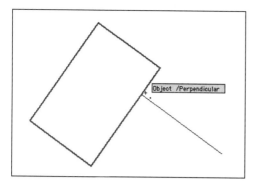

Figure 4.37 Drawing toward the object, look for the SmartPointer cue Object/Perpendicular, which signals that you have drawn the perpendicular from your starting point to the object.

The Snap to Angle constraint behaves slightly differently when you use it to draw a line to an object than when you draw a line from an object.

To draw a line perpendicular to an object:

1. On the Constraints palette, click the Snap to Angle and Snap to Object buttons.

2. Start a line anywhere in the drawing area and bring the pointer over the target object. Click when the cue is Object/Perpendicular showing that the snap is on the object and the line is perpendicular to it (**Figure 4.37**).

✔ Tips

- When you start a polygon by snapping on an object, all subsequent segments of the polygon refer to that initial snap for their Perpendicular or Parallel cues (**Figure 4.38**).

- When you start a polygon from a curved object, the initial Perpendicular Smart-Pointer cue means that the first segment would go through the center if it were extended. Tangent means that the line is perpendicular to the line from the center to the snap point (**Figure 4.39**).

- When you start a polygon from a curved object, the initial Perpendicular cue actually signifies that the line is aligned with the center of the curve. As you continue the polygon, the cue Tangent replaces the cue Parallel to refer to lines perpendicular to the initial line (**Figure 4.40**).

- When the SmartPointer cue reads Perpendicular to a curved segment of an open polyline, it is referring to the line between the start and end points of the polyline.

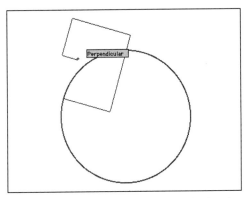

Figure 4.38 All the lines of a polygon refer back to the polygon's origin for their Perpendicular and Parallel cues.

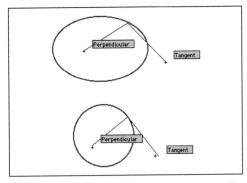

Figure 4.39 A line perpendicular to an oval isn't really perpendicular to the surface at the point of intersection, but is aligned with the center of the object.

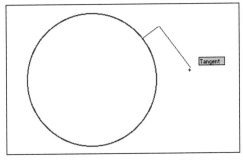

Figure 4.40 The SmartPointer refers to all lines perpendicular to the line from the center of a curve as Tangent.

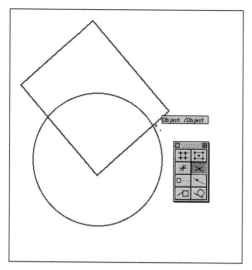

Figure 4.41 Object/Object is the SmartPointer cue for the intersection of two objects.

The Snap to Intersection Constraint

Another likely candidate for a snap point is the intersection of two lines. You can choose any intersection of 2D lines, including arc lines and polylines, as the starting or ending point for a drawing operation.

There are no special settings associated with this constraint—it's either on or off.

To use the Snap to Intersection constraint:

1. On the Constraints palette, click the Snap to Intersection button.

2. Choose a 2D drawing tool from the 2D Tools palette.

3. Move the pointer to the intersection of two lines.

The SmartPointer cue will be Object/Object when the pointer is within the snap radius of the intersection (**Figure 4.41**).

4. Click to place the point at the intersection.

Snap to Distance

Yet another option in the constraints department lets you snap to points on any straight line or segment of a polygon at specific distances between its end points and the middle. The constraint actually operates in two modes. In the first mode, the segment is divided into equal pieces and the pointer jumps to the ends of each piece. In the second, VectorWorks finds points at a specified distance (and multiples of that distance) from the end of the line, up to the midpoint of the line.

To set the Snap to Distance constraint as equal divisions:

1. On the Constraints palette, double-click the Snap to Distance button.

   The Snap Distance dialog box opens (**Figure 4.42**).

2. In the Snap By pane, to set the relationship between the distance from the end of the line to the snap point and the total length of the line:

   Click the Fraction radio button and type the ratio as a fraction

   or

   Click the Percent radio button and enter the ratio as a percentage of the length.

3. Click the Multiple Divisions checkbox to place snap points at multiples of the fraction or percentage.

   For example, if you set the fraction to 1/7 and choose the Multiple Divisions option, the pointer will also find the points 2/7 and 3/7 of the line length from each end (**Figure 4.43**).

4. Click OK.

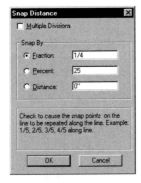

Figure 4.42 The Snap Distance dialog box sets up the way you snap to points other than just the ends and the middle on a line.

Figure 4.43 Choose Multiple Divisions to set up snaps at regular intervals all along the line.

Figure 4.44 Click the Snap to Distance button on the Constraints palette to cut a line into equal parts.

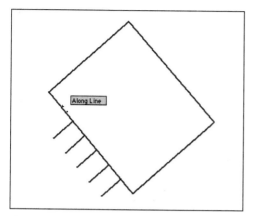

Figure 4.45 The SmartPointer cue Along Line belongs to the Snap to Distance constraint.

To set the Snap to Distance constraint for a fixed length:

1. On the Constraints palette, double-click the Snap to Distance button.

The Snap Distance dialog box opens.

2. In the Snap By pane, click the Distance radio button and type the distance you want a snap point from each end of the line.

3. Click the Multiple Divisions checkbox if you want to have snap points set at each multiple of that distance from the end of the line up to the center point.

4. Click OK to set the constraint and close the dialog box; click Cancel to close the dialog box without making any changes.

To use the Snap to Distance constraint:

1. On the Constraints palette, click the Snap to Distance button (**Figure 4.44**).

2. From the 2D Tools palette, click the drawing tool of your choice.

3. Bring the pointer up to the straight segment you want to divide.

As you move along the segment, the pointer shows the telltale dot and the SmartPointer cue reads Along Line when the you are within snapping distance of one of the divisions you have defined in the Snap Distance dialog box (**Figure 4.45**).

4. Click to place a point at the snap point.

SNAP TO DISTANCE

✔ Tips

- Distance snaps work from both ends of the segment toward the midpoint; choosing either a fraction or a fixed number that doesn't divide the line evenly will leave a long or short segment in the middle of the line (**Figure 4.46**).

- With the Snap to Distance button depressed on the Constraints palette, the pointer will appear to snap to a curve, showing the little dot and the cue Along Line, but the constraint doesn't really work on curved objects.

- The Snap to Distance constraint also works to set the reference points for tools on the Editing palette, specifically the 2D Mirror, 2D Rotate, Clip and Split tools (see Chapter 3, "Modifying 2D Objects").

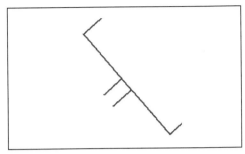

Figure 4.46 Setting the Snap Distance to 4/9 leaves only a small space (1/9 of the line length) between the two snap points.

Figure 4.47 Click the Constrain Tangent button on the Constraints palette when you want to draw lines tangent to a curve.

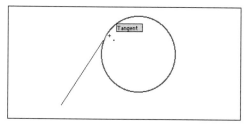

Figure 4.48 When the SmartPointer cue reads Tangent, the line to the curve will snap to its point of tangency.

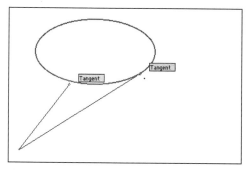

Figure 4.49 Don't be fooled when the SmartPointer seems to be telling you a line is a tangent (like the one on the left). VectorWorks is really detecting a line to the center of the object.

The Constrain Tangent Constraint

It's often important to draw a line tangent to an arc, and the Constrain Tangent constraint gives you two handy ways to do just that: coming and going.

The constraint works with circles; it has limited functionality with ovals and arcs. It doesn't work with polylines or quarter arcs (which are, in reality, polylines).

To draw a line tangent to an oval, an arc, or a circle:

1. On the Constraints palette, click the Constrain Tangent button (**Figure 4.47**).

2. On the 2D Tools palette, click the Line tool.

3. Click in the drawing area to start the line.

4. Bring the pointer to the edge of the oval, arc, or circle and move it along the edge until the cue reads Tangent (**Figure 4.48**).

   If the Constrain Angle button is also pressed, you will get the Tangent cue when the line is aligned with the center of the object as well, but it should be obvious that the line is not tangent to the surface of the object (**Figure 4.49**).

   continues on next page

5. Click the mouse to end the line at its point of tangency.

To extend the line, switch to the 2D Selection tool and drag the end point out as the SmartPointer displays the Parallel cue (**Figure 4.50**). (On the Mac, hold down the Shift key to lock the angle; the SmartPointer will read Angle.)

To draw a tangent from a circle, an oval, or an arc:

1. On the Constraints palette, click the Constrain Tangent button.

2. On the 2D Tools palette, click the Line tool.

3. Bring the pointer to the object from which you want the tangent to emerge, and click when the cue reads Object.

4. Click the mouse in the drawing area to end the line.

As you move the mouse, the starting point of the line will move along the arc to maintain the tangency of the line (**Figure 4.51**). To flip the line to the other side of the arc, hold down the Option (Mac) or Alt (Windows) key (**Figure 4.52**).

✔ Tips

■ You can use the Constrain Tangent constraint to draw the tangent between two circles, but it doesn't work with ovals or arcs.

■ You can use this constraint to place one edge of a rotated rectangle or other polygon tangent to an arc, with its corner at the point of tangency.

■ When you start a tangent from an arc, you can drag it around to where the arc would be if it were a full circle. Drawing to that arc, however, the constraint will not find those invisible points.

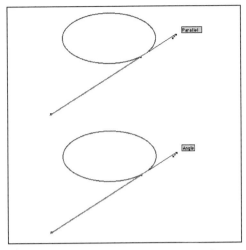

Figure 4.50 Extend the tangent by dragging it along its own axis; the Snap to Angle constraint keeps it aligned. On the Mac, use the Shift key to lock onto the angle.

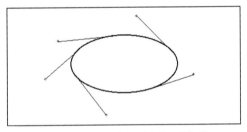

Figure 4.51 As you move the end point of the line around the curve, the point on the curve moves to maintain the tangency of the line.

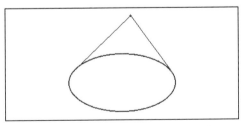

Figure 4.52 When you hold down the Alt or Option key, the tangent flips over to the other side of the curve while maintaining the end point where the cursor is placed.

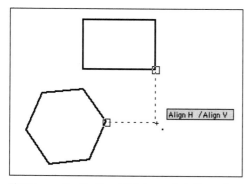

Figure 4.53 Use the Smart Points constraint to project extensions from snap points along the x and y axes as well as at whatever angles you have established in the Angle Snaps dialog box.

Smart Points

The Smart Points button doesn't really provide new snap points on the objects in your drawing; rather, it extends the ones you already have into the space between the objects along the various axes of your drawing—rotated grid, Alternate Coordinate System, and the usual horizontal and vertical axes (**Figure 4.53**).

SmartPoints draws extension lines from the points normally found by the Snap to Object and Snap to Intersection constraints

To select a point for extension, you must first identify it by putting the pointer over it so that the SmartPointer cue appears. Then, when you move the pointer away again, VectorWorks will draw a line to it along the horizontal and vertical axes, the axes of a rotated grid, or the angles set up in the Alternate Coordinate System (see above). You use the Smart Points dialog box to control which of these extensions is drawn.

Smart Point extensions operate in two basic modes. They can be drawn from a snap point on an object to the pointer whenever the line between them is one of the preset angles. And Smart Points can project perpendicular extensions from lines drawn at the selected angles when the extension intersects with one of the snap points on objects in your drawing. With both these options in operation, there are a lot of extensions being created as you move the pointer through the drawing area.

Also among the Smart Points settings is one for the datum (floating or otherwise). Other snap points depend on the geometry of the object, whereas you can put a datum anywhere. And when you do, you temporarily reset the Data Display bar to take its measurements from the datum rather than from the drawing's origin. This makes it easy to accurately place one point relative to another without resorting to the calculator.

You can even choose to give the datum an offset, so you can snap to points at a predetermined distance from it. You can use this offset in combination with other constraints to find a point on an object at a certain distance from the datum (**Figure 4.54**). Or, for example, you can snap to a series of points 48 inches from the center of a line in 30-degree increments by using the Offset Datum option in conjunction with the Snap to Angle constraint (**Figure 4.55**).

To set the Smart Points preferences:

1. On the Constraints palette, double-click the Smart Points button.

   The Smart Points dialog box opens (**Figure 4.56**).

2. Click the Horizontal/Vertical Extensions checkbox to enable the extension of lines from the pointer along the horizontal and vertical axes to points selected by the Object and Intersection constraints when they are selected (**Figure 4.57**).

   When this is the only box checked, the only extensions drawn will be along the x- and y-axes unless you've rotated the grid. In this case, extensions will be drawn on the i- and j-axes.

3. Click the Extensions Lines checkbox so that the pointer will find points projected perpendicularly off lines drawn at the preset angles selected in the Snap Angles dialog box when the Snap to Angle constraint is also active (**Figure 4.58**).

   The Extension Lines option in the Smart Points dialog box affects only the end point of a line; no extensions are projected unless the line you are drawing is snapped to one of the active angle constraints (30 or Δ30/±30, for example).

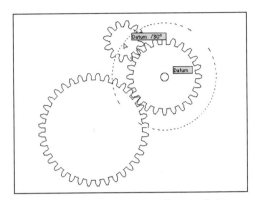

Figure 4.54 Press G to set a datum (surrounded by a small circle) in your drawing area. If you have set a datum offset, you will see a dotted circle at the preset radius from the datum when the pointer is at that distance.

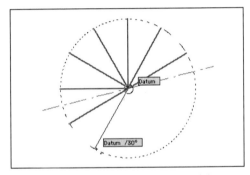

Figure 4.55 With both the Snap to Angle and the Smart Points constraints (and with the Offset Datum option), it's easy to create a series of lines of equal length and equal angular spacing.

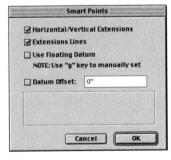

Figure 4.56 The Smart Points dialog box sets the preferences for the extensions from snap points and the operation of the datum.

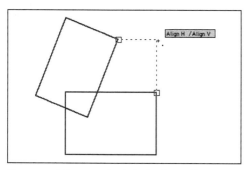

Figure 4.57 When you check the Horizontal/ Vertical Extensions checkbox, Smart Points will reach out to find intersections along the *x* and *y* axes from normal snap points.

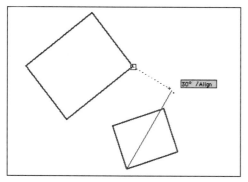

Figure 4.58 Click the Extensions Lines checkbox when you want to project points at the preset angles from the lines drawn at those angles.

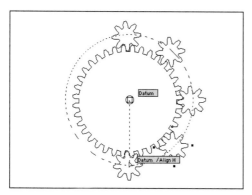

Figure 4.59 The Offset Datum feature creates snaps at a fixed distance from the datum that you place by pressing the G key. You can combine it with other constraints such as Constrain Angle.

4. Do not click the Use Floating Datum checkbox unless you want to have the datum set automatically when you pause the pointer over a snap point. Most users prefer the added control they have when they set the datum manually.

5. Click the Datum Offset checkbox and in the edit box enter the radius at which the offset extension line will lie if you want to use that feature.

The Datum Offset is a circular extension line that appears when the pointer is at approximately the set distance from the datum (**Figure 4.59**).

6. Click OK to close the Smart Points dialog box and impose its constraints.

✔ Tips

- Click both the Horizontal/Vertical Extensions checkbox and the Extensions Lines checkbox to present Horizontal and Vertical and I and J extensions when the grid is rotated.

- When you switch on the Smart Points constraint, you also see the extensions along the Alternate Coordinate System if you checked the Extensions Lines checkbox in the Angle Snaps dialog box (see above).

- In addition to the drawing tools from the 2D Tools palette, you can use some of the tools on the Editing palette: 2D Rotate, 2D Mirror, and Split.

Smart Edge

The Smart Edge button on the Constraints palette adds yet another level of control to the constraints picture. VectorWorks can extend the edges of objects to intersect with other objects or even with other extended edges (**Figure 4.60**). This option works only with straight lines, however; you can't extend arcs or other curves surfaces.

The Smart Edge feature also has a few special tricks that bear examination. First, you can define an offset distance along the extended edge to which you can snap at intersections with objects (or extension lines generated from other objects) and angle snaps (**Figure 4.61**). Second, you can select two edges to extend and then snap along the bisector of the angle between them (**Figure 4.62**). Third, open the Edge Snaps dialog box and turn on the Snap to Extensions Lines option, and the Smart Pointer will project points from objects perpendicular and parallel to the edges you designate with the Smart Edge option (**Figure 4.63**).

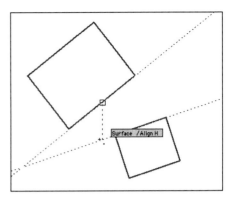

Figure 4.60 Smart Edges are created by snapping to the edge of an object and pressing T. The extension line can intersect another Smart Edge of any other snap in the drawing.

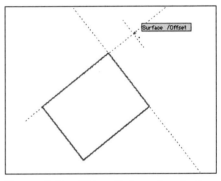

Figure 4.61 Smart Edge offsets create a short extension line offset from the selected edge extension.

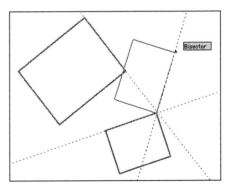

Figure 4.62 Choose the Snap to Bisector option in the Edge Snaps dialog box to produce yet another extension line when the pointer is midway between two edge extensions.

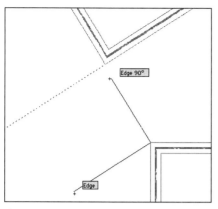

Figure 4.63 Click the Snap to Extension Lines checkbox, and the SmartPointer will detect when a line is perpendicular or parallel to the selected edge.

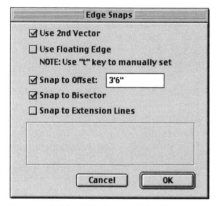

Figure 4.64 The Edge Snaps dialog box opens when you double-click the Smart Edges button on the Constraints palette.

To configure the options for the Smart Edge feature:

1. On the Constraints palette, double-click the Smart Edge button.

   The Edge Snaps dialog box opens (**Figure 4.64**).

2. In the Edge Snaps dialog box, click the Use 2nd Vector checkbox so that you can have two Smart Edge extensions at the same time.

   This is generally a good idea unless it is generating too much activity on the screen.

3. Leave the Use Floating Edge checkbox unchecked unless you want an edge snap extension line generated every time the pointer pauses over a line in the drawing.

   In the manual mode, you press the T key when the pointer snaps to any straight line (the pointer cue can be either Object or a more specific snap like Corner or Point) to select an edge for extension.

4. Click the Snap to Offset checkbox to generate an additional short extension line offset from the selected edge extension by a fixed amount.

   Enter the distance you want the offset line from the edge line in the edit box.

   The offset extension line will appear only when the pointer strays either side of the main extension line by approximately the offset distance.

5. Click the Snap to Bisector checkbox if you want the bisector of the angle between the two extensions to appear when your pointer is near it.

   You need to check the Use 2nd Vector checkbox for this option to be effective, but you don't need to have any other constraints selected.

   continues on next page

SMART EDGE

6. Click the Snap to Extension Lines checkbox if you want to use the edges you activate to temporarily define auxiliary axes (for the Snap to Angle constraint) along which assorted Smart Points are projected.

7. Click OK to set these snaps.

✔ Tip

■ To change the settings in the Edge Snaps dialog box without aborting the operation, double-press the F key quickly during a drawing operation.

To draw an offset polygon with the Smart Edge constraint:

1. On the 2D Tools palette, click the Polygon tool and draw an open polygon.

2. Leave the Polygon tool selected and set the Constraints palette so that only the Snap to Object, Smart Points, and Smart Edges constraints are active (**Figure 4.65**).

Snap to Object and SmartPoints are used only to align the start and end points; the bulk of the work is done by the Smart Edges constraint.

You could have other constraints active as well, but it would only confuse things by causing the pointer to snap to a lot more points.

3. Double-click the Smart Edge button, and in the Edge Snaps dialog box make sure Use 2nd Vector, Snap to Offset, and Snap to Extension Lines are checked. Type the offset in the edit box (**Figure 4.66**). Click OK to close the dialog box.

4. Bring the pointer up to the first edge of the polygon and press T to lock to this edge.

A dotted extension line appears along the first edge (**Figure 4.67**).

Figure 4.65 For this exercise, we will set the Constraints palette so that only three constraints are active.

Figure 4.66 Open the Edge Snaps dialog box and set it up to locate the corner points of the second polygon using the offsets from the two vectors. Snap to Extensions is used to locate the end points only.

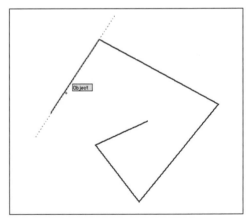

Figure 4.67 Start the process by selecting the first edge; snap to it anywhere and press T.

SMART EDGE

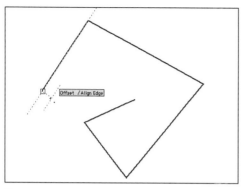

Figure 4.68 Now snap to the starting point of the original polygon and move the pointer off again until the offset extension appears and the cue Offset/Align Edge is displayed.

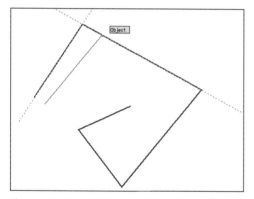

Figure 4.69 Snap to the second line and press T to create a second vector.

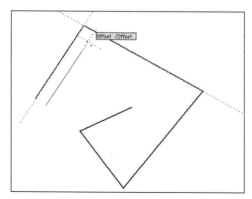

Figure 4.70 Bring the pointer to the offset distance from both lines so that both offset extensions appear with the SmartPointer cue Offset/Offset.

5. Bring the pointer to the starting point of the polygon so that the cue Point is displayed. Then move the pointer away at a right angle to the first segment of the polygon (either side will work) until it displays Offset/Align Edge (**Figure 4.68**). Click to place the first vertex of the second polygon.

6. Move the pointer to the second edge of the polygon (the cue will be Object) and press T to lock onto this segment.

A second dotted line appears (**Figure 4.69**).

7. Bring the pointer back down along the first line until the cue reads Offset/Offset (**Figure 4.70**). Click to place the second vertex at the intersection of the two offset extension lines.

continues on next page

8. Repeat the procedure (steps 6 and 7) all the way around the polygon (**Figure 4.71**).

9. When you get to the last point, bring the pointer to the end point of the master polygon so that the cue reads Point (**Figure 4.72**) and then move it away until it reads Offset/Align Edge (**Figure 4.73**) and double-click to end the polygon (**Figure 4.74**).

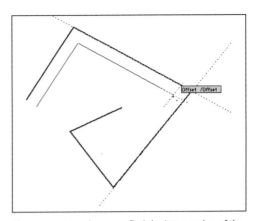

Figure 4.71 At each corner, find the intersection of the two offset extensions and click to place a vertex.

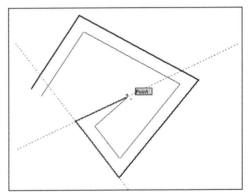

Figure 4.72 Repeat the process until you reach the end point, snapping to the end point of the original polygon.

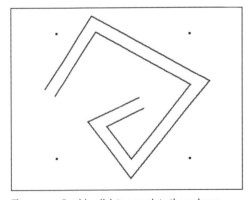

Figure 4.74 Double-click to complete the polygon.

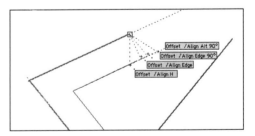

Figure 4.73 Note that there are a number of possible projections onto the offset. Choose the one labeled Align Edge. Align Edge 90° is the projection parallel to the previous segment; Align Alt 90° is the projection in the Alternate Coordinate System; Align H is the vertical projection along the y-axis.

Figure 4.75 The Parametric Constraints palette has buttons for imposing a range of controls that includes seven geometric constraints and five dimensional ones.

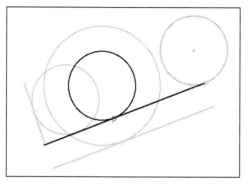

Figure 4.76 The Dynamic Tangent constraint keeps the line tangent to the circle even when the circle is moved or resized.

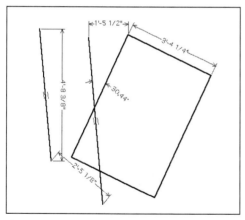

Figure 4.77 Imposing multiple constraints on a set of objects can define a pretty complex relationship. Changing the size or position of any of the three objects will change each of the others.

Parametric Constraints

The SmartPointer constraints are a tremendous expedient for creating objects in Vector-Works. Once objects have been put into the drawing, the Parametric constraints come into play (**Figure 4.75**). Their function is to lock in place specific geometric relationships among objects (or even within a single one) while you move things around in your drawing.

For example, you can create a line tangent to a circle using the Constrain Tangent constraint on the SmartPointer palette and then lock that line tangent to the curve with the Constrain Tangent parametric. They will then stay together—and the line will remain tangent to the circle—no matter how you resize the circle or the line or move them around the drawing (**Figure 4.76**).

Combine that with other parametric constraints (Constrain Radius, Constrain Perpendicular, Constrain Distance, and so on) and you can maintain specific dimensional and geometric relationships without inhibiting your ability to make changes to the objects in your drawing. In general, you can create a whole network of relationships among objects using Parametric constraints so that changing one object affects all the others in the set (**Figure 4.77**).

Note that Parametric constraints can't be placed between objects on different layers (a limitation that doesn't apply to SmartPointer constraints). In addition, they operate only on two-dimensional objects (although 3D objects like walls, plug-in objects, and hybrid symbols that contain 2D components do support parametric constraints).

VectorWorks divides the Parametric constraints into two groups, dimensional and geometric.

Dimensional constraints

Dimensional parametrics set a measurable quantity, such as the radius of a circle or the distance between two points. When you place one of these constraints, a red dimension (similar to the standard dimensional format) is placed to indicate that a constraint is in force. The dimensions indicating Parametric constraints are sized in pixels; unlike dimensions you place from the dimensions palette, they remain the same size on the screen as you zoom in and out (**Figure 4.78**).

The Constrain Angle constraint locks any two straight lines (free-standing lines, parts of polygons or polylines, or walls).

To constrain the angle between two lines:

1. Click the Constrain Angle button on the Parametric Constraints palette (**Figure 4.79**)

   The pointer will change to a small cross.

2. In the drawing area, click on one of the lines you want to constrain.

   The cross turns to a crosshairs to indicate that the first line has been selected (**Figure 4.80**)

3. In the drawing area, click on the second line.

   A red angular dimension is placed and the two lines are locked at that angle to one another (**Figure 4.81**). If you now change the angle one of the lines using the 2D Rotate tool, the 2D Reshape tool, or the 2D Selection tool, the other will rotate with it to maintain the constrained angle (**Figure 4.82**)

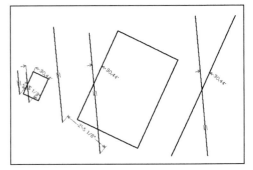

Figure 4.78 No matter how far you zoom in or out on a Parametric constraint, the text doesn't vary in size.

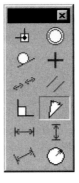

Figure 4.79 The Constrain angle button.

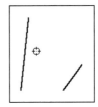

Figure 4.80 The pointer becomes a crosshairs when you have selected the first object for the constraint.

✔ Tip

■ Use the Snap to Object constraint on the SmartPointer Constraints palette to make sure the Parametric constraint is finding the objects to which you want to assign it.

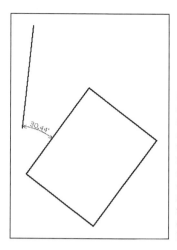

Figure 4.81
Once you have locked the angle between two lines, a red angle dimension is displayed as an indicator that the constraint is active.

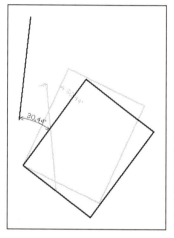

Figure 4.82
When you move the constrained objects (either by rotation or translation) the angle remains the same.

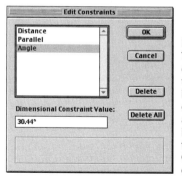

Figure 4.83
To change a constraint (or to eliminate it) select one of the objects affected by it and open the Edit Constraints dialog box.

To modify a constraint:

1. On the 2D Tools palette, click the 2D Selection tool.

2. In the drawing area, select one of the objects affected by the constraint you want to change.

3. Choose Edit > Edit Constraints.
   The Edit Constraints dialog box opens (**Figure 4.83**).

4. In the Edit Constraints dialog box, highlight the constraint you want to change.
   There may be several attached to the object you have selected. The selected constraint will change from red to cyan in the drawing to help you see which one it is.

5. Do one of the following:
   Click Delete to remove the constraint
   or
   Click Delete All to remove all constraints from the selected object
   or
   Enter a new value in the Dimensional Constraint Value edit box if you have selected a dimensional constraint.

6. Click OK.

PARAMETRIC CONSTRAINTS

To remove all constraints from an object (without using the dialog box):

1. On the 2D Tools palette, click the 2D Selection tool and select the object you want to unconstrain (**Figure 4.84**)

2. Choose Edit > Cut, or press Command-X (Mac) or Ctrl-X (Windows).

   The object is cut from the drawing (but saved to the clipboard) (**Figure 4.85**).

3. Choose Edit > Paste In Place, or press Command-Option-V (Mac) or Alt-Ctrl-V (Windows).

   The object is replaced without its constraints (**Figure 4.86**). The object will be placed on the active layer, whether or not that is the one from which it was cut.

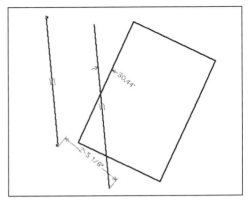

Figure 4.84 Select the object you want to emancipate from its constraints.

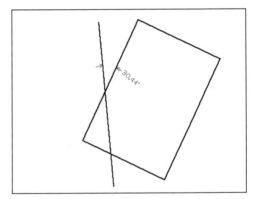

Figure 4.85 Remove the object temporarily from the drawing by cutting it.

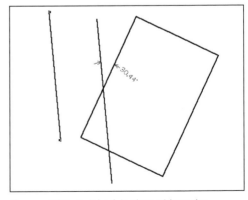

Figure 4.86 Paste it back in place without the constraints.

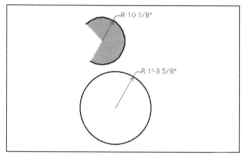

Figure 4.87 The Constrain Radius constraint locks the radius but lets you move the circle or arc around at will.

Figure 4.88 A simple radial dimension is the indicator that the Constrain Radius constraint is in force on the object.

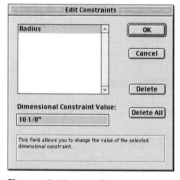

Figure 4.89 You can change or remove a constraint by selecting an object it controls and opening the Edit Constraints dialog box.

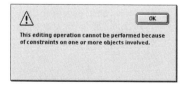

Figure 4.90 This Alert tells you that you are trying to contravene an active constraint.

To constrain the radius of a circle or arc:

1. On the Parametric Constraints palette, click the Constrain Radius button (**Figure 4.87**).

   The pointer turns into a small cross.

2. In the drawing area, click on the curve either at its center or somewhere on its circumference.

   The constraint is imposed and a radial dimension is drawn in the red style characteristic of constraints (**Figure 4.88**). You can't now change the radius of the circle except by removing the constraint or editing it in the Edit Constraints dialog box (**Figure 4.89**).

✔ Tip

- When you try to violate a constraint, an alert box pops up to explain that the editing operation can't be done. Sometimes, this refusal is not really mathematically justified, but there's not much you can do about it. (**Figure 4.90**)

There are three linear dimensional constraints available: You can fix the horizontal (X) distance between two points, the vertical (Y) distance, and/or the direct distance between them (**Figure 4.91**).

The only points these Parametric constraints recognize are end points of lines, corners of polylines and polygons, and centers of ovals, circle, and arcs.

To constrain the horizontal, vertical, or direct distance between two points:

1. On the SmartPointer Constraints palette, make sure the Snap to Object button is selected.

2. On the Parametric Constraints palette, click the Constrain Horizontal Distance, Constrain Vertical Distance, and Constrain Distance buttons (**Figure 4.92**).

   The pointer turns into a small cross.

3. In the drawing area, snap on either the end point of a line, the corner point of a polyline or polygon, or any point on a circle, arc, or oval (the constraint will locate the center).

   The pointer then changes to a crosshairs, indicating that it has captured the first point.

4. Click on the snap point you want to constrain relative to the first one.

   The constraint is recorded and the characteristic red dimension is drawn (**Figure 4.93**).

✔ Tips

■ A Quarter Arc is a polyline with two corner points; you can set distance constraints to them.

■ Apply any of the linear dimensional constraints to the length of a single line by clicking anywhere along its length except at an end point.

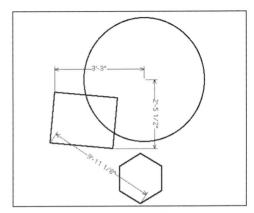

Figure 4.91 The Constrain Horizontal Distance constraint creates a locked dimension along the x-axis. The Constrain Vertical Distance constraint displays an invariable dimension along the y-axis. The plain Constrain Distance constraint locks the direct distance between two points.

Figure 4.92 To set a linear dimensional constraint, click the button on the Parametric Constraints palette for the dimension you want to lock.

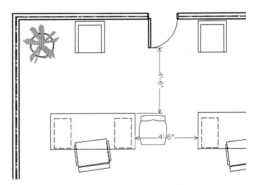

Figure 4.93 You can use linear constraints to anchor key dimensions while you try out a variety of design possibilities.

Figure 4.94 Geometric constraints define a slightly different kind of relationship between objects than the dimensional constraints.

Figure 4.95 You can lock a line to the *x* or *y* axis using the Constrain Horizontal/ Vertical constraint. If the line is not already aligned, the constraint will force it to the closest axis.

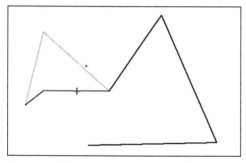

Figure 4.96 You can align one segment of a polygon to the *x*- or *y*-axis with the Constrain Horizontal/ Vertical constraint.

Figure 4.97 A small red cross appears on a segment when you constrain it to the horizontal or vertical axis.

Geometric constraints

Geometric constraints define relationships among objects on a more abstract level than the dimensional constraints (**Figure 4.94**). They also have the power to move objects to conform to the constraint. And unlike the dimensional constraints, the order in which you click on the objects makes a difference. When you bind two objects together, the first one you click will be the one that moves to conform to the constraint.

You will probably find the geometric Parametric constraints a little unpredictable. Sometimes objects will deform to conform to the constraints; other times they will simply move. Sometimes you will have to reverse the order in which you click on the objects to get the constraint to take hold. In general, you may have to experiment a bit to get them to work. Parametric constraints are new with VectorWorks 9 and may require a little more time to be certifiably bug-free.

To align a line to the *x*- or *y*-axis:

1. On the Parametric Constraints palette, click the Constrain Horizontal/Vertical button (**Figure 4.95**).

   The pointer becomes a small cross.

2. In the drawing area, click on the line (or a straight segment of an object).

   The line will rotate around its starting point to either the *x*- or the *y*-axis, depending on which axis is closer to the initial angle of the line (**Figure 4.96**).

   The line will show a red cross at its midpoint to indicate that it is now locked in the vertical or horizontal orientation (**Figure 4.97**).

To constrain a line parallel to another:

1. On the Parametric Constraints palette, click the Constrain Parallel button (**Figure 4.98**)

   The pointer becomes a small cross.

2. Click on the line you want to rotate to be parallel to the second line (if it isn't already parallel).

   The pointer becomes a crosshairs.

3. Click on the line to which you want the first line parallel.

   The second line moves to become parallel to the first (**Figure 4.99**). Both lines in the pair have little red icons consisting of a pair of parallel segments drawn at their midpoints (**Figure 4.100**).

✔ Tip

■ In general, you will find that geometric constraints are not really reciprocal. Moving or reshaping one of the objects in a constrained pair will cause the other to respond in a way that depends on whether it was the first or second object clicked when you set up the constraint. Sometimes VectorWorks doesn't allow you to modify one object but lets you do what you will to the other without protest.

Figure 4.98 The Constrain Parallel button on the Parametric Constraints palette forces a pair of lines to rotate together.

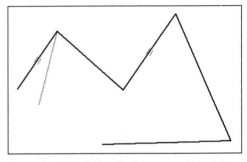

Figure 4.99 Click first on the line you want to rotate and then on the one you want to remain unchanged.

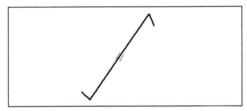

Figure 4.100 The indicator for lines constrained parallel is a pair or red lines at the center of the line.

Figure 4.101 The Constrain Collinear constraint forces two lines to be not only parallel, but also aligned along a common axis.

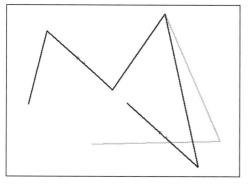

Figure 4.102 Imposing collinearity on a pair of lines moves the first one clicked into line with the second one.

Figure 4.103 The little double-headed arrows are the mark of lines constrained to be collinear.

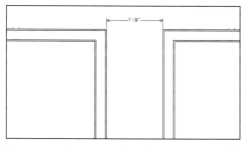

Figure 4.104 If you set up the walls as both collinear and constrained to a fixed spacing, you can pay attention to other details of the design without worrying about this one.

You can constrain a pair of lines to be collinear as well as parallel by using the Constrain Collinear constraint.

To constrain a pair of lines to be collinear:

1. On the Parametric Constraints palette, click the Constrain Collinear button (**Figure 4.101**).

   The pointer becomes a small cross.

2. Click on the line you want to move to become collinear to the second line.

   The pointer becomes a crosshairs, indicating that it has found the first line.

3. Click on the second line.

   The first line rotates around the point of intersection of the two lines to be collinear to the second (**Figure 4.102**). Each line of the pair now displays a double-headed arrow at its midpoint, signifying that is part of a collinear relationship (**Figure 4.103**).

✔ Tip

- You may find it useful to combine collinearity with the Constrain Distance constraint to maintain the spacing between your lines as well as their alignment with one another (**Figure 4.104**).

PARAMETRIC CONSTRAINTS

To constrain a line perpendicular to another:

1. On the Parametric Constraints palette, click the Constrain Perpendicular button (**Figure 4.105**).

   The pointer becomes a small cross.

2. Click on the line you want to move to become perpendicular to the second line.

   The pointer becomes a crosshairs, indicating that it has found the first line.

3. Click on the second line.

   The first line rotates around the point of intersection of the two lines to be perpendicular to the second (**Figure 4.106**). The two lines are now connected by red intersecting extension lines that have a small square at their intersection (**Figure 4.107**).

✔ Tip

■ If the point of intersection between the two lines you constrain perpendicular is distant, the lines are going to be displaced significantly. And if the lines are parallel, VectorWorks throws up its hands and declares the constraint invalid.

Figure 4.105 The obvious companion to the Constrain Parallel option is Constrain Perpendicular.

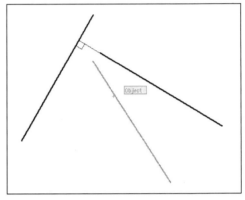

Figure 4.106 The first line you click will rotate about its intersection with the second as it lines itself up perpendicular to it.

Figure 4.107 Lines constrained perpendicular have a little square at their actual or projected intersection.

PARAMETRIC CONSTRAINTS

Figure 4.108 The Constrain Coincident button starts you on your way to locking two objects together at one of their key points.

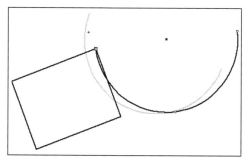

Figure 4.109 Click on the point you want to move to coincide with a second point.

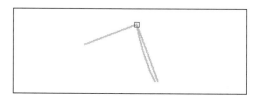

Figure 4.110 A small red square marks the point at which two objects coincide.

You can also constrain two points to be coincident.

To constrain two points coincident:

1. On the Parametric Constraints palette, click the Constrain Coincident button (**Figure 4.108**).

   The pointer becomes a small cross.

2. Click on the point you want to move to become coincident with a second one.

   The pointer becomes a crosshairs, indicating that it has found the first point.

3. Click on the second point.

   The first object moves so that its selected point coincides with the selected point on the second object (**Figure 4.109**)

   With arcs, you can constrain a point to lie on the arc, but not at the center or an end point. Straight lines and segments of polygons and polylines work from their end points.

   The concentric points are marked by a little red square (**Figure 4.110**).

✔ Tips

- For circles, you can only click at their centers, not along their circumferences, for the first click. On the second click, you can choose either the circumference or the center.

- An oval operates only from its center, but you have to click the circumference to select it.

- You can constrain a line's end point to the circumference of a circle by clicking first on the end point and then on the circumference of the circle. You can then move the line anywhere around the circumference (**Figure 4.111**).

- To set a point coincident with the center of an arc, try using the 2D Selection tool to select the arc and then click on the center point. Sometimes, the Constrain Coincident constraint will recognize the end point of the curve but not the starting point.

The Constrain Concentric constraint works with circle and arcs, but not with ovals.

To constrain two arcs concentric:

1. On the Parametric Constraints palette, click the Constrain Concentric button (**Figure 4.112**).

   The pointer becomes a small cross.

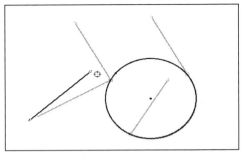

Figure 4.111 A line constrained coincident to a curve can be moved anywhere as long as the end remains on the arc.

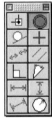

Figure 4.112 The Constrain Concentric constraint button works with both circle and arcs.

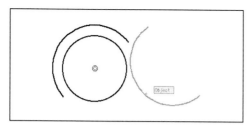

Figure 4.113 When you move an arc or circle to be concentric with another, a pair of little red circles appears at their common center.

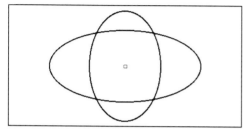

Figure 4.114 The Constrain Concentric constraint doesn't work with ovals, but Constrain Coincident does.

2. Click on the object you want to move to become concentric with a second one.

You can click either the circumference or the center of the object. The pointer becomes a crosshairs, indicating that it has found the first point.

3. Click on the second object.

The first object moves so that its center is coincident with the center of the second object (**Figure 4.113**). The centers are marked by red concentric circles to indicate they are constrained.

✔ Tip

■ Use the Constrain Coincident constraint to line up the centers of two ovals; Constrain Concentric doesn't work with them (**Figure 4.114**).

The Constrain Tangent constraint will create and lock a tangency relationship between two circles or arcs or between a straight line (or the edge of a polygon) and a circle or curve. Unlike the SmartPointer tangent constraint, it doesn't work with ovals.

To constrain two objects tangent:

1. On the Parametric Constraints palette, click the Constrain Tangent button (**Figure 4.115**).

   The pointer becomes a small cross.

2. Click on the object you want to move to become tangent with a second one.

   You can click either the circumference or the center of a circle or curve. The pointer becomes a crosshairs, indicating that it has found the first point.

3. Click on the second object.

   The first object moves so that the line is tangent to the curve or the curves are tangent to one another (See **Figure 4.76**, above). There is a circle with an extending line at the point of tangency to indicate the objects are constrained (**Figure 4.116**).

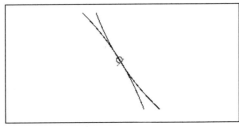

Figure 4.115 The Constrain Tangent constraint puts two arcs or an arc and a line into tangency and holds them there.

Figure 4.116 The mark of the Constrain Tangent constraint is a little circle with a line extending along its edge.

USING LAYERS AND CLASSES

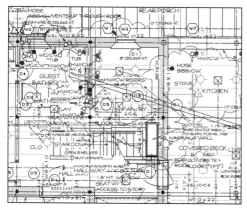

Figure 5.1 When all the layers and classes in a VectorWorks drawing are visible, you might as well be looking at a plate of spaghetti.

The first four chapters of this book have dealt with setting up the drawing space, then creating objects and editing and arranging those objects relative to one another. But the problem still remains—especially when the number of objects on the page starts to grow—of presenting documents that are actually useful. The paradox presented by a powerful application like VectorWorks is that you can put *so* much useful information into a single drawing that it becomes unintelligible (**Figure 5.1**).

VectorWorks's solution to this quandary is its clever use of *layers* and *classes* to control the visibility of sets of elements. Both let you to make all the objects in them visible or invisible at once. There are myriad ways to group objects into classes and layers, but some are more practical than others. You can also assign layers to entities other than the objects themselves, items like notes, parts lists, bills of materials, door schedules, and so on, so that you can display them as part of the drawing or not, according to your needs.

Layers

Layers are often described as analogous to sheets of acetate or tracing paper that can be stacked in various combinations according to what you want to display. Layers share with their real-world equivalents the property that the ones on the top of the stack can hide what lies below. In the electronic environment, however, you can also handle overlapping elements in a variety of other ways, including transparency and color inversion.

The active layer is shown on the Data Display bar (**Figure 5.2**).

To choose the active layer:

◆ Click on the Layer menu in the Data Display bar and drag down to the layer you want to make active.

The Layer menu shows the visibility setting of each layer as well as whether visible and gray layers are in Plan view or not (**Figure 5.3**). (VectorWorks also refers to Plan view as Top/Plan view; the two terms are synonymous.).

Layers (unlike classes) locate 3D objects in 3D space, and you can define them so that things wind up in the right relationships when you assemble the 3D elements of a model.

Figure 5.2 The Data Display bar shows both the active layer and the active class.

Figure 5.3 From the Layer menu you select which layer is active (which is where the objects you create will be placed). The visibility and view orientation of each layer is indicated by the icons (Mac version is at left).

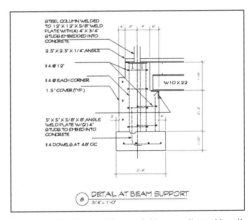

Figure 5.4 Working on the model is complicated by all the extra information in the notes and dimensions.

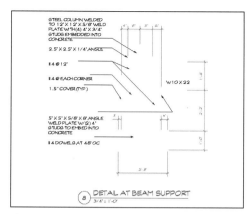

Figure 5.5 Putting the dimensions and notes on a separate layer lets you turn them on and off as you go.

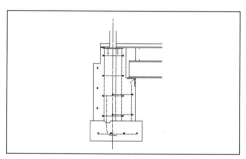

Figure 5.6 The drawing is easier to work on when you hide the layer of extraneous material and show only the design elements.

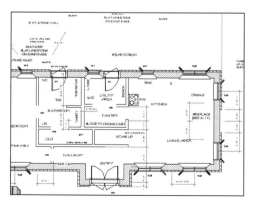

Figure 5.7 When you view an area of a drawing in Plan view with all the notation and dimensions visible, that 2D information makes sense.

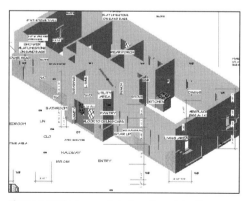

Figure 5.8 When you rotate the 3D model, 2D elements in the drawing remain fixed and no longer make much sense.

Architects commonly assign several layers to each floor of a building so that they can put the design components on certain layers and the notes and dimensions on another. That way, you can hide all the annotations and dimensions while you're doing the actual design work (**Figures 5.4**, **5.5**, and **5.6**). Then you can select only the layers made up of 3D elements when you link layers to form a complete (or partial) model (see Chapter 10, "Worksheets, Reports, and Presentations").

Two-dimensional elements in a layer don't move as you rotate the 3D model. You will usually want to hide them when viewing a rendered 3D representation of the design (**Figures 5.7** and **5.8**).

LAYERS

In mechanical drawings individual sub-assemblies are sometimes put on separate layers. Instead of drawing each subassembly on its own sheet (as you might with paper drawings), you can put each on its own layer or layers in a single document so you can display and print each by itself, in combination with others, and finally as part of a complete assembly (**Figure 5.9**). You can also set up multiple layers to create alternative configurations that you can view by turning on and off the affected layers (**Figure 5.10**).

Each layer in a drawing can have its own scale, so you can set up layers at a larger scale for details and at a reduced scale for the site plan. Some users like to set up their drawing stationery in a layer of its own at a 1:1 scale. In general, the use of layers is a pretty personal thing; different offices use them in different ways.

To create a new layer:

1. Choose Organize > Layers

   or

   Choose Layers from the Layers drop-down menu in the Data Display bar (**Figure 5.11**). The Layers Setup dialog box opens (**Figure 5.12**).

2. Click New.

   The Layer Options dialog box opens (**Figure 5.13**).

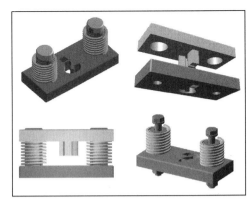

Figure 5.9 Displaying and hiding layers lets you put together as many variant subassembly drawings as you want.

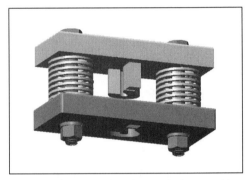

Figure 5.10 You can replace the pins in the assembly with screws and nuts by turning off the pin layer and displaying the screw layer instead.

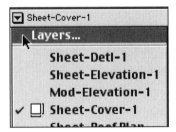

Figure 5.11 Choosing the Layers command from the Layers menu in the Data Display bar opens the Layers Setup dialog box.

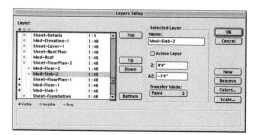

Figure 5.12 The Layers Setup dialog box is where you create new layers and edit existing ones.

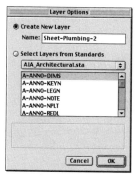

Figure 5.13 The Layer Options dialog box presents two options for naming a new layer.

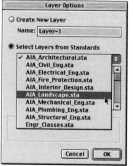

Figure 5.14 When you click the Select Layers from Standards radio button, you can choose from a long list of layer names (though this list is really better suited to setting up Class names). that accord with the AIA format.

3. Give the new layer a name by doing one of the following:

Select the Select Layers from Standards radio button, choose a standard from the pop-up menu, and then pick a layer name from the list that opens in the window (**Figure 5.14**)

or

Select the Create New Layer radio button and type a name for the new layer in the Name field.

4. Click OK.

The Layer Options dialog box closes and the Layers Setup dialog box displays the name of the new layer at the top of the list with the same scale as the layer below it.

5. Use the Top, Up, Down, and Bottom buttons to move the new layer to its proper place in the stack. The visibility of objects in a layer depends on what is above and below it in the stack (see below).

6. Check the Active Layer box if you want the new layer to be the active one when you finish its creation.

7. Set both the Z and the ΔZ (Mac) or $\pm Z$ (Windows) values for the layer.

The Z value sets the elevation above the ground plane at which the whole layer will be placed when you create a model using the Create Layer Link command (see Chapter 10, "Worksheets, Reports, and Presentations").

Set the $\Delta Z/\pm Z$ field to specify the default height of walls and extrusions in the layer.

By default, the Z value of a new layer is set so that the Ground plane of the layer will sit neatly on top of walls (and other objects that extend the default height above the Ground plane) created in the layers already in the document; the $\Delta Z/\pm Z$ value is the same as that of the layer below it.

continues on next page

LAYERS

8. Choose a Transfer mode from the drop-down menu (**Figure 5.15**).

The Transfer mode controls the way objects within a layer are displayed when they overlap and how the objects interact with objects in layers below their layer. Most people use the default Paint mode. In this mode, lines and fills hide objects in the layers below (**Figure 5.16**).

The Overlay mode simulates the use of transparent inks, allowing you to see objects in layers below the transparent layer. (**Figure 5.17**).

The other choices are used much less frequently. The term Not in this menu (as in Not Paint or Not Overlay) means that the colors of the layer are inverted and then painted, overlaid, and so forth onto the stack.

Transfer modes also affect how you see overlapping objects within a single layer. By default, as objects are drawn in a layer, they are placed one on top of the other. Rearranging the stacking order of objects within a layer is pretty simple (see below).

Figure 5.15 The pop-up menu for Transfer mode sets how VectorWorks displays objects that overlap one another.

Figure 5.16 When you stay with the default Paint mode, it's like drawing on clear acetate layers with opaque inks.

Figure 5.17 The Overlay mode simulates transparent inks on clear acetates. Colors in overlay layers blend with the colors of objects behind them.

LAYERS

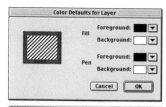

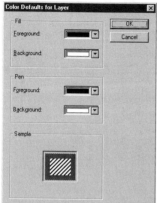

Figure 5.18 The Color Defaults for Layer dialog box sets the colors that will be used if you choose the Use Layer Colors option (Windows version is on the bottom).

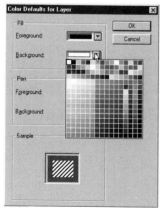

Figure 5.19 You pick each color for the layer colors option from pop-up palettes on the Color Defaults for Layer dialog box.

9. Click the Colors button.

   The Color Defaults for Layer dialog box opens (**Figure 5.18**).

10. Use the pop-up color palettes to set the Foreground and Background colors for the Fill and Pen (**Figure 5.19**).

    These are the colors that will be used to display the objects in the layer only when you select the Use Layer Colors option in the Document Preferences. Otherwise, the colors will be controlled by the Attributes palette.

    Click OK to close the Color Defaults for Layer dialog box.

continues on next page

11. Click the Scale button on the Layers Setup dialog box.

    The Layer Scale dialog box opens (**Figure 5.20**).

12. Set the Layer Scale options by picking one of the two following options:

    In the Layer Scale dialog box, select the radio button next to one of the preset scales

    or

    Type a value into the Paper Scale field.
    Check the All Layers checkbox to apply the new scale to all the layers in the document. Otherwise the setting controls only the selected layer.

    Check the Scale Text checkbox to have any text already in the layer or text you move in from another layer scaled along with the other objects.

    Click OK to close the Layer Scale dialog box.

13. Set the visibility of the layer when it's not the active layer by clicking in one of the three narrow columns to the left of the layer's name on the Layers Setup dialog box as follows:

    Click in the leftmost column to set the layer as visible. When the layer is inactive, objects in the layer appear normally when the Layer Options are set to Show Others, Show/Snap Others

    or

    Show/Snap/Modify Others. It will display only gray outlines when you select Gray Others in the Layer Options and will be invisible when you pick Active Only (**Figure 5.21**).

    Click in the right column to make objects in the layer fully visible only when it's active. Otherwise the objects in the layer will be gray outlines (unless you choose Organize > Layer Options > Active Only) (**Figure 5.22**).

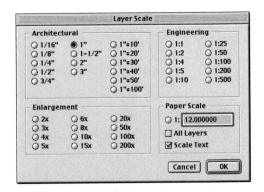

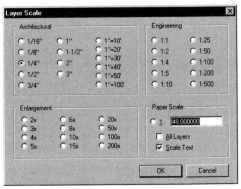

Figure 5.20 To set the scale for each layer (or all of them if you click the All Layers checkbox), use the Layer Scale dialog box (Mac version on the top).

Figure 5.21 The number "2" is not in the active layer, but it is set as a visible layer in the Layers Setup dialog box, so it shows up as normal.

Figure 5.22 The number "2" is in an inactive layer and is set to gray in the visibility section of the Layer Settings dialog box.

Figure 5.23 When a layer is set to invisible, its contents are hidden until that layer is made active.

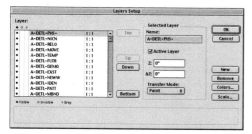

Figure 5.24 The AIA layer names are designed to facilitate the exchange of files.

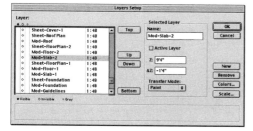

Figure 5.25 Many architects prefer to stick with traditional naming conventions for CAD layers.

Click in the middle column to keep the layer invisible except when it's the active layer (**Figure 5.23**).

The captions for the visibility of the layers are shown below the layer names box. Visibility settings can be changed either by going back to the Layers Setup dialog box or through the Saved Sheet procedures (see below).

14. Click OK to close the Layers Setup dialog box and add the new layer to the drawing.

✔ Tips

- Many people prefer to use a system of descriptive layer names or those adopted by their offices rather than those in the AIA Standard list (**Figures 5.24** and **5.25**).

- Usually, you don't have to start from scratch every time you start a new drawing because the layer and class structures (as well as such things as the title block, text style, dimension standard, and even a library of symbols) are part of the templates you used as the basis for the drawing. Therefore, you should probably stick with the standardized names for Classes since they designate types of objects (A-FURN-STOR, for example, designates Furniture System Storage Components) rather than spatial relationships.

LAYERS

Once you have created a layer, you may have cause to modify it. Sometimes you just want to change its name or its place in the stacking order; other times, you realize that a change of scale or Z value is called for.

To edit a layer:

1. Choose Organize > Layers

   or

   Choose Layers from the Layers drop-down menu in the Data Display bar.

   The Layers Setup dialog box opens.

2. In the list at the left, highlight the layer you want to modify.

3. Follow steps 5 through 13 above.

✔ Tips

- To remove a layer, open the Layers Setup dialog box, highlight the layer you want to eliminate, and click Remove. As the removal of a layer deletes everything in that layer, VectorWorks gives you a chance to rethink your decision (**Figure 5.26**). Click Yes only if you really want to go ahead.

- You can't modify or snap to objects in a layer that's set at a different scale than the active layer, even if you've set the Layer Options to Show/Snap/Modify Others.

- You also can't work with objects in other layers unless both the active and the inactive layers are in Plan view (see Chapter 7, "Creating 3D Objects").

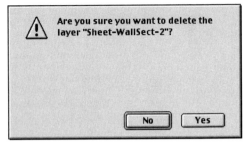

Figure 5.26 When you delete a layer, everything in the layer disappears from the drawing. VectorWorks lets you reconsider.

The AIA Standard

The standard list of layer and class names VectorWorks offers is derived from the American Institute of Architects AIA CAD Layer Guidelines. This document was designed to accommodate the transfer of files between offices and between CAD applications. It reflects a certain bias toward the most common protocol for file translation, DWG/DXF, which is based on AutoCAD.

The AutoCAD legacy is bound to create some confusion for VectorWorks users, because VectorWorks's dialog boxes use the same standardized names for both layers and classes. AutoCAD, on the other hand, doesn't have anything like VectorWorks's layer structure, but it does use something like VectorWorks's classes—except it calls them *layers*.

LAYERS

Managing Objects in Layers

When you create an object, it is automatically placed in whatever layer is active. Sometimes you will want to change the layer that an object or set of objects inhabits.

To move objects from one layer to another:

1. Open the Object Info palette by choosing Palettes > Object Info, or by pressing Command-I (Mac) or Ctrl-I (Windows).

2. Use the 2D Selection tool to select the objects you want to move to another layer.

3. On the Object Info palette, select the name of the destination layer from the drop-down list of layers.

   The objects are placed in the new layer. If that layer isn't visible, the objects disappear from sight. If the layer is visible, how the objects are displayed depends on the stacking order and the Transfer modes of the layers involved.

   An object retains its size in the units of the drawing. This means that its apparent size may change dramatically when it moves to a layer with a different scale.

✔ Tip

■ When you group objects from different layers, the group becomes part of the active layer. If you then ungroup the objects, they remain in that layer rather than reverting to the layers they came from before they were grouped.

Dimensions and Layers

With earlier versions of VectorWorks, it was usual to put dimensions into a layer separate from the model's. In architectural offices, this meant putting them on a sheet layer rather than on the model layer. But VectorWorks 9 now offers *associative dimensioning*, which ties the dimension to the objects in the drawing so that the dimension updates automatically when the objects are moved or reshaped (see Chapter 10, "Worksheets, Reports, and Presentations").

Associative dimensions are a kind of Parametric constraint (see Chapter 4, "Drawing with Constraints") and don't work across layers. So you have to choose between using associative dimensions and putting the dimensions onto another layer. Since dimensions are automatically placed into their own class, which you can show or hide, the best compromise may be to leave them on the model layer and control their visibility with the class settings.

Object are stacked in a layer in the order in which you create them. Newer objects are treated as being "in front" of the older ones and can obscure the view and complicate the selection of those already in the layer. You move objects forward and backward in the stack via the Send commands.

Figure 5.27 When you draw an object overlapping one already in the document, the one below may be obscured.

To change the stacking order of objects within a layer:

1. Make the layer you want to rearrange active by clicking the Layers menu on the Data Display bar and dragging down to its name.

2. Use the 2D Selection tool to select the objects you want to move forward or backward within the layer (**Figure 5.27**).

Figure 5.28 Moving an object forward within a layer brings it out from behind one that hid it.

3. Choose Tool > Send and select an option from the list as follows:

   Send to Front or press Command-F (Mac) or Ctrl-F (Windows) to move the objects to the front of the stack within the layer (**Figure 5.28**).

   Send Forward or press Command-Option-F (Mac) or Alt-Ctrl+F (Windows) to move the objects one level forward in the stack.

   Send to Back or press Command-B (Mac) or Ctrl-B (Windows) to move the objects to the back of the stack within the layer.

   Send Backward or press Command-Option-B (Mac) or Alt-Ctrl-B (Windows) to move the objects one level back in the stack.

✔ Tip

- When you select several objects to move forward and backward at once, they retain their order relative to one another as they move relative to the other items in the layer.

MANAGING OBJECTS IN LAYERS

Classes and Layers

Since both layers and classes let you control the visibility and selectability of the objects in your drawing, it might seem like a matter of whim whether to group like objects as one or the other. But layers and classes each have some additional features that you should take into account when setting up a document.

Here are reasons for setting up a new *layer*:

1. A layer has an inherent spatial dimension that you assign in the Layers Setup dialog box when you create it. This makes the design of multi-storied buildings simpler and can be useful when you work with mechanical models as well.

2. Objects affect the visibility of others in the layers below them. Putting objects closer to the viewer in higher layers helps you visualize complex constructions even when they are drawn in only two dimensions.

3. You can give each layer its own scale. This is useful when you want to create details at an enlarged scale or set up the border and title block at 1:1.

4. When you set up workgroup referencing, which allows several people to work from a common document, you can specify which layers from the master document are placed in the target document and which are not, so you don't have to import such large files.

5. The Wall tool and the Extrude command both use the $\Delta Z/\pm Z$ setting of the layer as a default height. Setting the Z values for a layer can save a lot of time, especially if you are doing a lot of walls.

6. When you build a 3D model by linking several layers of your document, you should do it in a new layer created just for that purpose so that the layers will array themselves correctly along the z axis.

Classes, on the other hand, have a few handy tricks of their own:

1. Classes are good for grouping things that may appear on several layers (plumbing fixtures in an architectural drawing or bearings in a mechanical one). You can show or hide, select or deselect, all the members of a class in one action.

2. You can use membership in a class as a criterion by which data is automatically entered into a worksheet that can total up the quantities of various items, calculate square footage or costs, and export the information to other applications.

3. Classes can be organized hierarchically into subclasses and even sub-subclasses for easier selection from the menus.

4. You can have all objects in a class override the active settings in the Attributes palette and take on those assigned to the class (including texture if you have RenderWorks installed). For example, all the objects in the sub-subclass Furniture-Desk-Executive can be drawn in purple lines with a green and blue patterned fill and rendered in walnut. Those in the sub-subclass Furniture-Desk-Peon can be drawn in brown and rendered as beige laminate (**Figure 5.29**).

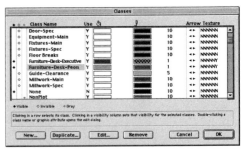

Figure 5.29 You can easily set up a class structure to draw Executive and Peon desks with different graphic attributes and render them in the appropriate materials.

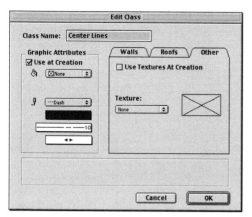

Figure 5.30 Use classes to control the line styles in your drawings.

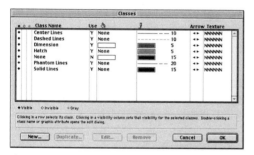

Figure 5.31 The ME templates included with Vector-Works are designed to use classes to assign line styles.

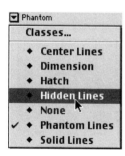

Figure 5.32 Choose the class you want to make active by dragging down the Data Display bar's Class menu.

Classes

Classes don't have any dimensional characteristics, but each class has a set of graphic attributes that you can set to be automatically applied to every object created in the class. Because classes are applied to objects irrespective of their layers, you can display a number of layers (all the floors of a building, say) and still have control over which classes (plumbing and electrical, for example) are displayed and which (structural framing and furniture, say) are hidden.

Setting up classes is similar to setting up layers. You first name the class and create it, then you edit its variables.

Some designers use classes as a quick way of managing distinctive line styles in a drawing: Create a class for each line style, and click the Use at Creation checkbox. (**Figure 5.30**). Changing styles then is as simple as selecting a class from the Data Display bar menu.

The ME (mechanical engineering) templates provided with VectorWorks include a set of line style classes (**Figure 5.31**).

Objects are members of whatever class is active when you create them. Make sure the class you want an object to belong to is the active class before you create it; this will save yourself the nuisance of having to change it later. The active class is shown in the Data Display bar.

To set the active class:

◆ Click on the Class menu in the Data Display bar, and drag down to the name of the class you want to make active (**Figure 5.32**).

CLASSES

Setting up and editing classes

To create a new class:

1. Choose Organize > Classes

   or

   Choose Classes from the Classes drop-down menu in the Data Display bar.

   The Classes dialog box opens (**Figures 5.33** and **5.34**).

2. Click New.

   The Class Options dialog box opens (**Figure 5.35**).

3. Do one of the following:

   Select the Create New Class radio button and type a name for the new class in the Name field

   or

   Select the Select Classes from the Standards radio button, choose a standard from the pop-up menu, and pick a class name from the AIA standards list (**Figure 5.36**).

4. Click OK.

   The class is added to the list alphabetically, with default attributes.

5. Set the class visibility by clicking in one of the three columns on the left to specify the display of a class when it's not the active class (see Chapter 10, "Worksheets, Reports, and Presentations").

   When you choose Organize > Class Options > Show/Snap/Modify Others, classes you have designated as Visible are visible, classes designated Gray are gray, and classes marked Invisible are marked invisible, and so on.

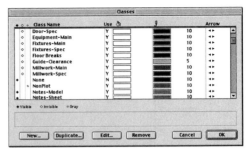

Figure 5.33 When RenderWorks isn't installed, the Classes dialog box lacks a Texture column.

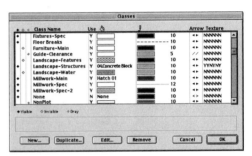

Figure 5.34 All the classes in the document are listed alphabetically in the Classes dialog box.

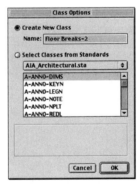

Figure 5.35 The Class Options dialog box is where you name a new class.

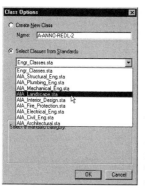

Figure 5.36 The list of AIA standards drops down when you click the button next to Select Classes from Standards field of the Class Options dialog box.

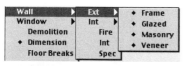

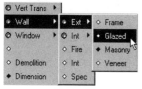

Figure 5.37 When you drag down the Class menu on the Data Display bar, a class that has subclasses attached to it is marked by an arrow (Mac) or a radio button (Windows).

Figure 5.38 The Assign Name dialog box opens when you duplicate a class from the class name list.

✔ Tip

■ Giving classes hyphenated names is a way of grouping them under common headings. On the Data Display bar's Class menu, classes with subclasses cascade out to reveal the full extent of the repertoire (**Figure 5.37**).

If you need to create a new class with characteristics similar to one you already have, you can save yourself valuable time by using the existing class as the starting point.

To create a new class by duplication:

1. Open the Classes dialog box by doing one of the following:

   Choose Organize > Classes

   or

   Choose Classes > from the Classes drop-down menu in the Data Display bar.

   The Classes dialog box opens.

2. Click on the name of the class you want to duplicate.

   The class name is highlighted.

3. Click the Duplicate button below the Class Name list.

   The Assign Name dialog box opens (**Figure 5.38**).

4. Type a name for the new class in the edit box and click OK.

   A new class, with attributes identical to the original's, is placed in the Class Name list.

CLASSES

To edit a class:

1. Choose Organize > Classes

   or

   Choose Classes from the Classes drop-down menu in the Data Display bar.

   The Classes dialog box opens.

2. Highlight the class you want to modify and click the Edit button.

   The Edit Class dialog box opens (**Figure 5.39**).

3. In the Edit Class dialog box, you can enter a new class name in the Class Name field.

4. In the Graphic Attributes area, check the Use at Creation checkbox if you want the attributes in the panel to override the default attributes in the Attributes palette.

   Classes that use their graphic attributes at creation display a Y in the Use column in the Classes dialog box. Otherwise, an N is shown.

5. Set the Class Attributes for Fill (style and colors) and for Pen (style, thickness, and colors) as well as for the style of terminator to be used where that applies.

   The arrow style for the class is displayed under the heading Arrow in the Classes dialog box.

6. If you've installed RenderWorks, the Edit Class dialog box will have an additional area with three tabs for configuring textures (**Figure 5.40**).

   You can set the textures independently for the walls, roofs and other objects in the class.

7. Click OK to make the changes to the Edit Class dialog box.

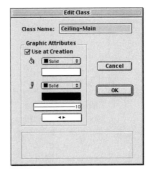

Figure 5.39 The Edit Class dialog box allows you to change the attributes of a class and to choose the option of using the attributes whenever an object is created in the class.

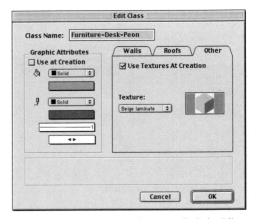

Figure 5.40 When RenderWorks is installed, the Edit Class dialog box has an additional section for setting class textures.

✔ Tips

- If you don't select the Use at Creation option for the class's attributes, you can still apply them by choosing the Class Style, Class Thickness, or Class Color option from the Attributes palette.

- If you go back and check the Use at Creation option in the Edit Class dialog box, you will be offered the option of retroactively setting all the objects already part of the class to these attributes.

- Removing a class does not delete the objects within it (as you *can* do with layers, which are sometimes said to "contain" objects and not just to classify them). The objects just become members of the default class None.

- When you bring an object into a drawing from another drawing, the classes associated with it are imported at the same time. A symbol, for example, may be constructed from objects of several classes; once it's constructed, those objects become part of the file into which they are brought.

- Symbols don't take their attributes from the class to which they are assigned; their size and appearance are fixed at the time that they are created (see Chapter 6, "2D Symbols and PIOs").

Managing Objects in Classes

An object is a member of whatever class is active when it is created. The exceptions are dimensions, which always go into the Dimensions class, and some plug-in objects that go into the default class None. These are the two default classes that exist when you open a blank document, and they can't be removed. You can, however, edit them to change their names and attributes.

Changing the class to which an object or set of objects is assigned is simple enough. Often you will create a new class in the course of the design process and then need to go back and change the class membership of objects you have already drawn.

Unlike layers, the stacking order of classes in the menu has no impact on their visibility; they are arranged alphabetically.

Figure 5.41 From the pull-down menu in the Object Info palette, select the class into which you want to place the selected objects.

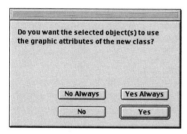

Figure 5.42 When you change the class of an object to one that uses its graphic attributes at creation, an alert box pops up to let you choose this option.

Figure 5.43 Little arrows in the fields of the Attributes palette signify that the attribute is controlled by class settings (Windows version is on the left).

To change the class of an object:

1. Open the Object Info palette by choosing Palettes > Object Info, or press Command-I (Mac) or Ctrl-I (Windows).

2. Use the 2D Selection tool to select the objects you want to move to another class.

3. In the Object Info palette, choose the destination class from the drop-down list of Classes (**Figure 5.41**).

    The selected objects will be placed in the new class. If the objects are not now using class attributes but the new class was set up to use its graphic attributes when objects are created in it, you will be asked if you want to use those attributes (**Figure 5.42**).

    Click No if you don't want to change them, but you want the choice next time you change the class of an object.

    Click No Always if you don't want to change the attributes of the object and don't want the message to pop up again.

    Click Yes if you want to change the attributes this time, but want the option to not change them when you make other changes.

    Click Yes Always if you want to change the attributes to those of the class and you want the attributes to change every time you change the class of an object.

✔ Tips

■ When you make an Always or Never selection, it remains in force until you exit and restart the application.

■ In general, a change of class will automatically change whichever attributes of an object are already controlled by the Class settings (as shown by the little arrow in the Attributes palette) (**Figure 5.43**).

Using Saved Sheets

You can use VectorWorks's Saved Sheets function to preserve for later recall a particular combination of visible, gray layer, and class settings; a view; or a perspective.

This is important because it often takes a while to get those settings just right. Remember that a saved sheet records only the conditions of the view. The content continues to change as you develop the drawing file.

A drawing often has lots of layers and classes. It is very useful to be able to quickly set all their visibilities at once. But a saved sheet doesn't have to dictate all the settings. For example, you could choose to save only the layer settings, leaving the view unchanged. You could even choose to affect only some of the layers and classes and leave the rest as they are.

Once you have saved and edited a sheet, you can view it by clicking the Saved Sheet button on the View bar and selecting the one you want from the pop-up list.

To Save a Sheet:

1. Choose Page > Save Sheet

   or

   From the View bar a the bottom of the window, click the Sheets Menu button and choose Save Sheet from the pop-up menu (**Figure 5.44**).

   The Save Sheet dialog box opens (**Figure 5.45**).

2. In the Save Sheet dialog box, type a name into the Sheet Name field.

3. Check the Save View checkbox if you want to revert to the current view (as opposed to just the layer and/or class settings) when this saved sheet is recalled.

Figure 5.44 When you click the Sheets menu button in the View bar, the list of sheets you've already saved is displayed below the Save Sheet and Edit Sheet commands.

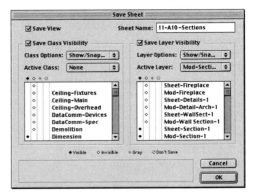

Figure 5.45 The Save Sheet dialog box contains the settings for creating a saved sheet for future reference.

4. If you want to save any settings relating to Class, check the Save Class Visibility checkbox.

If you want to save the class settings as-is, you're done with this part. Otherwise, choose the Class Options and the Active Class you want from their respective pop-up menus.

Then you can go through the list of classes used in the drawing file and individually tweak their visibility, setting them as Visible, Gray, or Invisible. Or select the Don't Save option to leave them as they were when you selected the saved sheet.

5. If you want to save any settings relating to Layer, check the Save Layer Visibility checkbox.

If you want to save the layer settings as-is, you're done with this part. Otherwise, choose the Layer Options and the Active Layer you want from their respective popup menus.

Then you can go through the list of layers used in the drawing file and individually tweak their visibility, setting them Visible, Gray, or Invisible. Or, select the Don't Save option to leave them as they were when you selected the saved sheet.

6. Click OK.

The dialog box closes and the new sheet is added to the list in the View bar.

To Open a Saved Sheet:

1. On the View bar, click the Saved Sheet button (the down arrow) and drag down to highlight the sheet you want.

2. Release the mouse. The view will change to show the saved sheet, using whatever criteria you established when you created it.

Sometimes you will find it easier to edit a saved sheet than to create a new one.

To edit a Saved Sheet:

1. Click on the Saved Sheet button in the View bar and drag up to Edit Sheet.

   The Edit Save Sheet dialog box opens (**Figure 5.46**).

2. Make whatever changes in the configuration are necessary. Click OK to close the Edit Save Sheet dialog box.

✔ Tips

- When you add new layers and classes to a drawing, they remain invisible in existing saved sheets until you edit the sheet to make them either visible or gray.

- The Save Sheet command is also available on the Page menu, but you can edit sheets or access previously saved ones only from the View bar.

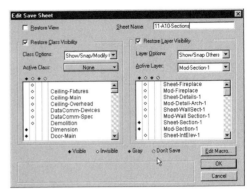

Figure 5.46 The Edit Saved Sheet dialog box is pretty much the same as the Save Sheet one except for its title bar.

2D SYMBOLS AND PIOS

VectorWorks comes with a number of ready-made objects you can use to save yourself a lot of time. Some of these are symbols and some of them are *plug-in objects* (PIOs). Both are placed in the drawing either from the Resources palette (using the 2D Symbol Insertion tool) or directly from the Object Browser.

It is important to grasp the differences between symbols and PIOs—and it's not always immediately obvious which is which.

Basically, every instance of a symbol in a drawing is a visible copy of an object that inhabits a hidden layer in the drawing (that object is the *symbol definition*). When you edit a symbol, you leave the visible drawing and enter this hidden realm. The symbol definition is part of the drawing file.

A PIO, on the other hand, is drawn by an interactive script (a bit of programming magic) that is stored in the Plug-Ins folder in the VectorWorks folder on your hard drive. When you use one of those scripts, you create a unique object, but you can't edit it as you would an object you draw yourself. Instead, the Object Info palette becomes a sort of control panel for the object, offering a variety of menus and edit boxes that reshape the object as you adjust its parameters.

Symbols

The symbols in a drawing are "instances" of their definitions. That is, all their properties (other than their positions and their layer and class assignments) are copied from an object that does not appear in the drawing itself.

The symbol definition has to be part of the drawing file in which the symbol is used, but you can quickly import symbol definitions from other drawing files, including the ones VectorWorks supplies.

If you've created multiple objects from the same symbol definition and you need to make a global change to them, changing the symbol definition changes every instance in the drawing. If you just cut and paste a lot of copies of an object (or group) all over your drawing, you have to change them one at a time. Symbols are easy to create from objects in your drawing and they are easy to modify (see below).

Symbols (and PIOs) have a very special relationship to wall objects: Walls open up to make a space for them, so that the insertion of windows, doors, and the like is relatively effortless. This is a very important feature of VectorWorks. Insertion of objects into walls is covered in Chapter 9, "Architectural Applications."

The most direct way to place a symbol is from the Object Browser, but you can also select a symbol from the Resources palette or pick one up from the drawing itself using the 2D Symbol Insertion tool's Pick Up Symbol mode.

To place a symbol using the Object Browser:

1. Choose Palettes > Object Browser, or press Command-H (Windows) or Ctrl-H (Mac).

   The Object Browser opens (**Figure 6.1**).

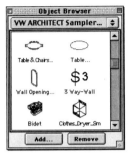

Figure 6.1 The Object Browser is a streamlined interface between you and all the objects you can put into the drawing using the symbol insertion tools.

Figure 6.2 Choose among all the available files from the drop-down menu at the top of the Object Browser.

Figure 6.3 You can't see it here in black and white, but the first five objects are shown in red, indicating they're PIOs. The others are in black; they are static symbols. Any editable objects would appear in blue.

Figure 6.4 When you choose a symbol (or other insertable object in the Object Browser), it is highlighted in the Object Browser window.

Figure 6.5 The Mode bar has buttons that temporarily shift the insertion point of a symbol.

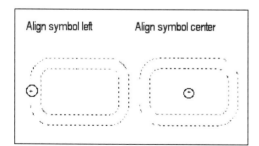

Figure 6.6 The position of the symbol relative to the cursor depends on which button you chose on the Mode bar.

2. From the drop-down menu at the top of the Object Browser, choose a file from which you want to use a symbol (**Figure 6.2**).

The Browser window will display thumbnails and names for all the symbols in the selected file. The symbols are black, while other kinds of objects are red or blue (**Figure 6.3**).

3. In the Object Browser window, scroll to the symbol you want to insert and click it.

The Insert 2D Symbol tool is selected and the symbol is highlighted (**Figure 6.4**).

4. On the Mode bar, choose an insertion mode button that moves the symbol's insertion point. For example, click the Align Symbol Left button to temporarily shift the insertion point of the symbol along the x-axis all the way to the left edge of the symbol.

Click the last button to use the insertion point as it exists in the symbol definition (**Figure 6.5**).

5. Move the cursor in the drawing area where you want to place the symbol.

As you move the cursor in the drawing area, the cursor marks the insertion point and the symbol is positioned relative to it according to the setting on the Mode bar (**Figure 6.6**).

continues on next page

SYMBOLS

6. Click to set the insertion point.

The symbol is shown in a preview mode; moving the cursor sets the rotation of the symbol around the insertion point (**Figure 6.7**).

7. Click again to complete the placement of the symbol at the desired rotation (**Figure 6.8**).

✔ Tips

■ Press the I key to toggle the insertion point mode among the mode choices.

■ If you select a 3D or hybrid symbol while in a 3D view, the 3D Symbol Insertion tool is selected and the object is placed relative to the working plane (see Chapter 7, "Creating 3D Objects").

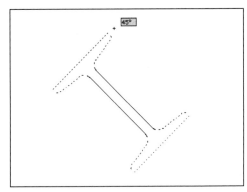

Figure 6.7 After you click to place the insertion point for the symbol, drag the cursor around to set the angle.

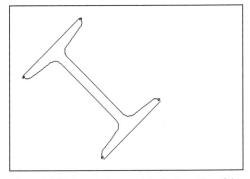

Figure 6.8 Click again to complete the insertion of the symbol.

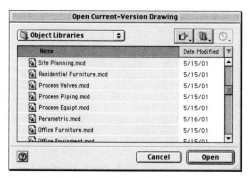

Figure 6.9 To add more files to the Object Browser, click the Add button at the bottom to open the Open Current-Version Drawing navigation box.

By default, the Object Browser's drop-down menu lists the drawing files VectorWorks provides in the Object Libraries folder. In addition, it gives you access to the symbols residing in all open drawing files; however, these libraries close when the file is closed. You can also add files that stay on the list until you remove them.

To add symbols to the Object Browser:

1. At the bottom of the Object Browser, click Add.

The Open Current-Version Drawing navigation box opens (**Figure 6.9**).

2. In the Open Current-Version Drawing navigation box, select the drawing file from which you want to use symbols.

3. Click Open.

The symbols (as well as the plug-in objects and editable groups) from the file are added to the Object Browser.

These files will remain part of the Object Browser and are available to all drawing files until you remove them.

To remove files from the Object Browser:

1. On the Object Browser, select the file you want to remove.

2. Click Remove.

The file is removed from the Object Browser.

SYMBOLS

Working from the Resources Palette

You can also place symbols using the Resources palette. The advantage of using this palette is that you can see which symbols are 2D, 3D, and hybrid. But you can't distinguish symbols from PIOs or editable groups, as you can with the Object Browser's color coding.

To place a symbol from the Resources palette:

1. Open the Resources palette by choosing Palettes > Resources or pressing Command-R (Mac) or Ctrl-R (Windows) (**Figure 6.10**).

2. On the Resources palette, use the pop-up menu at the top to select an open file listed at the bottom of the pane

   or

   Navigate to another drawing file and press Enter (**Figure 6.11**).

   The resources of the selected drawing file (including the symbols) are listed in the menu.

3. Click on the symbol you want to place.

   The symbol is previewed in the right window at the bottom of the palette.

4. Click the Select button at the bottom center to activate the symbol (**Figure 6.12**). The symbol is displayed in the left window.

5. Click the 2D Symbol Insertion tool on the 2D Tools palette (**Figure 6.13**).

Figure 6.10 The Resources palette is the nerve center of a drawing file. That's where you can import, select, and edit symbols and record formats as well as hatches and commands.

Figure 6.11 Use the drop-down menu at the top of the Resources palette to navigate your way to other files so you can import their resources into the active file.

Figure 6.12 When you click a symbol (or PIO) from the menu in the Resources palette, it appears in the right window at the bottom. Click the Select arrow to make it the active symbol.

Figure 6.13 The 2D Symbol Insertion tool on the 2D Tools palette.

6. On the Mode bar, choose an insertion mode button that moves the symbol's insertion point along the *x*-axis from where it lies in the symbol definition. For example, click the Align Symbol Left button to temporarily shift the insertion point of the symbol along the *x*-axis all the way to the left edge of the symbol.

Click the last button to use the insertion point as it exists in the symbol definition.

7. Move the cursor in the drawing area where you want to place the symbol.

As you move the cursor in the drawing area, the cursor marks the insertion point and the symbol is positioned relative to it according to the setting on the Mode bar.

8. Click to set the insertion point.

The symbol is shown in a preview mode; moving the cursor sets the rotation of the symbol around the insertion point.

9. Click again to complete the placement of the symbol at the desired rotation.

✔ Tips

■ You can select a symbol in one step by double-clicking it on the Resources menu. It will immediately appear in both windows at the bottom of the palette.

■ Once a symbol has been used in a drawing, it becomes part of that drawing's resources. You can also import a symbol (or other resource) from another drawing by navigating to it in the Resources palette and clicking Import.

WORKING FROM THE RESOURCES PALETTE

Organizing Symbols

When you have a large number of symbols in a drawing, you should consider organizing them into folders. Not only does this reduce visual clutter and make it easier for you to find the symbol you're looking for, but it also makes it easier to import a relevant set of symbols from one file to another.

To create a new symbol folder:

1. On the Resources palette, click New.

   The Create Resource dialog box opens (**Figure 6.14**).

2. On the Create Resource dialog box, click the Symbol Folder radio button and click Create.

   The Assign Name dialog box opens (**Figure 6.15**).

3. Type the name you want to give the folder in the edit box and click OK.

   The new folder is placed on the menu on the Resources palette (**Figure 6.16**).

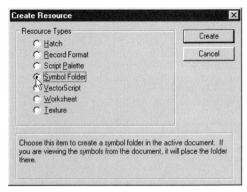

Figure 6.14 Click New on the Resources palette to open the Create Resource dialog box.

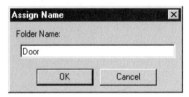

Figure 6.15 When the Assign Name dialog box opens, choose a name for the symbol folder you are creating.

Figure 6.16 The new folder now appears among the other resources on the Resources palette.

Figure 6.17 Use the Move Symbol (Mac) or Move (Windows) dialog box to put symbols into folders on the Resources palette.

To move symbols into a folder:

1. On the Resources palette, select the symbol you want to put into a folder.

   To move more than one symbol, hold down the Command (Mac) or Ctrl (Windows) key and make multiple selections.

2. On the Resources palette, click Move.

   The Move Symbol dialog box opens (**Figure 6.17**).

3. In the Move Symbol dialog box, navigate to the folder into which you want to place the selected symbols (on the Mac, you have to open the folder), and click OK.

   The symbol or symbols are moved into the selected folder.

✔ Tip

■ You can nest folders within one another (putting, say, Set Screws inside Screws inside the Fasteners folder).

Creating 2D Symbols

VectorWorks provides a pretty good set of symbols to start with (and don't overlook the files included as samples in the Resources folder for some extras), but building your own symbols is so easy that even the most timid should give it a try.

All kinds of things can be turned into symbols: ordinary objects, text, PIOs, groups, or even selections of multiple objects. Symbols can even be created from other symbols.

To create a 2D Symbol:

1. Select the object or group of objects you want to make into a symbol.

2. Choose Organize > Create Symbol.
   The Create Symbol dialog box opens (**Figure 6.18**).

3. Type a name for your new symbol in the Name field.

4. Check the Leave Instance In-Place box if you want the selection left where it is, so that it becomes the first instance of the new symbol.
   Otherwise, the objects are removed when the symbol is created.

5. Click either the Plan Projection Center or the Next Mouse Click radio button to set the default insertion point (see above).
   If you are using a symbol or a plug-in object as the basis for your new symbol, the dialog box will say Plug-in Center instead of Plan Projection Center.

6. Click Options.
   The Insertion Options dialog box opens (**Figure 6.19**).

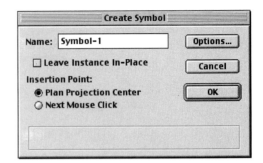

Figure 6.18 The Create Symbol dialog box.

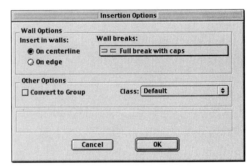

Figure 6.19 The Insertion Options dialog box, where you define the placement of your symbol in walls, choose a class, and specify whether or not it will remain a symbol once it's inserted.

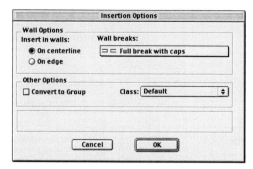

Figure 6.20 There are four possible treatments of the wall into which a symbol is inserted.

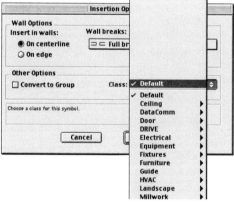

Figure 6.21 Use the Class drop-down menu to either make a class assignment part of the symbol definition or to let the symbol join the class that is active when it is placed.

7. In the Wall Options pane of the Insertion Options dialog box, select either the On centerline or the On edge radio button to set how the insertion point of the symbol will be placed within a wall object.

8. Under Wall breaks, choose an option from the drop-down menu (**Figure 6.20**).

The Wall breaks options come into play when you insert a symbol (a window or door, for example) into a wall (see Chapter 9, "Architectural Applications").

9. In the Other Options pane, check Convert to Group if you want to immediately convert the inserted object to an editable group.

An editable group is not linked to the definition that created it and can be modified by the usual methods.

If you are using a plug-in object as your original, the option will be Convert to Plug-in Object and you will be able to edit it using the Object Info palette.

10. Use the Class drop-down menu to choose a class for the new symbol; your choices are either to let it default to whatever class is active when you insert it or to assign the symbol to one of the classes in the drawing file (**Figure 6.21**).

Note that if your new symbol contains some PIOs, they may have internal class assignments that you can't change.

11. Click OK to close the Insertion Options dialog box and again to close the Create Symbol dialog box.

Click in the drawing area to set the insertion point if that option was chosen; otherwise the symbol is automatically created.

If the Leave Instance In-Place checkbox was not checked, the original object is removed from the drawing.

CREATING 2D SYMBOLS

Editing 2D Symbols

There are several ways to edit symbols. When you edit an instance of a symbol, you are in fact editing the symbol definition unless you separate—forever—the instance from its definition.

To edit a symbol in the drawing:

1. In the drawing, select the symbol you want to edit.

2. Choose Organize > Edit Symbol, or press Command-[(Mac) or Ctrl-[(Windows).

   The screen changes to show the unrotated symbol with vertical and horizontal dotted lines intersecting at the insertion point (**Figure 6.22**).

3. Edit the object that constitutes the symbol definition as follows:

   If the object is a plug-in, use the Object Info palette to make the required changes.

   If the object is a group or a nested symbol, you can edit its individual parts by selecting it and either choosing Organize > Edit Group or pressing Command-[(Mac) or Ctrl-[(Windows).

   You can move down through the levels of a symbol by choosing the Edit Group (or Edit Symbol command and move back up again either by choosing Exit Group (or Exit Symbol) or by pressing Command-] (Mac) or Ctrl-] (Windows).

4. Move the entire symbol relative to the origin to change the default insertion point.

5. When you have completed your changes, choose Organize > Top Level or click the Exit Symbol button on the Data Display bar until you have returned to the drawing.

   The screen returns to the drawing with the selected symbol, its definition, and all other instances modified.

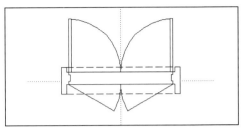

Figure 6.22 When you edit a 2D symbol, you move into a special layer and the symbol is shown unrotated. The insertion point is at the intersection of the dotted lines.

Hybrid and 3D Symbols

VectorWorks lets you place 3D objects in the symbol definitions to create 3D symbols. When you see a 3D object in the 2D (Plan view) space, what you see is the top view of the object (see Chapter 7, "Creating 3D Objects").

But you can also build what are called hybrid symbols by combining a 2D symbol with a 3D symbol. Hybrid symbols contain two different objects: The 2D one is displayed in Plan view, and the 3D one appears in all other views. This allows you to use a schematic symbol in the 2D Plan view that is automatically replaced by an object you can model in 3D when you go to a different view (a front or isometric view, for example) (**Figure 6.23**).

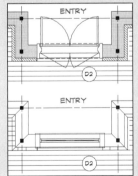

Figure 6.23 Hybrid symbols can look very different in Plan view than in Top view. The 2D symbol for a door (above) shows the doors with their swing; the Top orthogonal view (below) depicts the object as if you were looking down on it with the doors closed.

EDITING 2D SYMBOLS

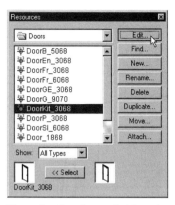

Figure 6.24 To edit a symbol from the Resources palette, highlight it and click Edit.

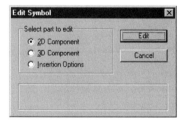

Figure 6.25 The Edit Symbol dialog box lets you edit the insertion options —something you can't do by choosing a symbol in the drawing area.

You can perform the same editing functions by selecting the symbol in the Resources palette. An advantage of using the Resources palette is that you can also edit the insertion options (see above), something you can't do by editing the instance in the drawing. And from the Resources palette you can add a 3D component to a 2D symbol or vice versa to create a hybrid symbol (see below), which you can't do from the drawing.

To edit a symbol from the Resources palette:

1. On the Resources palette, highlight the symbol definition you want to edit. You can only edit symbols in the active drawing file, although those symbols don't need to be in use in the drawing itself. (**Figure 6.24**).

2. Click Edit.
   The Edit Symbol dialog box opens (**Figure 6.25**).

3. In the Edit Symbol dialog box, select the component you want to modify or select the Insertion Options radio button.

4. Click Edit.
   If you selected the 2D component of a 2D or hybrid symbol, that component will be displayed on its own sublayer as discussed earlier. Click Exit Symbol on the Data Display bar or choose Organize > Top Level when you are finished.

   If you selected Insertion Options, the Insertion Options dialog box will open. Click OK when you are finished.

EDITING 2D SYMBOLS

Sometimes you want to edit just the selected instance of the symbol without changing all the other instances or the definition. This requires that the instance be cut loose from the definition; to do this, you choose the Convert to Group command.

To convert an instance of a symbol to a group:

1. Select the symbol you want to modify.

2. Choose Organize > Convert to Group.

    If the symbol contains other symbols or plug-in objects, the Convert to Group Options dialog box opens (**Figure 6.26**).

    If the symbol consists only of editable objects, it becomes a group (or, if it is only a single object, just an object).

3. In the Convert to Group Options dialog box, choose an option as follows:

    Click Don't convert sub-objects to groups if you want to break down the symbol only part way, leaving all its components intact.

    Click Convert nested symbols and plug-in objects to reduce the objects within the symbol to the level of directly editable objects.

    Click Convert all sub-objects to dissolve the symbol to its most primitive elements.

4. Click OK.

    The symbol instance is changed to a group that, depending on the choice made in the Convert to Group Options dialog box, may or may not contain other symbols or PIOs.

✔ Tip

■ If the symbol consists of a single object, it reverts to being just an object and does not become a group.

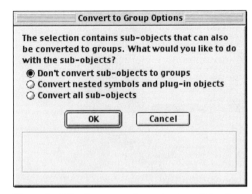

Figure 6.26 The Convert to Group Options dialog box opens to let you decide what to do with nested symbols or plug-in objects.

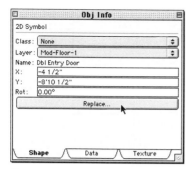

Figure 6.27 In the drawing area, you first select the symbol you want to replace and then go to the Object Info palette and click Replace.

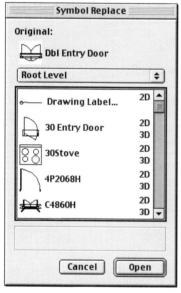

Figure 6.28 In the Symbol Replace dialog box, choose the symbol you want to swap for the existing one.

Replacing Symbols

Another advantage of symbols is that you can replace them from the Object Info palette with another symbol in the drawing file.

To replace symbols in the drawing:

1. Select the symbols you want to replace.

2. On the Object Info palette, click Replace (**Figure 6.27**).

   The Symbol Replace dialog box opens (**Figure 6.28**).

3. In the Symbol Replace dialog box, choose the symbol from the menu.

   If the replacement symbol is in a folder, highlight the folder and click Open (or double-click the folder in the menu).

4. Click Replace (or double-click the symbol).

   The new symbol replaces the old one(s) but retains its insertion point and rotation.

Deleting Symbols

If you find that your drawing file is so over-loaded with symbol definitions that finding the ones you want is a problem, it's time for some housecleaning.

To delete symbols from a drawing file:

1. On the Resources palette, select the symbols you want to delete. Use the Command (Mac) or Ctrl (Windows) key to select more than one.

2. Click the Delete button on the right side of the Resources palette.

   An alert pops up asking if you really want to delete the selected resources (**Figure 6.29**).

3. Click OK.

   The symbols are removed from the drawing.

   If you delete the definition of a symbol that is in use in the drawing, all that will remain will be a 3D locus at its insertion point (**Figure 6.30**).

✔ Tip

■ Plug-in objects do not use any resources within the drawing file, so deleting instances leaves no residue.

You can go all the way and remove all the symbols that are not in use in the drawing by *purging* the file of those symbols.

To purge the file of unused symbols:

1. Choose Edit > Purge Unused Objects. The Purge Unused Objects dialog box opens.

2. Click the Symbols checkbox and click OK.

   The unused symbols are removed, and so is the undo history of the file, making this procedure truly irreversible.

Figure 6.29 VectorWorks gives you a chance to change your mind before you delete resources from a drawing file.

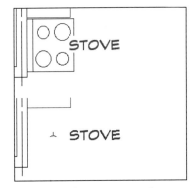

Figure 6.30 When you remove the symbol definition for a symbol in use in the drawing (top), a 3D locus replaces the symbol (bottom).

Records and Symbols

Another useful feature of symbols is their relationship with the database functions VectorWorks offers. You can attach database records to symbols so that you can generate spreadsheets and databases tracking all their instances —to create a door schedule, for example. Any object can have a record format (see Chapter 10, "Worksheets, Reports, and Presentations") attached to it, but symbols can include that record along with all relevant information associated with that symbol.

When you import a symbol from another document, it comes complete with both the record format and whatever information is part of the symbol definition. You can use other fields in the record format to enter other data pertaining to the specific instance of the symbol, such as its ID number, finish details, notes, or a location.

When you attach a record format to a symbol, it differs from other modifications to the symbol in that it is not retroactive. Only symbol instances placed after the fact will automatically have the new format. Instances already in the drawing have to be updated manually.

What's With These Records, Anyhow?

Any object in a VectorWorks drawing can carry a whole raft of information in the form of a *record*. But first a *record format* has to be attached to the object.

The record format sets up data fields that contain the information you want to record for each object. You can have many record formats in a drawing file, and an object can have more than one. For example, a lighting fixture could carry both a record format specific to electrical fixtures (manufacturer, voltage, finish, and so on) and a circuit information record containing data relating to wire size, breaker panels, switching, and so forth.

Once you've created a record format, you can attach it to a symbol with the fields that apply to all instances completed but with other fields left open for the individual instances. You can change the information in the record for each instance; records do not affect the symbol definition.

Records and their formats are covered more fully in Chapter 10, "Worksheets, Reports, and Presentations."

To attach a record format to a symbol definition:

1. On the Resources palette, highlight the symbol to which you want to attach a record format.

2. On the Resources palette, click Attach.

   The Attach Record dialog box opens (**Figure 6.31**).

3. In the Attach Record dialog box, highlight the record format you want to attach and click the Attached checkbox.

   A diamond marks the record formats attached to the symbol.

4. Click OK to close the dialog box and attach the record formats to the symbol definition.

   On the Object Info palette, the Data tab shows the records attached to the object selected in the drawing area (**Figure 6.32**).

✔ Tip

■ Remove record formats from symbol definitions by following the same procedure of highlighting the record formats on the Attach Record dialog box, except that you *uncheck* the Attached checkbox.

Figure 6.31 The Attach Record dialog box let you select one or more records to attach to the selected symbol.

Figure 6.32 You can change the record for any symbol that has a record format attached by entering data on the Data tab of the Object Info palette.

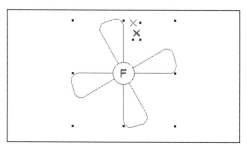

Figure 6.33 Once the type is placed relative to the symbol (and you're sure you like its alignment and other formatting), select them both.

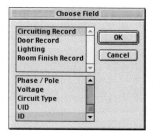

Figure 6.34 When you link the text of a record to a symbol, you have to tell the application which field in the record (lower menu) controls the text block.

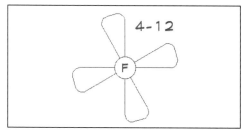

Figure 6.35 Once the text block is linked to the symbol's record, it shows whatever is entered into the selected field.

✔ Tip

- You can use the Eyedropper tool to pick up the record from one instance and apply it to other instances of the symbol (or even to other symbols) in the drawing.

Once a symbol has a record format attached, you can use the record to couple a text object to its instances. The text is derived from one of the fields of the record, so you can set it to a default value and then change it as you see fit. For instance, you can tag a tree symbol "spruce" and then change the instances for pines and larches from the Data tab of the Object Info palette.

To link text to a symbol:

1. Click the Type tool on the 2D Tool and click next to the symbol with which you want to associate the text.

   A text box appears with a blinking cursor.

2. Type in any character—an x will do—and click Enter to complete the entry.

3. Adjust the position and format of the text and make sure the symbol is not rotated.

4. Select both the text block and the symbol with which it is to be associated (**Figure 6.33**).

5. Choose Organize > Link Text to Record.

   The Choose Field dialog box opens (**Figure 6.34**).

6. From the upper menu, choose the record format for the record you want to attach.

7. From the lower menu, choose the particular record field that will control the text attached to the symbol.

8. Click OK to close the Choose Field dialog box and attach the text to the record to the symbol.

   The text block becomes part of the symbol definition, and in each instance the text block next to the symbol will change to whatever text is in the record for that symbol (**Figure 6.35**).

To edit the text attached to a record:

1. Select the symbol you want edit.

2. Choose Organize > Edit Symbol, or press Command-[(Mac) or Ctrl-[(Windows), and change the position and formatting of the text object component of the symbol.

   Click Exit Symbol to apply the changes to the symbol definition and all the instances in the drawing.

3. On the Data tab of the Object Info palette, highlight the record format name in the top pane and the record field in the middle pane.

   The value assigned to that record for the selected symbol appears in the bottom pane, which is where you'll change that value (**Figure 6.36**).

4. Once you've edited the text in the bottom pane, click Enter to change the value for the selected symbol (**Figure 6.37**).

Figure 6.36
The record for an individual symbol can be edited in the Object Info palette when the symbol is selected.

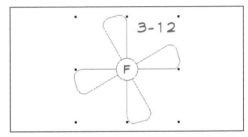

Figure 6.37 Changing the value in one of the record fields changes the text attached to the symbol.

Obj Info

Simple Window 2

Class:	None
Layer:	Layer-2
X:	-9'11 1/2"
Y:	11'0"
Z:	0"
Rot:	0.00°
3D:	Draw Using 3D Polys

☐ Installation settings ----------
☐ Ceiling View

Sill Depth:	4"
Stool Depth:	4"
☑ Has Trim1	
Trim1 Width:	4"
☑ Has Trim2	
Trim2 Width:	4"
Offset:	0"

☐ Config settings ----
Config: | Cased Opening
          | • Fixed Glass
          | Single Hung
          | Double Hung
Unit Width: | Casement
Unit Height: | Biparting Casement
Elevation: | Horizontal Slider
Elev set at: | Awning
Frame Face: | Hopper
Frame Depth: | 6

☐ Use Wall Depth

Sash Th:	2"
Manuf./Supplier:	
Stock #:	

☐ Other settings --------------
☐ Draw Wall Lines
☐ Clerestory

Num H Muntins:	2
Num V Muntins:	2

| Shape | Data | Texture |

Figure 6.38 Plug-in objects are edited by changing the parameters on their Object Info palettes. Some are quite simple; others are extremely versatile, with many options and editable fields.

Figure 6.39 The same PIO creates both these sets of tables and chairs.

Plug-in Objects (PIOs)

A plug-in object, or PIO, is a special kind of object generated from a script stored in VectorWorks' Plug-Ins folder. Once you have placed a PIO in the drawing, you will see all its defining parameters displayed (and editable) on the Object Info palette with checkboxes, pop-up menus, and editing fields for its many variables (**Figure 6.38**).

You will find PIOs to be a remarkable tool. Generally, a PIO script can create a whole species of object and, once you have placed it in the drawing, you can tailor it to your needs. A single plug-in object, for example, can draw (in 3D, no less) a conference table in a choice of shapes and leg styles and any dimensions, complete with chairs in a variety of styles (**Figure 6.39**).

Except to move or rotate it, you can't edit a plug-in the way you would another kind of object, by dragging its handles or with any of the other tools or commands discussed in the last chapter. Your ability to control its appearance with the Attributes palette or by means of its class setting depends on how the script has been crafted, but some PIOs let you assign styles (modifiable in the Edit Class dialog box) to various components so that you can have, say, upholstered chairs and veneered tables with chrome legs. Or doors finished inside in cherry and outside in a painted trim color and glazed with rippled blue glass, if that's what you want.

You can't even enter a PIO as you would a symbol to make changes. Plug-in objects *can* be converted to groups and then ungrouped into ordinary objects if you feel compelled to edit them that way. But once you have done so, they are forever stripped of their script and the tremendous flexibility it offers. You *can* write your own PIO scripts, but it isn't an easy task, and beyond the scope of this book).

To insert a plug-in object:

1. Click the 2D Symbol Insertion tool on the 2D Tools palette and then go to the Resources palette and choose the plug-in object you want to place in the drawing

   or

   Go to the Object Browser and double-click the PIO you want.

   The selected PIO (in its default configuration) is shown as dotted lines with the cursor at its insertion point (**Figure 6.40**).

2. Click in the drawing area to define the insertion point of the PIO.

3. Move the cursor around the insertion point to set the angle of the PIO.

   Click to complete the placement of the object (**Figure 6.41**).

   The Object Info palette shows the location and angle of the object, as well as all the parameters available for configuring the object (**Figure 6.42**).

4. On the Object Info palette, use the edit fields and the drop-down menus to shape the object to your needs.

   A single PIO often allows you to create a whole family of objects—2D views of bolts of various sizes and styles viewed from top, bottom, front, and side, for example (**Figure 6.43**).

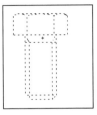

Figure 6.40 Inserting a plug-in object is much like inserting a symbol. The object is shown dotted and positioned relative to the insertion point.

Figure 6.41 After setting the insertion point and the rotation, the default object is placed.

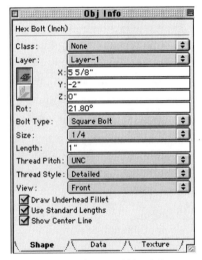

Figure 6.42 You then use Object Info palette to shape the object.

Figure 6.43 Changing the settings in the Object Info palette (as in Figure 6.42) changes the object.

PLUG-IN OBJECTS (PIOs)

CREATING 3D OBJECTS

So far, our discussion has centered on creating and manipulating two-dimensional objects, and for the many people who use VectorWorks only as a drafting tool, never bothering to delve into its modeling capabilities, that's fine. But those modeling capabilities are useful in both design and presentation. Three-dimensional primitives and *hybrid objects* (a scheme for creating 3D objects while working in the 2D drawing environment) make the development of sophisticated models relatively painless.

Let's first get clear about one thing: Vector-Works does not create *real* 3D objects, just virtual ones. You can virtually move around and even through them. But nothing is really moving in space—the computer is just feverishly (and, to my mind, miraculously) calculating pixel colors to simulate the appearance of an object moving relative to the observer.

In order to make full use of the 3D modeling potential VectorWorks offers, we need to be able to comfortably navigate in the space in which our 3D objects exist. Virtually, of course.

In VectorWorks, 2D and 3D objects exist in completely different realms. The space inhabited by 2D objects is relatively simple: You can move left and right and up and down, and change the magnification of the view, but you are always working in the non-space of the drawing area (as opposed to the virtual space of 3D).

Operating in 3D space is a lot more complicated. View changes—such as view rotations and perspective changes—affect only the layer in which they are performed. As a result, layers containing 3D objects can become misaligned with other layers; their rotations or perspective settings are different, so viewing more than one layer at a time no longer adds up to a coherent presentation of your design. (The 2D objects in the layers remain unaffected by view changes.)

And even though you may have chosen Show/Snap/Modify Others as your Layer Option on the Organize menu, you can't select or snap to objects in an inactive layer unless both it and the active layer are in Top/Plan view.

Rotating a view isn't the same as rotating an object. When you set the rotation of a view, everything moves together. You aren't modifying the relationships among the objects in the model or their relationship to the working plane. Rotating an object, on the other hand, changes its position in the space and its relationship with the other objects in the design (**Figure 7.1**).

Remember, 2D objects aren't attached to the working plane and don't move when the space is rotated. They have no depth and so aren't affected by changes of perspective (**Figure 7.2**).

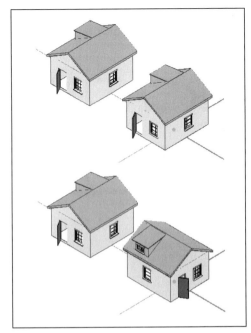

Figure 7.1 Rotating a view (top) leaves relationships within the drawing intact. Rotating an object (bottom) changes the content of the drawing.

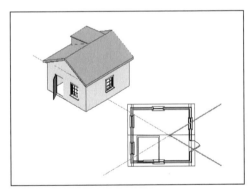

Figure 7.2 A 2D floor plan doesn't move when you rotate the view of the 3D model.

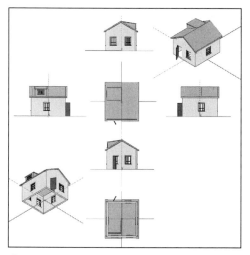

Figure 7.3 The standard orthographic views are based on a viewer looking directly at the faces of a cube. The *isometrics* are based on a viewer looking at the cube on the diagonal.

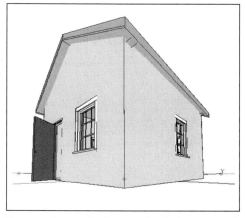

Figure 7.4 Perspective lets you give the impression of real space, even from a worm's point of view.

Rotating the View

This chapter is about creating 3D objects, and will cover only the basic orthogonal views that you'll need in order to see what you're doing here. In Chapter 10, "Worksheets, Reports, and Presentations," we'll deal with the presentation of the design, including things like perspectives, flyovers, and walkthroughs, as well as lighting and rendering.

The standard views are based on the idea of a cube drawn on the working plane (**Figure 7.3**). When you change the view, you are looking at the cube from a different direction. In orthogonal projection, there is no sense of the distance from the viewer to the object—only of the direction. Zooming in magnifies the view, but it doesn't alter the form of the objects to create a sense of being closer (a sense of perspective) (**Figure 7.4**).

Standard views place the origin of the Ground plane (or working plane) at the center of the screen and rotate it according to the view chosen.

To choose a standard 3D view:

Choose View > Standard Views and from the menu choose one of the following 15 standard views (**Figures 7.5** and **7.6**):

Top/Plan view is always orthogonal (meaning parallel lines do not converge and so do not provide a sense of perspective), is always oriented to the ground plane, and is always drawn in wireframe rather than rendered. Hybrid objects (see below) are displayed in their 2D guises, while 3D objects are seen from the top (looking along the z-axis in the negative direction) (**Figure 7.7**).

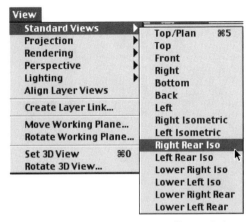

Figure 7.5 The Standard Views menu offers 15 choices.

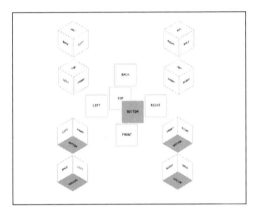

Figure 7.6 The standard views as translated into views of the standard cube.

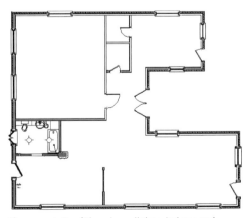

Figure 7.7 In Top/Plan view, all the windows and doors are displayed in their symbolic forms.

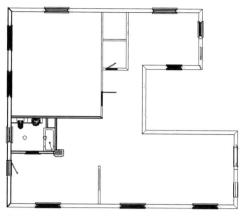

Figure 7.8 In the orthogonal Top view, windows and doors are shown representationally.

▽	X: -24'2"	Y: 27'4"	Z: 0"
	I: -24'2"	J: 27'4"	K: 0"

Figure 7.9 Unless you have a big monitor, some of the fields in the Data Display bar may not be visible unless you open it up by clicking on the arrow head in the upper left corner.

Unless you have moved the working plane (see Chapter 8, "Editing 3D Objects") Top view is a 3D view much like Top/Plan except that hybrid objects are shown as 3D objects (**Figure 7.8**). Bottom view looks at the same cube from the opposite direction. These views (and all the rest except Top/Plan) can be rendered in a variety of ways, and they can be either orthogonal or perspective. The direction of the view is perpendicular to the ground plane along the z-axis (or an alternative working plane along its k-axis).

The Front and Back views display 3D objects as if you were viewing them (again in opposite directions) along the y-axis of the Ground plane (or the j-axis of the working plane).

The Left and Right views complete the "view cube" with vistas of the objects along the x-axis of the ground plane (or the i-axis of the working plane).

VectorWorks's isometric views are diagonal views from the perspective of a viewer looking along a line from one corner of the view cube through the center to the opposite corner.

There are eight isometric views, one for each corner of the cube.

✔ Tip

- When you are using any of the tools on the 3D Tools palette, you may want to click the little arrow head in the upper left-hand corner of the Data Display bar to open a set of edit fields for the $i, j,$ and k coordinates that may not show up on a smaller screen (**Figure 7.9**). If you are working relative to the ground plane, these coordinates will be the same as the $x, y,$ and z coordinates.

Projections

In the real world, we are continuously processing information (generally without even being aware of it) about the size and spatial location of objects near and far on the basis of the way lines that we assume are parallel seem to converge at the horizon (making distant objects seem smaller), and by the degree to which surfaces that are more or less parallel to our line of sight seem to be foreshortened. Many familiar optical illusions depend on simulating or exaggerating these kinds of distortions to fool the viewer.

When you view 3D objects on the flat screen, you can put the objects into a perspective space that you can vary to suggest a reasonably normal experience of a person walking though a building, say, or to mimic the viewpoint of an ant crawling up a skyscraper or a giant looking down on it. Perspective views set up vanishing points toward which parallel lines converge; they also automatically adjust the image itself to foreshorten it.

Alternatively, you can present objects in *paraline* drawings so that, regardless of the rotation of the view, all the lines that are parallel in the object remain parallel in the drawing. Paraline drawings favor the true shapes of objects, whereas perspective drawings create a more lifelike rendition of an object.

Orthogonal views form a small subset of the nonperspective projections, in which the angles between lines in the drawing are the same as the corresponding angles in the object itself.

It is common practice to use a simple cube to represent the generic object. Those views that are directed at one of the faces (top, left, front, and so on); and show the cube without distorting its angles or dimensions are referred to as *orthogonal* views.

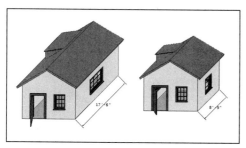

Figure 7.10 Objects in Cavalier projection look distorted, but give true measurements along the axes. Cabinet projections look more reasonable, but the measurements on the oblique axis are 50 percent of the true value.

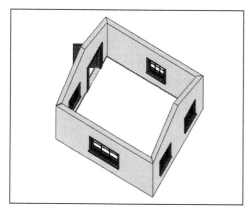

Figure 7.11 When you rotate a Cabinet projection of the Top view, you get a plan axonometric.

In VectorWorks, however, the term *orthogonal* includes not only the traditional six orthogonal views, but also all the other rotations of the cube in which lines parallel to one another in one plane remain so in the drawing.

Among these rotations, the eight views that look directly at the corners of the cube are called *isometrics*. VectorWorks's use of this term differs from the usual usage, in which isometric means that dimensions along all three axes are drawn to scale.

The most popular isometric layout is drawn with the *z*-axis vertical and the *x*- and *y*-axes at 30 degrees from the horizontal. The Vector-Works isometric views are drawn on those 30-degree axes, but they aren't scalable.

The Projections menu does, however, offer Cavalier projections, which are in fact isometrics, and Cabinet projections, which (in a compromise with a more natural appearance) are directly scalable on two axes and scalable at half scale on the third (a *diametric projection*).

The object, particularly in Cavalier projection, will look odd, but it will be dimensionally correct (**Figure 7.10**). Architects sometimes favor a Cabinet projection displaying the plan rotated but undistorted so that the verticals align with the *y*-axis of the drawing; they often call this an *axonometric* view (**Figure 7.11**).

PROJECTIONS

Controlling Layers in 3D

Since each layer is rendered and rotated independently, when you modify the view of one layer it may no longer correspond to the objects with which it was meant to align in the other layers (**Figure 7.12**).

To align layer views:

1. From the Layers drop-down menu on the Data Display bar, choose the layer to which you want to align the others.

   The layer to which all other will be aligned becomes the active layer.

2. Choose View > Align Layer Views.

   All layers (even those not visible) are rotated to the same viewpoint, and their projections (orthogonal, perspective, or one of the Cavalier or Cabinet projections) are likewise given identical settings (**Figure 7.13**).

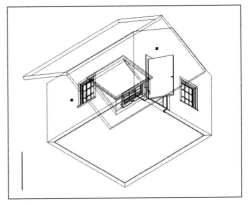

Figure 7.12 Rotating layers in a drawing can lead to visual confusion. The roof layer in a left isometric and the wall layer in a lower-left isometric make it hard to see what's really going on.

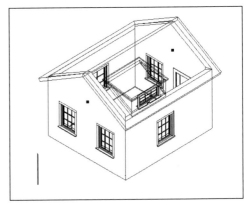

Figure 7.13 Once the layers are aligned, the drawing no longer looks like conceptual architecture.

Creating Objects in 3D

You can take three basic routes to creating 3D objects: choose a primitive from the 3D Tools palette; draw a 2D object (or objects) and then project it into three dimensions as either an extrusion or a sweep; or make a hybrid object using the Wall tool or one of the commands on the Model menu.

You can also delve into the bowels of the VectorWorks folder and add some plug-in object scripts to your workspace to draw a torus (or a pyramid, cylinder, ellipsoid, paraboloid, or box object); these objects are manipulated from the Object Info palette.

All those primitives are really just shortcuts to creating objects you could have created by other means, starting with 2D elements. You can turn those elements into extrusions in a variety of modalities. The simplest extrusions are things like the extruded rectangle and polygon; multiple extrusion produces a pyramid (although tapered extrusion works as well). The rest of the objects (spheres, hemispheres, cones, toruses, cylinders) are the result of sweeping a 2D object around a center axis.

CREATING OBJECTS IN 3D

Two More Snap Constraints

There's no getting around the fact that drawing in 3D is tricky. To help, VectorWorks provides an extra pair of constraints to control where in space the points you click with the mouse will lie.

When you select any of the tools on the 3D Tools palette, the Constraints palette changes, replacing the last two buttons with two new ones (**Figure 7.14**). When you draw in 3D, the default condition is that all points you define with the mouse lie on the working plane. When you snap to a point on a 3D object, however, that condition can be overridden.

These two constraints function when a working plane other than the Ground plane is active (working planes are discussed in Chapter 8, "Editing 3D Objects").

Constrain Working Plane

The first button is the Constrain Working plane constraint. Once this button is pressed, all points, regardless of what they are snapped to, project onto the working plane along the current angle of view.

But the angle of projection isn't perpendicular to the plane, as you might expect; it is determined by the position of the observer. For this reason, you will usually choose to use the constraint when you are looking directly at the plane.

Constrain Perpendicular

The second button is the Constrain Perpendicular constraint. With this constraint active, points can be placed only along the k-axis. When editing, this constraint allows you to move points only perpendicular to the working plane.

Figure 7.14 The two constraints added to the Constraints palette when you select a tool from the 3D Tools palette are Constrain Working Plane and Constrain Perpendicular.

TWO MORE SNAP CONSTRAINTS

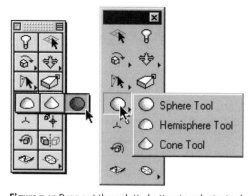

Figure 7.15 Drag out the palette button to select a tool not visible at first inspection (Mac left, Windows right).

Primitives

VectorWorks makes your life easy by providing a set of tools for creating basic 3D objects— spheres, hemispheres, cones, extruded rectangles, and polygons. The objects created with these tools are called *primitives*. They are the building blocks for the more complex objects you are working so hard to model.

Each of these primitives can be created from 2D objects (more on that later in the chapter). Using the primitive*s* is generally quicker than starting from scratch, although sometimes the long way turns out not to be so long after all. With experience, you'll learn which method works best for you.

The Sphere, Hemisphere, and Cone tools share a single location on the 3D Tools palette. Drag on the location to access the hidden tools (**Figure 7.15**). The objects these tools produce are called *solids* and only their radii and heights (as well, of course, as their positions) can be changed. A sphere can't be changed into an ellipsoid without first converting it into a different *kind* of object (see Chapter 8, "Editing 3D Objects").

The 3D Polygon tool makes a polygon that has no thickness but, unlike its 2D cousin, inhabits the 3D space and moves with the other 3D objects as you change the view.

The Sphere by Radius tool centers a sphere on a location on the working plane defined by the mouse or by the coordinates you enter in the Data Display bar.

To draw a sphere by its radius:

1. On the 3D Tools palette, choose the Sphere tool.

   In the default workspace, it shares its place on the palette with the Hemisphere and Cone tools; you may need to click and drag on the tool location to select the desired tool.

2. On the Mode bar, click the Sphere by Radius button (**Figure 7.16**).

   The 3D tools, including the Sphere tool, work only in 3D views. If you are in Plan view, an alert will ask you if you want to switch to the corresponding (Top) orthogonal view. (**Figure 7.17**). Click Yes to change. If you click Yes Always, Vector-Works will automatically switch without posting the alert.

   The Constrain Working Plane constraint is automatically selected; the sphere is always placed with its center on the ground plane (or other working plane) by default.

3. Click in the drawing area to set the center of the sphere.

   If you snap to a point in the drawing, that point will be projected onto the working plane.

4. Drag the cursor to set the radius of the sphere, and click again to complete the operation (**Figure 7.18**).

   As you move the cursor, the sphere will be previewed. You can use the Data Display bar to set any of the coordinates relative to the Ground plane.

5. Click to complete the sphere.

   If you snap to a point in the drawing, that point will be projected onto the working plane.

Figure 7.16 The Sphere tool operates in three modes.

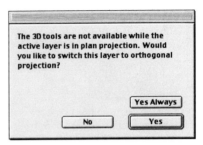

Figure 7.17 Click Yes to switch to the Top view; click Always to avoid seeing this alert every time you select a 3D tool without first choosing a 3D view.

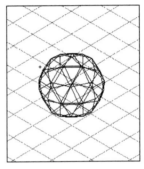

Figure 7.18 Once you've clicked to set the center of the sphere, click again to set its radius.

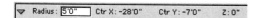

Figure 7.19 Press Tab to switch focus to the Data Display bar, where you can enter a radius for the sphere.

To draw a sphere by diameter:

1. In the 3D Tools palette, click the Sphere tool and then choose the Sphere by Diameter mode from the Mode bar.

2. In the drawing area, click to set one end of the diameter that defines the sphere.

3. Move the cursor to define the length and orientation of the sphere.

   As you move the cursor, the sphere is sketched. You can fix the radius in the Data Display bar (**Figure 7.19**) and then use the mouse to pivot the sphere around the first point.

4. Click again to complete the sphere.

✔ Tip

- Use the Sphere by Diameter tool if you want to use the Snap to Grid constraint to control the size of the sphere. The Sphere by Radius tool lets you snap to a center point, but you can't set the radius on the snap grid. You can, however, use the Snap to Object constraint to set the radius.

To draw a sphere by center and radius:

1. In the 3D Tools palette, click the Sphere tool and then choose the Sphere by Center and Radius mode from the Mode bar.

   For the most predictable results, it's best to work off the Ground plane; using an alternative working plane can prove extremely frustrating. This is probably a bug that will be eliminated in later versions of the software.

2. In the drawing area, click on the Ground plane to set the *x* and *y* coordinates for the center of the sphere.

3. Drag the mouse to set the distance from the plane to the center of the sphere.

   As you drag the mouse, a dotted line is drawn perpendicular to the plane. Click to set the center point (**Figure 7.20**).

4. Drag the mouse to set the radius of the sphere, and click to complete its creation (**Figure 7.21**).

✔ Tips

- In either the Sphere by Radius or the Sphere by Center and Radius mode, you can use the Data Display bar to place points where you can't snap them. Entering a *z* or *k* value (even though there's a field for it) before you've made the first click has no effect. But once you have clicked anywhere to begin creating a sphere, you can completely control its size and location from the Data Display bar (**Figure 7.22**).

- To place a sphere with control points (its center or edges) off the Ground plane, you have to create a working plane on which both points lie (see Chapter 8, "Editing 3D Objects").

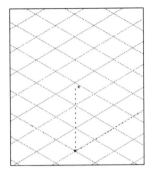

Figure 7.20 Click to set the *x-y* (or *i-j*) position of the sphere and then drag to set the *z* or *k* distance above or below the working plane.

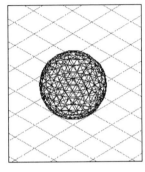

Figure 7.21 Once you've set the distance of the sphere's center above the working plane, you drag to set its radius and click to complete the object.

Figure 7.22 Use the Data Display bar to make sure you get exactly the sphere you intend.

PRIMITIVES

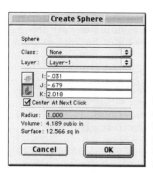

Figure 7.23 Double-click the Sphere tool on the 3D Tools palette to open the Create Sphere dialog box.

■ You can also sometimes override the Constrain Working Plane constraint on the Sphere tool by momentarily switching into Front view (press 2 on the number pad) and then back into the view in which you want to draw. But you can't then pan the view, or the constraint will trip back into effect.

■ Use the Sphere tool in its Sphere by Diameter or by Sphere by Radius mode combined with the Constrain Perpendicular constraint to construct the sphere using points projected up from the working plane.

■ Double-click the Sphere tool to open the Create Sphere dialog box, where you can place a sphere of any radius anywhere in the drawing area. You can also set its layer and class (**Figure 7.23**).

■ When you choose the Center At Next Click option in the Create Sphere dialog box, keep in mind that when you exit the dialog box, you will be in 2D space, so you won't be able to click on any 3D object or use the Snap to Grid constraint to pick a point in 3D space on either the Ground plane or any other working plane. In general, it's best to ignore this option and enter coordinates for the object in the dialog box.

The same holds true for the Create Hemisphere and Create Cone dialog boxes as well.

PRIMITIVES

To create a hemisphere by radius:

1. On the 3D Tools palette, click the Hemisphere tool (**Figure 7.24**).

2. On the Mode bar, click the Hemisphere by Radius button (**Figure 7.25**).

3. Click in the drawing area to place the center of the hemisphere.

   Unless you have tricked VectorWorks as outlined in the Tips above, the center will be placed on the working plane.

4. Drag the mouse to set the radius relative to the first point, and click again to complete the hemisphere (**Figure 7.26**).

   As you drag the mouse, the hemisphere is previewed.

To create a hemisphere by diameter:

1. On the 3D Tools palette, click the Hemisphere tool.

2. On the Mode bar, click the Hemisphere by Diameter button.

3. Click in the drawing area to place one edge of the hemisphere.

   Unless you have tricked VectorWorks as outlined in the Tips above, the point will be placed on the working plane.

4. Drag the mouse to set the diameter and direction relative to the first point, and click again to complete the hemisphere (**Figure 7.27**).

✔ Tips

- Use the Hemisphere by Diameter tool if you want to use the Snap to Grid constraint to control the size of the sphere. The Hemisphere by Radius tool lets you snap to a center point, but you can't set the radius on the snap grid if you are in an oblique view. You can, however, snap to a point to set the radius.

Figure 7.24 Click the Hemisphere tool on the 3D Tools palette to draw a hemisphere in one of three modes.

Figure 7.25 The three modes in which the Hemisphere tool operates are selected on the Mode bar.

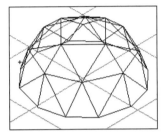

Figure 7.26 The radius of the hemisphere is set by a second click of the mouse.

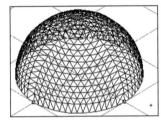

Figure 7.27 The hemisphere is completed when you click again in the drawing area. You can use either the grid or another object as the snap point.

- The Hemisphere by Height tool creates a hemisphere relative to the view, not to the working plane. The hemisphere is always drawn so that you are looking edge-on at the plane of its base, and it both pivots around the center point of the base and changes the radius of the base as you move the mouse.

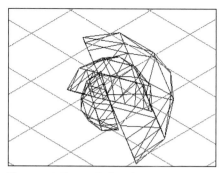

Figure 7.28 The Hemisphere by Up Radius mode creates a hemisphere that you always see edge-on unless you tip the object over by snapping to a point on another object.

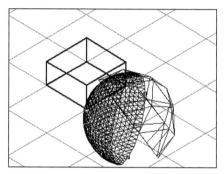

Figure 7.29 When you snap to an object to set the height of a hemisphere, the hemisphere can rotate out of the plane about its center point.

Figure 7.30 The Create Hemisphere dialog box is another way of creating a hemisphere in the drawing area.

To create a hemisphere by height:

1. On the 3D Tools palette, click the Hemisphere tool.

2. On the Mode bar, click the Hemisphere by Height button.

3. Click in the drawing area to place the center of the hemisphere.

4. Drag the mouse to set the radius and its direction perpendicular to the plane of the base (**Figure 7.28**).

   As you drag the mouse, the hemisphere is previewed.

   If you snap to an object, the hemisphere rotates freely around its center point; otherwise, it remains comfortably seated on the plane perpendicular to the screen plane (**Figure 7.29**).

✔ Tips

- Double-click the Hemisphere tool to open the Create Hemisphere dialog box (**Figure 7.30**).

- When you use the dialog box approach to creating the hemisphere (or the sphere or cone) the Center at Next Click option works only on the Ground plane.

- The Hemisphere by Diameter mode will snap to the grid of the working plane regardless of its orientation; in the Hemisphere by Radius mode, it works only when a view is directly aligned with one of the axes (for instance, Front or Right view but not any of the isometric or other oblique views).

PRIMITIVES

To create a cone:

1. On the 3D Tools palette, click the Cone tool.

2. On the Mode bar, choose either the Cone by Radius and Height or the Cone by Radius and Tip mode (**Figure 7.31**).

3. Click in the drawing area to place the center of the cone's base on the working plane.

4. Drag the mouse to define the radius of the base and click again (**Figure 7.32**).

5. Drag the mouse to set the height of the cone.

   If you are in Cone by Radius and Tip mode, when you snap to an object in the drawing, the cone will tip over, pivoting around the center of its base, so that the tip of the cone lies on the snap point (**Figure 7.33**).

   Click to complete the cone.

✔ Tips

- In views in which you are looking directly at the working plane (in other words, non-oblique views), the Cone tool works differently; when you click to set the center of the cone, you set the height of the cone via a dialog box before you drag the cursor to set the radius.

- The Snap to Grid constraint lets you locate the center of the cone on the grid but doesn't work to set the radius unless you are in one of the *true* orthogonal views (Top, Bottom, Front, and so on). Use the edit box in the Data Display bar instead (**Figure 7.34**).

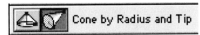

Figure 7.31 The Cone tool has two modes, Cone by Radius and Height (left) and Cone by Radius and Tip (right).

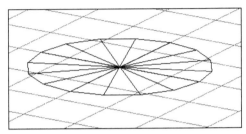

Figure 7.32 After you set the center of the cone, drag out the radius and click again.

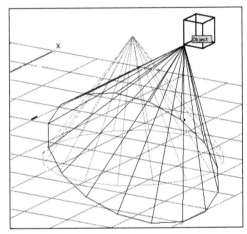

Figure 7.33 Drag again and click to set the height of the cone. If you're in Radius and Tip mode, the cone will abruptly tip from the working plane when you snap to a point on another object.

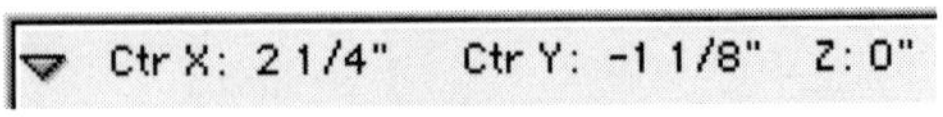

Ctr X: 2 1/4"   Ctr Y: -1 1/8"   Z: 0"

Figure 7.34 As with the Sphere and Hemisphere tools, the snap grid doesn't always work to set the radius of the cone. Use the edit box on the Data Display bar.

PRIMITIVES

Figure 7.35 The Extruded Rectangle tool on the 3D Tools palette.

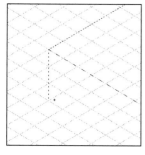

Figure 7.36 Once you've set the first corner of the extruded rectangle, drag the mouse to set its thickness.

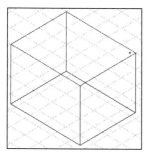

Figure 7.37 Complete the extruded rectangle by drawing the diagonal of the rectangle you are extruding.

■ To project points onto the working plane, choose one of the non-oblique views with Snap to Object and Constrain Working Plane selected. Clicking on an object will place the point on the plane. If Constrain Working Plane isn't active, the points will be placed where they are snapped.

Extruded Primitives

Extrusion is a manufacturing process that squeezes metal or plastic through a shaped opening to create a long piece of material with its cross-section determined by the hole it came out of. Cookie presses are a domestic version of the same thing. VectorWorks uses an analogous approach to create solids by extending 2D objects into three dimensions.

The button position next to the one occupied by the Sphere, Hemisphere, and Cone tools is likewise the home of a trio of tools for creating rectilinear objects. Two of the tools create solid objects; the third tool lets you draw 3D polygons by snapping to points in the drawing. Three-dimensional polygons can be non-planar: For example, they can be bent to follow the contour of a roof line.

To create an extruded rectangle:

1. On the 3D Tools palette, click the Extruded Rectangle tool (**Figure 7.35**).

2. Click in the drawing area to place one corner of the rectangle.

3. Drag the cursor to set the distance the rectangle will be extruded (its k dimension, or thickness) and click again (**Figure 7.36**).
   The first edge will be drawn perpendicular to the working plane.

4. Drag the cursor to define the diagonal of the rectangle you are extruding, thereby completing the rectangle (**Figure 7.37**).

✔ Tips

■ In the oblique views, the Snap to Point constraint works only on points lying on the plane when the Constrain Working Plane constraint is also active.

EXTRUDED PRIMITIVES

To create an extruded polygon:

1. On the 3D Tools palette, click the Extruded Polygon tool (**Figure 7.38**).

2. Click in the drawing area to place the first vertex of the polygon.

3. Drag the cursor to adjust the distance the polygon will be extruded (its *k* dimension, or thickness) and click to set it.

4. Define each of the subsequent corners of the polygon by clicking in the drawing area.

   As you draw, the polygon is sketched (**Figure 7.39**).

5. Close the polygon by snapping to the starting point (**Figure 7.40**)

   or

   Double-click the mouse. The polygon will automatically add a side between the last click vertex and the starting point.

   The completed extruded polygon (mesh) is drawn (**Figure 7.41**).

✔ Tips

- Snap to points of varying heights above and below the working plane to create a mesh object with non-planar top and bottom surfaces. The thickness of the object's section will still be set by the second mouse click (**Figure 7.42**).

- You can draw meshes that twist back and pass through themselves, but they don't have much use in modeling real-world objects, and you can't use them as building blocks for more complex objects (**Figure 7.43**).

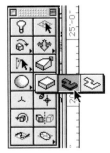

Figure 7.38 In the default condition, the Extruded Polygon tool lies under the Extruded Rectangle. Drag the button to open the flyout palette.

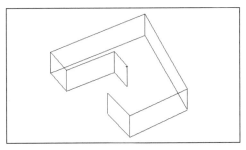

Figure 7.39 As you draw the polygon, the edges are sketched.

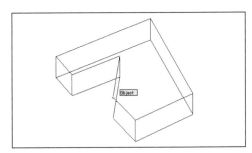

Figure 7.40 Close the polygon by returning to the starting point.

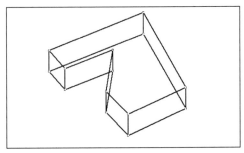

Figure 7.41 The complete extruded polygon is drawn with the attributes.

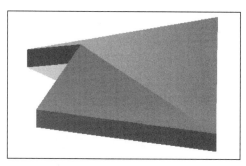

Figure 7.42 Non-planar extrusions can be drawn by using snap points above or below the working plane.

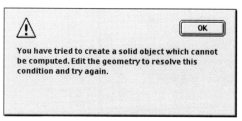

Figure 7.43 If you try to use a polygon that twists back through itself, VectorWorks will post this alert.

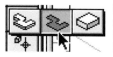

Figure 7.44 The 3D Polygon tool resides with the Extruded Rectangle and Extruded Polygon as a flyout on the 3D Tools palette.

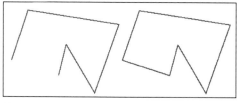

Figure 7.45 A 3D polygon can be either open or closed (unlike Extruded polygons, which are always closed).

To create a 3D polygon:

1. On the 3D Tools palette, click the 3D Polygon tool (**Figure 7.44**).

2. Click in the drawing area to place the first vertex of the polygon.

3. Continue clicking to place the other vertices.

4. Complete the polygon by snapping to the starting point or double-clicking the mouse.

   Like their 2D counterparts, 3D polygons can be either open or closed (**Figure 7.45**).

✔ Tips

- Turn off the Constrain Working Plane constraint and snap to objects in the drawing area to create nonplanar polygons.

- To create a 3D polygon, select a 2D polygon and choose Model > Convert to 3D Polys. The converted polygon will lie in a plane parallel to the screen, not on the working plane.

Using the Plug-in Objects

VectorWorks provides eight plug-in object scripts that create 3D objects in yet another way. They don't come installed in the workspace, but adding them isn't difficult.

To insert a 3D Primitive PIO:

1. Choose View > Standard Views > Top/Plan; or press Command-5 (Mac) or Ctrl-5 (Windows); or press 0 on the keypad.

    The view changes to Top/Plan.

2. Click one of the 3D PIO Primitive tools from whatever palette you have put it on (**Figure 7.46**).

    The Mode bar will show buttons for insertion of the PIO into a wall object (which may not be relevant), a Preferences button, and the name of the chosen tool (**Figure 7.47**).

3. Click the Preferences button. The Preferences dialog box for the selected object opens (**Figure 7.48**).

4. In the Preferences dialog box, type values for the various parameters. In some instances, the parameters won't apply, depending on the object type you've selected.

    Choose Sector or Segment to control how spheres and toruses will be constructed when the circular sections on which they are based are swept less than 360 degrees. *Segments* are slices of the swept section perpendicular to the axis of the sweep; *sectors* are constructed from radii from the center of the object (**Figure 7.49**).

    Choose Regular or Frustrum in the Cone or Pyramid dialog box (**Figure 7.50**). (A *frustrum* is what is left of a cone or pyramid after you slice off the top, cutting parallel to the base.)

Figure 7.46 You can collect all the 3D primitive PIOs on a single palette of their own, or you can add them to existing palettes.

Figure 7.47 The Mode bar lets you set the preferences for the PIO before you place it. You can always make changes later in the Object Info palette.

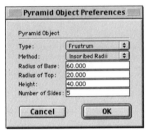

Figure 7.48 Each PIO has its own Preferences dialog box. This one is for the Pyramid object.

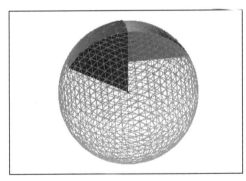

Figure 7.49 The choice of the segment or sector parameter matters only if you are creating a PIO for just a partial sweep of the object. Sectors (left) include the center point; segments (right) take the shortcut to the axis of rotation.

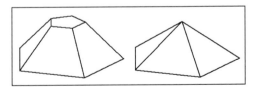

Figure 7.50 Cones and pyramids can either come to points or be sliced off, leaving only a frustrum.

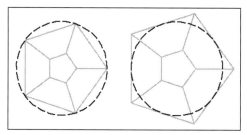

Figure 7.51 A pyramid can be either inscribed (left) or circumscribed (right) in a circle.

Figure 7.52 The Cylinder PIO can create both solid and hollow cylinders.

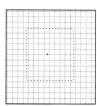

Figure 7.53 Once you have set the preferences, the boundaries of plug-in object are outlined.

Figure 7.54 PIOs can be rotated around their insertion points (like symbols) before they are placed.

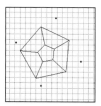

Figure 7.55 When the object is finally placed, the outline boundaries are replaced by the thing itself.

Choose Inscribed Radii or Circumscribed Radii in the Pyramid dialog box to define the dimensions of the base and top of the pyramid (**Figure 7.51**).

Choose Solid or Hollow in the Cylinder dialog box (**Figure 7.52**).

5. Click OK to close the dialog box.

A dotted rectangular box delimiting the object surrounds the cursor (**Figure 7.53**).

6. Click in the drawing area to set the *x* and *y* coordinates of the insertion point (the center point of the base of a flat-bottomed object or the center point of a sphere, paraboloid, or torus object)

7. Rotate the object to the desired orientation in the *x-y* plane and click again (**Figure 7.54**).

The object is placed (**Figure 7.55**).

✔ Tip

- The first time you use one of the tools, the Preferences dialog box will open automatically. Thereafter, each tool will apply the last-used preferences until you reset it.

USING THE PLUG-IN OBJECTS

3D and Hybrid Symbols and Other PIOs

In Chapter 6, we talked about working with 2D symbols. VectorWorks also has 3D symbols that work pretty much the same way. We also briefly touched on hybrid symbols, which consist of a 2D symbol linked to a 3D symbol. When you select the Top/Plan view, the 2D symbol replaces the 3D one that is displayed in all other views. This allows you to use a symbolic representation of an object in the Top/Plan view and a more illustrative image in the other views.

A 3D symbol can be placed with either the 2D Symbol Insertion tool (in Top/Plan view) or the 3D Symbol Insertion tool (in all other views). Hybrid symbols insert the 2D symbol when you use the 2D Symbol Insertion tool and require you to work in Top/Plan view. When you use the Object Browser, it automatically chooses the insertion tool to suit the current view.

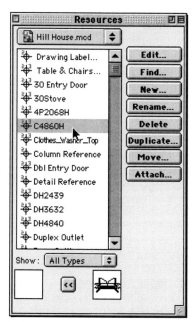

Figure 7.56 Symbols can be chosen from the list in the Resources palette. A 2D symbol has a 2 on the symbol mark, a 3D symbol has a 3, and a hybrid has both.

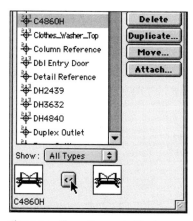

Figure 7.57 The active symbol is shown in the left-hand window at the bottom of the Resources palette.

To place a 3D symbol from the Resources palette:

1. On the Resources palette, click the symbol you want to insert.

   The symbol's name is highlighted and an image is displayed in the right-hand window at the bottom of the Resources palette (**Figure 7.56**).

2. Click the Select (or arrow) button to the left of the window.

   The symbol is selected and appears in the left-hand window (**Figure 7.57**).

3. On the 3D Tools palette, click the 3D Symbol Insertion tool.

   The cursor becomes a cross representing the insertion point of the symbol, but the symbol isn't previewed.

4. Click in the drawing area to set the insertion point of the symbol

or

On the Data Display bar, you can enter values for two (but not all three) of the *i, j,* and *k* coordinates for the insertion point. Click to define the third coordinate and set the insertion point.

The symbol (a double bed) is displayed in the drawing (**Figure 7.58**).

5. In the drawing area, drag the mouse to define the rotation of the symbol and click to finish the insertion (**Figure 7.59**).

✔ Tip

■ By default, a symbol is placed so that its insertion points lies on the working plane, but you can use the Snap to Object constraint to place it exactly where you want it.

To insert a 3D symbol from the Object Browser:

1. Open the Object Browser by choosing Palettes > Object Browser, or press Command-H (Mac) or Ctrl-H (Windows) (**Figure 7.60**).

2. In the Object Browser, click the symbol you want to insert.

The symbol is highlighted and one of the two Symbol Insertion tools is selected from the tool palettes: If you've selected a 3D symbol and you are in a 3D view, the 3D Symbol Insertion tool is selected; otherwise, the 2D tool is activated.

3. Follow steps 4 and 5 above.

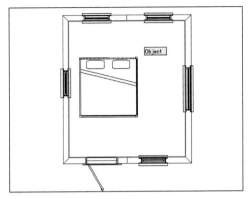

Figure 7.58 A 3D symbol is inserted in the drawing with its *k*-axis orientation set by the working plane.

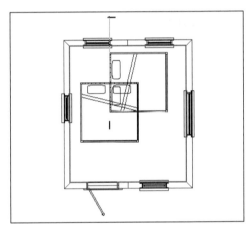

Figure 7.59 After you set the symbol's rotation in the *i*- and *j*-plane, click to finish the insertion process.

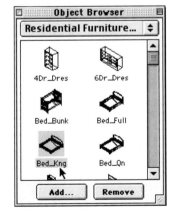

Figure 7.60 The Object Browser is a quick way to place symbols in the drawing.

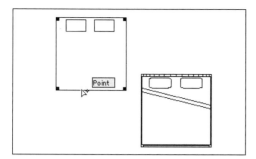

Figure 7.61 Creating a hybrid symbol involves creating a symbol from a 2D object (left) and a 3D object (right) at the same time. Position the 2D and 3D components (in most cases, you'll center the 2D and 3D objects over one another) before you choose Organize > Create Symbol.

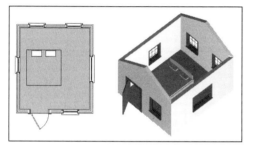

Figure 7.62 Hybrid symbols have two separate objects in their definitions. The 2D element is shown in Top/Plan view, and the 3D element in all other views.

As with 2D symbols, creating your own 3D and hybrid symbols is easy and well worth your time.

To create a 3D or hybrid symbol:

1. Select the objects you want to include in the symbol definition.

   To create a hybrid symbol, you have to include both 2D and 3D objects and be in Top/Plan view. Make sure the 2D and 3D elements are in the desired relationship (**Figure 7.61**).

2. Follow the steps for creating a 2D symbol in Chapter 6, "2D Symbols and PIOs."

   The symbol is created. The hybrid symbol will display its 2D object in Top/Plan view and its 3D object in 3D views (**Figure 7.62**).

✔ Tip

- An easy way to transform a 3D symbol into a hybrid one is to edit the symbol and then just draw in the 2D element before exiting the symbol's sublayer. The alignment will always be just what you wanted. To edit the symbol, either select it in the drawing and choose Organize > Edit Symbol, or press Command-[(Mac) or Ctrl-[(Windows). Or you can edit it from the Resources palette by choosing 3D Component in the Edit Symbol dialog box.

3D AND HYBRID SYMBOLS AND OTHER PIOS

Extrusions

As mentioned earlier, extruding shapes is a lot like using a cookie press, whose nozzle imparts the shape of its opening to the dough you squeeze through it. So a star-shaped hole creates a star-shaped cookie of whatever thickness you want.

VectorWorks extrusions (and sweeps as well) depend on the view in which they are created; 2D objects are extruded perpendicular to the plane of the screen. Unlike primitives, they aren't placed relative to the working plane.

To create a simple extrusion:

1. Select the 2D object you want to extrude (**Figure 7.63**).

2. Choose Model > Extrude, or press Command-E (Mac) or Ctrl-E (Windows). The Create Extrude dialog box opens (**Figure 7.64**).

3. In the Create Extrude dialog box, adjust the proportions of the extrusion using the ΔX and ΔY (Mac) or ±X and ±Y (Windows) fields and set the length of the extrusion in the Extrusion field.

   Click OK to create the extrusion (**Figure 7.65**).

✔ Tip

- You can select more than one object; the result will be a group of extrusions you can then ungroup if you so desire (**Figure 7.66**).

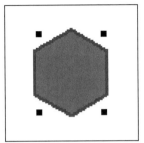

Figure 7.63 Extrusions begin with a selection of 2D objects.

Figure 7.64 Choose the Extrude command to open the Create Extrude dialog box.

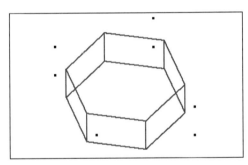

Figure 7.65 An extrusion can be any length.

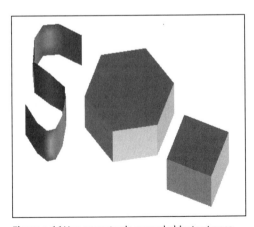

Figure 7.66 You can extrude several objects at once.

EXTRUSIONS

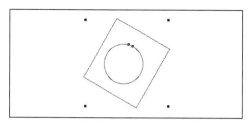

Figure 7.67 Select several objects and position them as required. You may also want to change their stacking order.

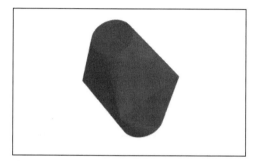

Figure 7.68 Multiple extrusions change their profiles as they go.

Multiple extrusions are blends over the distance of the extrusion from one 2D section to another. And you aren't limited to just two sections.

To create a multiple extrusion:

1. Select the objects you want to combine in a multiple extrusion (**Figure 7.67**).

   The objects will be evenly spaced in the extrusion according to their places in the stacking order. If they aren't aligned, the extrusion will zigzag through space to include them.

2. Choose Model > Multiple Extrude, or press Command-Option-E (Mac) or Alt-Ctrl-E (Windows).

   The Create Extrude dialog box opens.

3. In the Create Extrude dialog box, adjust the proportions of the extrusion using the ΔX and ΔY (Mac) or ±X and ±Y (Windows) fields and set the length of the extrusion in the Extrusion field.

   Click OK to complete the extrusion (**Figure 7.68**).

EXTRUSIONS

Tapered extrusions are one more possibility.

To make a tapered extrusion:

1. Select the object you want to extrude (**Figure 7.69**).

2. Choose Model > Tapered Extrude.

   The Set Tapered Angle and Extrude Height dialog box opens (**Figure 7.70**).

3. In the Set Tapered Angle and Extrude Height dialog box, set the angle of the taper and the length of the extrusion.

4. Click OK.

   The extrusion is created (**Figure 7.71**).

The Extrude Along Path mode of extrusion is the most powerful of the extrusion tools. With it, you can create complex 3D objects such as a railing or a v-belt. In VectorWorks 9 you can work with NURBS curves (see below) to extrude a section along a non-planar path.

The objects chosen as *profile* objects are extruded along the *path* object. Profile objects define the form of the section and must be 2D objects or planar 3D polygons or NURBS objects; path objects can be open or closed but can't cross themselves.

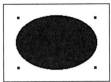

Figure 7.69 A tapered extrude scales the profile as it extends. (You could accomplish the same thing with a multiple extrude).

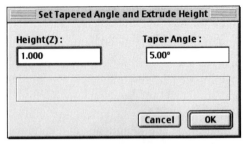

Figure 7.70 Set the angle of the taper and the length of the extrusion in the Set Tapered Angle and Extrude Height dialog box.

Figure 7.71 Tapered extrusions become cones or pyramids if the angle is too great for the length of the extrusion.

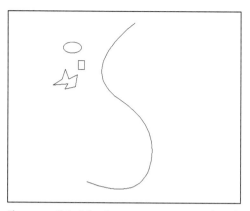

Figure 7.72 Select the shapes you want to extrude and the path along which their profiles will be translated.

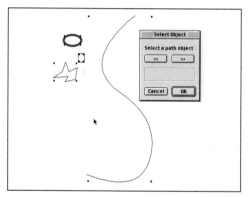

Figure 7.73 You have to tell VectorWorks which of the selected objects is the path object and which are the profile objects.

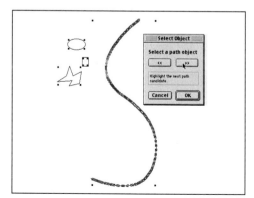

Figure 7.74 As you click the arrow buttons, the selected objects are highlighted one after another until you get to the one you want.

To extrude a shape along a path:

1. Select both the shapes and the path along which you want to extrude them (**Figure 7.72**).

2. Choose Model > Extrude Along Path.

   The Select Object dialog box opens, and one of the selected objects is highlighted in the drawing area (**Figure 7.73**).

3. In the Select Object dialog box, use the arrow buttons to select which of the selected objects is to be the path along which the other is extruded.

   As you click the arrow buttons, the objects are highlighted one after another (**Figure 7.74**).

4. Click OK.

   The Select Object dialog box closes and the extrusion is drawn (**Figure 7.75**).

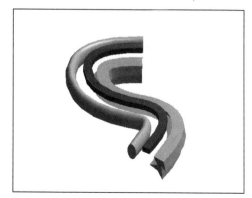

Figure 7.75 Once you select the path and click OK, the object is created.

EXTRUSIONS

Sweeps

Sweeps are like extrusions around a central axis or a shape repeated many times around the axis (**Figure 7.76**).

The center of the sweep can be outside the boundary of the swept shape, creating a donut-like object. And you can specify a *pitch* so that the sweep is corkscrew-like, instead of coming back onto itself. Or you can choose to sweep an object less than the full 360 degrees to get the effect of an apple with a slice cut out of it—or of the slice itself.

Sweeps are always made around the vertical axis of the screen, regardless of the rotation of the view.

To create a sweep from a 2D object:

1. Select the object that you want to sweep (**Figure 7.77**).

2. Choose Model > Sweep.

   The Create Sweep dialog box opens (**Figure 7.78**).

3. In the Size area of the Create Sweep dialog box, adjust the height and radius values to scale the objects you have selected.

   Height is the vertical dimension of the section of the sweep; radius is the distance from the axis around which the sweep is made to the outer edge of the swept section (**Figure 7.79**).

4. On the right side of the Create Sweep dialog box, do the following:

   Set the Start Angle and the Arc Angle. The default settings (0.00° for Start Angle and 360.00° for Arc Angle) create a complete sweep. To create a helix—like a coil spring or a screw thread—you will want multiple revolutions (you can enter the value as an arithmetic expression like 360°*3.5) (**Figure 7.80**).

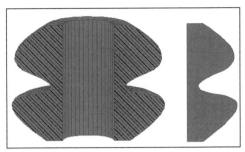

Figure 7.76 A shape (right) repeated over and over around a center axis produces a sweep. The smaller the angle between the slices, the smoother the object.

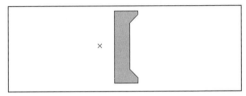

Figure 7.77 Sweeps take a 2D form and wrap it around a center axis.

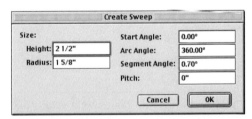

Figure 7.78 The Create Sweep dialog box is more complicated than those for the extrusion commands.

Figure 7.79 Changing the Radius (left) or Height (right) scales the section of the objects swept around the axis and changes the proportions of the spool in the center.

SWEEPS

Figure 7.80 Three-and-a-half revolutions of the helix is achieved by typing 360*3.5 in the Arc Angle field of the Create Sweep dialog box.

Figure 7.81 Set the pitch of the sweep to open or close the turns of the helix. On the left, the pitch is 2.75"; on the right it's 4".

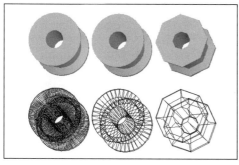

Figure 7.82 Small segment values make smooth objects, but their demands on memory and rendering time may unnecessarily bog down the whole system.

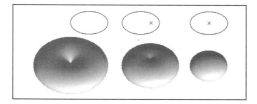

Figure 7.83 If you don't want to sweep around the left edge of the selected objects (as with the leftmost object), include a locus object in the selection.

Set the Pitch value. The default is 0, which means that there is no vertical displacement of the section as it sweeps around the central axis. Increasing the pitch increases the spacing between the turns of the helix (**Figure 7.81**).

Set the Segment Angle. The segment angle controls how smoothly VectorWorks attempts to draw the object. Smaller segments create a smoother image, but it takes more time and memory to render it. The default (5.63 degrees) translates into 64 segments for a full circle (**Figure 7.82**).

As you change the settings in the Create Sweep dialog box, the image is previewed in the drawing. Click OK to close the dialog box and create the sweep.

✔ Tip

- In general, it's a good idea to include a 2D locus defining the axis of the sweep with the objects you select for a sweep. Otherwise, the axis is always the left edge of 2D shape (**Figure 7.83**).

NURBS Objects

NURBS stands for Non-Uniform Rational B-Spline, which probably doesn't tell you very much. Suffice it to say that NURBS objects are paths in three dimensions that move with the other 3D objects in the drawing. They can be used as paths for extrusions or as line elements in 3D space. They do not, however, define a shape, and they can't be filled or rendered.

By default, NURBS objects are drawn on the working plane, but you can snap points to objects in the drawing to create them as non-planar objects. You can also convert 2D objects and 3D polygons to NURBS objects by choosing the Convert to NURBS command from the Model menu.

There are three tools for NURBS creation. Two of them create circle and arc objects (they aren't true circles or arcs, but they're close enough for most purposes); the free-form NURBS tool lets you draw 3D lines by setting control points wherever you click.

To draw a NURBS circle:

1. On the 3D Tools palette, click the NURBS Circle tool (**Figure 7.84**).

2. On the Mode bar, choose one of the three modes corresponding to the 2D Ellipse tool's circular modes (**Figure 7.85**).

3. Do one of the following:

    With the NURBS Circle by Radius mode chosen, click to set the center of the circle

    With the NURBS Circle by Diameter or NURBS Circle by Three Points mode chosen, click to place the first point on the circle's circumference (**Figure 7.86**).

Figure 7.84 Click the NURBS Circle tool on the 3D Tools palette to create the NURBS equivalent of a circle.

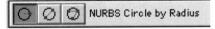

Figure 7.85 There are thee modes for NURBS circle creation on the Mode bar.

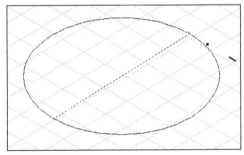

Figure 7.86 A NURBS circle begins with the first point on either its circumference or its center. As you move the mouse, the circle is previewed.

NURBS OBJECTS

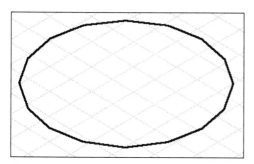

Figure 7.87 One or two more clicks and the circle is complete. Its relative lumpiness depends on the 3D Conversion Resolution setting in the VectorWorks Preferences dialog box.

Figure 7.88 The NURBS Arc tool is under the NURBS Circle tool on the default 3D Tools palette.

Figure 7.89 The Mode bar for NURBS arcs has four modes.

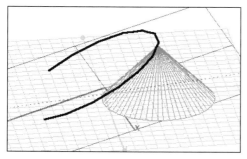

Figure 7.90 A NURBS arc is drawn on the working plane unless you snap to points off the plane (as shown here).

4. Click to place the remaining points that define the circle. In some cases, (for instance, if you are working in an oblique view and drawing the circle on the working plane), the circle will be viewed at an angle and appear as an ellipse (**Figure 7.87**).

   The NURBS object is completed on the working plane unless you have snapped elsewhere.

To draw a NURBS arc:

1. On the 3D Tools palette, click the NURBS Arc tool (**Figure 7.88**).

2. On the Mode bar, choose one of the four modes corresponding to the 2D Arc tool's modes (not including the 2 Points and Radius mode) (**Figure 7.89**).

3. Proceed as if you were drawing in 2D.

   As in the case of NURBS circles, you may find yourself drawing the arc in a plane oblique to the viewer's line of sight, in which case the curve will be shown somewhat flattened.

   When you place the last point, the object is completed (**Figure 7.90**).

NURBS OBJECTS

273

To draw a NURBS curve freehand:

1. On the 3D Tools palette, click the NURBS tool (**Figure 7.91**).

2. On the Mode bar, choose one of two drawing modes:

   The Interpolation Point mode places a free-form curve (according to some rather complicated mathematics) through the points you define with the mouse. The curves you draw in this mode are somewhat like polylines drawn with Cubic Spline points (**Figure 7.92**).

   In the Control Point mode, the points you place lie outside the curve—which is again defined by the math. Compare it to the Bézier and Arc point modes of the Polyline tool in the 2D environment.

3. Click in the drawing area to place each successive control point.

   As you draw, the curve is sketched. Each control point affects not only the segment within which it lies, but the segments on either side of it, so the whole curve changes continuously as you draw (**Figure 7.93**).

4. Complete the curve by double-clicking or by clicking on the starting point of the curve (**Figure 7.94**).

✔ Tip

- As with other tools in the 3D drawing environment, you may need to trick the Constraints palette into letting you disable the Constrain Working Plane constraint. Try switching into one of the non-oblique views and back again.

Figure 7.91 The NURBS tool for freehand curves has its own place on the 3D Tools palette.

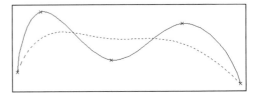

Figure 7.92 Interpolation points lie on the NURBS object (solid line). Control points aren't on the line, but they control the shape of the NURBS object (broken line).

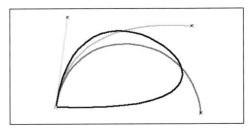

Figure 7.93 The curve changes continuously as you create new points. As you click the four control points in succession, the shape of the whole curve is affected.

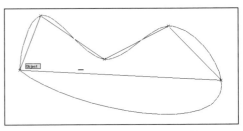

Figure 7.94 The NURBS object is completed by double-clicking or bringing it back to its starting point.

EDITING
3D OBJECTS

The objects we created in Chapter 7 are all very well, but if we're trying to model some real-world object, we need to use them as basic building blocks that we can move around in 3D space, reshape and combine.

With the notable exception of extrusions and sweeps—which begin life tied to the plane of the screen where their 2D antecedents were drawn—3D objects are created with reference to the working plane.

By default, the Ground plane is the working plane, and you must be in Plan view to create and place the 3D plug-in objects that come with VectorWorks (see Chapter 10, "Architectural Applications") on the Ground plane. But other 3D tools let you work on planes that are offset or rotated relative to the Ground plane.

Once you have created a 3D object, you are free to move it around the space as required. You can move and rotate objects using the 2D and 3D Rotation and Selection tools or the commands under the Tools menu. But it's often more expeditious to set up a working plane using other objects in the view as reference points, especially if you have a number of objects that you want to orient to a single reference plane.

To keep the coordinate systems distinct, VectorWorks employs the convention that the Ground plane uses *x, y,* and *z* to name its axes and other working planes use *i, j,* and *k* (**Figure 8.1**). In the 2D world, you use *i* and *j* coordinates when you rotate the grid (see Chapter 4, "Drawing with Constraints"), but it's an entirely distinct system and there is no link between the 2D grid and the 3D working plane.

In the Object Information palette, you can choose between displaying a 3D object's coordinates relative to the Ground plane (*x, y, z*) or to the working plane (*i, j, k*) (**Figure 8.2**).

When the Ground plane is the working plane, only one coordinate system is in force, and the I, J, and K edit boxes in the Data Display bar and the Object Info palette will display the x, y, and z values.

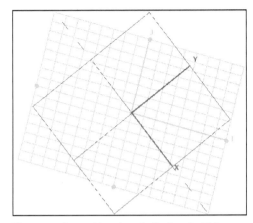

Figure 8.1 The working plane is displayed with its axes labeled I and J (K is the vertical axis) while the Ground plane is always the XYZ system.

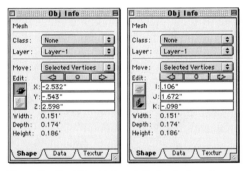

Figure 8.2 The Object Info palette has buttons to switch back and forth between the coordinate systems when a 3D object is selected.

Figure 8.3 You can store specific working planes by naming them and adding them to the list. You can also leaf through the history of the working planes you've used but not saved with the buttons below the list.

Working with Working Planes

Up to this point, we have pretty much skipped over the subject of alternate working planes. As you probably don't recall from high school, but we have to tackle it now, it takes three points to define a plane. In VectorWorks, working planes (other than the default Ground plane, which is always there) can be established by clicking three points in the drawing.

Because many of VectorWorks's 3D tools operate relative to whatever working plane is currently active, setting up a working plane before you create an object can save you the time it would take you to come in afterward and orient it the way you really wanted it in the first place. Alternatively, you can align one of the surfaces of an existing object to whatever plane is active.

The Working Planes palette maintains a history of the last ten working planes you have used in the drawing. It's much like the view history you access in the View bar at the bottom of the drawing area (**Figure 8.3**).

Any plane can be named and stored as a *temporary plane* in the Working Planes palette for future reference. As with Saved Sheets, you can go through them using the arrows at the bottom of the list.

Use the buttons at the bottom of the palette to switch between Ground plane mode and the working plane mode (assuming you have chosen a working plane other than the Ground plane) and to orient the view with the *x-y* plane or the *i-j* plane to the plane of the screen.

Creating and Saving Working Planes

When you draw in the VectorWorks 3D environment, you are working on some working plane or other. By default, that plane is the Ground plane, but you will often want to set the plane to one more convenient to the task at hand. That plane can then be saved for later use.

To set the working plane:

1. On the 3D Tools palette, click the Set Working Plane tool (**Figure 8.4**).

   The pointer turns to an open cross with a dot in the center.

2. On the Constraints palette, make the Snap to Point constraint active and the Constrain Working Plane and Constrain Perpendicular constraints inactive (**Figure 8.5**).

   The other constraints can be either active or not.

3. Click on the point you want to make the origin of the new working plane.

   When the pointer snaps to an object (such as a vertex, a 3D locus, or a point along a segment line of a PIO), the pointer changes to a cross with thickened endpoints and displays the (not very helpful) cue "Object" (**Figure 8.6**).

4. Click at a second point in the drawing, either on an object or on the current working plane to set the *i*-axis relative to the first point.

   The pointer will be the open cross until it snaps to an object and becomes the thickened cross. It will have an I next to it to remind you that the line between the first snap and the second is the *i*-axis.

Figure 8.4 The Set Working Plane tool on the 3D Tools palette.

Figure 8.5 When you want to define the working plane, disable the Constrain Working Plane and Constrain Perpendicular constraints and activate the Snap to Point constraint.

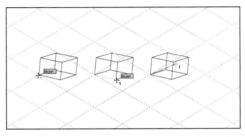

Figure 8.6 Defining a new working plane is as simple as clicking on three points in the drawing.

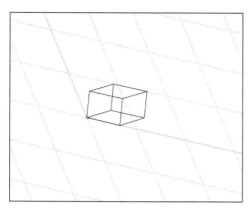

Figure 8.7 When you have defined the new working plane, it will be displayed with its origin at the point of your first click and its *i*-axis extending through the second click.

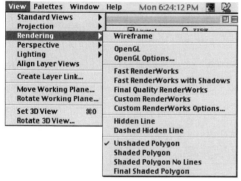

Figure 8.8 The Rendering menu has four options that let you set a working plane with a single click.

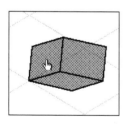

Figure 8.9 Define the working plane with a single click of the finger pointer on a surface rendered as a polygon.

5. Click at a third point to define the *i-j* plane on which all three snaps lie.

The pointer will again be an open cross until it snaps to an object and turns into the lumpy cross. This time the pointer has a J next to it.

The working plane then moves to the newly defined configuration (**Figure 8.7**). If the Show Grid Lines option in the Set Grid dialog box is checked, you will see the new grid; otherwise it will be displayed only when you are using the view control tools on the 3D Tools palette (see Chapter 10, "Worksheets, Reports, and Presentations").

✔ Tips

- Render the drawing in one of the polygon modes at the bottom of the Rendering menu (**Figure 8.8**). and click on one of the surfaces when the pointer turns to finger to set the working plane with one click (**Figure 8.9**).

- If your first click with the Set Working Plane tool isn't on an object, the working plane reverts to the Ground plane.

CREATING AND SAVING WORKING PLANES

279

To save a new active working plane:

1. On the Working Planes palette, click Add.
   The Assign Name dialog box opens
   (**Figure 8.10**).

2. In the Name Working Plane field, type the
   name by which you want this new plane
   to be known and click OK.

   The dialog box closes and the name is
   added to the alphabetical list (**Figure 8.11**).

Some Pointers on Using the Working Planes Palette

◆ To activate a working plane from the list
  of saved planes, double-click its name on
  the list.

◆ To rename one of the saved planes, click
  its name on the list, click Rename, and
  follow the steps above.

◆ To delete a working plane from the list,
  click its name and click Delete.

◆ To switch the active working plane
  between from a selected alternate working plane to the Ground plane, click the
  Ground Plane Mode button at the bottom of the Working Planes palette.

  To switch from Ground Plane mode to
  Working Plane mode, click the Working
  Plane Mode button.

  In either case, the working plane is still
  displayed if the Show Grid Lines option is
  chosen.

◆ To view the selected working plane from
  the top (downward along its *k*-axis), click
  the View Working Plane button at the
  bottom of the palette.

You can both translate the working plane
and rotate it on its origin in order to position
it as a reference for your drawing and editing
operations.

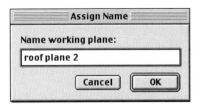

Figure 8.10 A working plane can be added
to the list on the palette by giving it a name.

Figure 8.11 When you save a
working plane, you can recall it
any time by double-clicking its
name on the Working Planes
palette.

Figure 8.12 The 3D Selection tool on the 3D Tools palette.

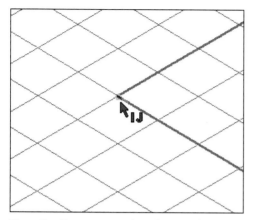
Figure 8.13 The cue next to the pointer toggles back and forth between IJ and XY as you move the pointer around the center handle of the working plane.

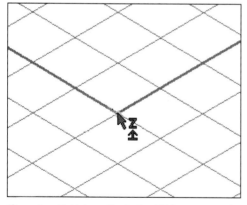
Figure 8.14 Hold down the Option/Alt key to move the working plane along the *z* or *k* axis.

■ When you choose the 3D Selection tool, the Constrain Working Plane constraint is automatically invoked. You may want to disable it so you can snap to points off the working plane.

To move the working plane by its center handle:

1. On the 3D Tools palette, click the 3D Selection tool (**Figure 8.12**).

2. Move the pointer to the center handle of the working plane.

   If you haven't created a working plane, the Ground plane is the working plane.

   As you move the mouse over the handle, the cue will change between IJ and XY (**Figure 8.13**).

3. Choose the axis of movement by doing one of the following:

   Click the mouse while the pointer reads IJ to move the plane in the *i-j* plane with the *k* coordinate remaining unchanged.

   Click the mouse when the pointer reads XY to move the mouse in the *x-y* plane so that the plane's *z* coordinate doesn't change.

   Hold down the Option/Alt key and click when the pointer reads K to move only along its own *k*-axis (**Figure 8.14**).

   Hold down the Option/Alt key and click when the pointer reads Z to move the plane perpendicular to the *x-y* plane.

4. Drag the origin of the plane to its new location and click again (assuming you're using the click-drag mode of drawing).

   You can use the Snap to Point, Snap to Grid, Constrain Angle, Constrain Working Plane and Constrain Perpendicular constraints to help you move the origin of the plane where you want it.

✔ Tips

■ Working planes are part of the 3D environment; you can't work with them in Top/Plan view.

There are two modes of rotation for the working plane. The first uses the origin of the *i-j* plane as a pivot; the other uses either the *i*- or the *j*-axis as the hinge around which the plane turns.

To rotate a working plane by one of its handles:

1. On the 3D Tools palette, click the 3D Selection tool.

2. Move the pointer to one of the handles on the edge of the working plane. In the default condition, the working plane and the ground plane are one and the same.

   As you move the mouse over the handle, the cue will change between K and I (if you are on the J handle) or K and J (if you are on the I handle).

3. Choose the axis of rotation by doing one of the following:

   To rotate the plane on the *k*-axis, click the mouse when the pointer cue reads K at any of the handles (**Figure 8.15**).

   To rotate the plane on the *i*-axis, click when the pointer cue reads I (**Figure 8.16**).

   To rotate the plane on the *j*-axis, click the mouse when the pointer cue reads J.

4. Move the pivot handle to its new position (you can use the snap constraints to help align it) and click again.

   The plane is moved. If you want ready access to it, you can then add it to the list on the Working Planes palette.

✔ Tips

- Choose View > Move Working Plane or View > Rotate Working Plane to manipulate the position of the working plane by typing new values into the dialog boxes that open (**Figure 8.17**).

- Displacing or rotating the working plane is a good way to establish simple spatial relationships among 3D objects.

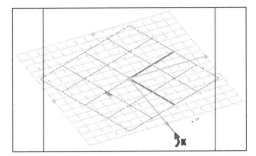

Figure 8.15 Click on the edge handle of the working plane when the pointer cue is K to rotate the plane around its center point.

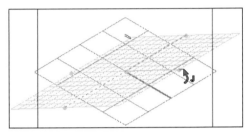

Figure 8.16 Click on the edge hand of the plane when the pointer says I or J to tilt the plane on the other axis.

Figure 8.17 The Move Working Plane (left) and Rotate Working Plane (right) dialog boxes allow you to manipulate the working plane by entering values in edit boxes.

- Hold down the Option/Alt key when you click on one of the edge handles and the cue reads Z. Then the plane rotates about the drawing's *z*-axis rather than its own *k*-axis.

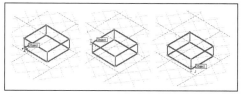

Figure 8.18 The Align Plane tool is under the Set Working Plane tool in the default condition.

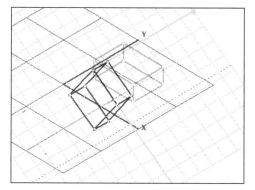

Figure 8.19 Three snaps on an object and you have aligned it to the working plane.

Figure 8.20 The object moves so that the first point you clicked is at the origin of the working plane and the second one lies on the *i-* (or *y-*) axis.

When you create an object relative to one working plane but then want it oriented to another, the solution is simple: align the object to the new plane.

To align objects a the working plane:

1. Select the object you want to reorient.

2. On the 3D Tools palette, choose the Align Plane tool (**Figure 8.18**).

   The Align Plane tool shares its location on the 3D Tools palette with the Set Working Plane tool.

   The pointer becomes an open cross with a dot in the center until it snaps to the first point and becomes a cross with enlarged ends (in heraldry, it would be a *cross formeé*).

3. Click on the point of a selected object you want to place at the origin of the working plane.

   The pointer then becomes the I-beam you're used to when working with text.

4. Snap to a second point and click it to show which way the object rotates.

   This point will lie on the *i*-axis.

5. The third point defines which plane of the object will lie on the working plane (**Figure 8.19**).

   The object will move to its new location and orientation (**Figure 8.20**).

CREATING AND SAVING WORKING PLANES

✔ Tips

■ As with the Set Working Plane tool, if you render the level in one of the polygon modes, you can select a surface with a single click of the mouse.

■ Check to be sure the Constrain Working Plane constraint isn't active if you want to place one surfaces of the object on the working plane. The points you click don't have to be on selected objects, but if they aren't, what you align to the working plane may not be what you had expected.

■ You can align several objects at once by selecting them and then proceeding as above. They will keep their orientation relative to one another and be grouped temporarily while you align them (**Figure 8.21**).

■ Be sure to select all the points of a mesh object or only those you have selected will be moved and the object will be reshaped (**Figure 8.22**).

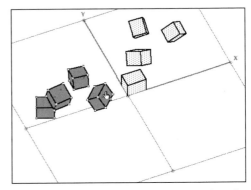

Figure 8.21 Clicking a surface on one of the selected objects (rendered as unshaded solid polygons) aligns them as a group (shown here as textured objects) to the working plane.

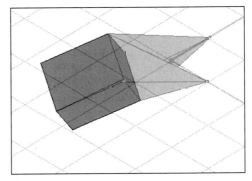

Figure 8.22 If only some of the points of a mesh are selected (in this example, two points), they alone will be moved to align with the working plane.

The 2D and 3D Selection Tools

The 3D and the 2D Selection tools both work in both the 3D and the 2D drawing environments. Differently, of course.

You can use either tool, in either the Marquee or Lasso modes, to select entire objects or individual vertices of mesh objects and then to move them. The difference is that the 2D Selection tool moves objects or vertices in the screen plane without regard to the consequences in the 3D space (as if they were 2D objects) while the 3D Selection tool moves them relative to the working plane which may be parallel to the screen plane, but often isn't. Keep in mind that a very small apparent movement on the screen may in fact be a very large movement in the 3D space, particularly if you are snapping to the grid or to another object.

The 2D Selection tool moves 3D objects in the screen plane without reference to the working plane. When you are in top or bottom view, the 2D tool changes the x and y values, but not the z value; right and left views are y-z views, and in front or back view, the screen plane is the x-z plane. Other views may line up with an alternative working plane's i-j-k system and allow you to move objects along those coordinates in a predictable way.

To select an object with either selection tool:

1. Choose either the 2D Selection tool on the 2D Tools palette or the 3D Selection tool on the 3D Tools palette (**Figure 8.23**).

2. On the Mode bar, click either the Marquee mode or the Lasso mode button to define how objects will be selected by dragging (**Figure 8.24**).

3. Do one of the following:

   Click on one of the vertices of a mesh object to select only that vertex

   or

   Draw a marquee or lasso around a selection of vertices to select only part of a mesh object (**Figure 8.25**)

   or

   Click on the object at a point other than a vertex to select the entire object.

✔ Tip

■ The same methods that work with 2D objects also apply here. You can draw a marquee or lasso with the Option/Alt key pressed to select all those objects even partially within the selection area. Hold the Shift key down to add to or subtract from a selection already made.

To move 3D objects with the 2D Selection tool:

1. Once you have selected the objects you want to move, choose the 2D Selection tool from the 2D Tools palette.

2. With the 2D Selection tool, click somewhere on one of the selected objects and move it to a new location.

Figure 8.23 The 2D Selection (left) and 3D Selection (right) tools.

Figure 8.24 Both the 2D and 3D Selection tools operate in either Marquee or Lasso mode. The Mode bar for the 3D Selection tool also includes buttons for quick switches to Top, Front, Right and Right and Left Isometric views.

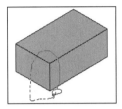

Figure 8.25 Drawing a marquee or lasso around some but not all the vertices of an object lets you reshape the object.

✔ Tips

■ Moving 3D objects with the 2D Selection tool when you are in a non-oblique view (top, front, left, and so forth) moves the object only in the plane parallel to the screen without affecting the third coordinate. Unless the working plane is aligned with the screen plane, moving an object with the 2D Selection tool has the effect of moving it in all three dimensions of the working plane. The results in the 3D space may be hard to foresee.

■ When you use the 2D Selection tool, VectorWorks doesn't distinguish between 2D and 3D objects. You can make use any of the 2D constraints and you can enter either absolute or relative coordinates on the Data Display bar as well.

■ Parametric constraints don't work on 3D objects.

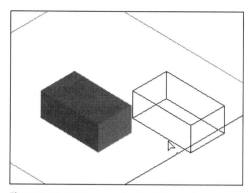

Figure 8.26 To move an object in all three dimensions, first drag it to a new position on the working plane.

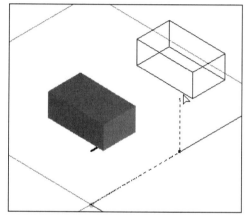

Figure 8.27 Once you've moved the object to the correct i-j position, press R to lock those coordinates and then drag the object along the *k* dimension.

- Move an object by one of its vertices and it will snap to a key point in the drawing if the Snap to Point constraint is active.

- Move an object by one of its edges (the pointer won't change to a cross) and it won't snap to the grid or to a point but move parallel to the working plane without any change in its *k* coordinate.

- The 3D Selection tool selects 2D objects, but it doesn't move them.

The 3D Selection tool moves objects relative to the working plane, not the screen plane. Dragging objects with the mouse has three modes. With the object snapped along one of its surfaces (or with Constrain Working Plane active) and Constrain Perpendicular inactive, you can drag it around without changing its *k* coordinate. With the Constrain Working Plane constraint off and the object snapped by a vertex, you can move it along the *k*-axis by snapping it to another object or to the grid (with the appropriate constraints active). But, with the Constrain Perpendicular constraint active, you can move the object only along the *k*-axis.

To move 3D objects with the 3D Selection tool:

1. With the objects you want to move selected (see above), choose the 3D Selection tool from the 3D Tools palette.

2. With the 3D Selection tool, click on one of the selected objects and drag it to a new *i-j* position (**Figure 8.26**).

3. Press R to engage the Constrain Perpendicular constraint, locking the *i-j* position, and move the objects along the *k*-axis perpendicular to the working plane (**Figure 8.27**).

   Release the mouse to place the object.

✔ Tips

- Constrain Working Plane lets you move an object by one of its vertices without having it snap down to the working plane (*k*=0). With this constraint active, the pointer won't turn to a cross even when you click at a vertex.

- Move an object by one of its vertices and it will snap to the Ground plane if the Snap to Grid constraint is active.

Rotating objects

As is the case with the Selection tools, you can use both the 2D and 3D Rotate tools to rotate 3D objects. The 3D version of the tool is more complicated than the 2D one; it has two pairs of buttons on the Mode bar to control its options (**Figure 8.28**).

The 2D Rotation tool treats an object as though it were just a collection of lines or polygons and rotates it in the screen plane. Snaps to other objects are actually snaps to their projections onto the screen plane. Thus, when you rotate the view after rotating objects in 2D, you may discover that edges that appeared to be aligned in the screen plane really aren't.

To rotate a 3D object with the 3D Rotation tool:

1. With the object selected, click the 3D Rotation tool on the 3D Tools palette (**Figure 8.29**).

   The pointer becomes a small cross.

2. On the Mode bar, choose either Rotate Selected Objects mode or Rotate Duplicate Objects mode.

   Rotate Selected Objects mode lets you click to set a pivot point and then define the angle through which the object is rotated.

   Rotate Duplicate Objects does the same thing except it creates a duplicate object and leaves the original in its original state.

3. On the Mode bar, choose either Standard Rotation mode or Alignment Rotation mode.

   In the Standard mode, the object is rotated on an axis perpendicular to the working plane.

   In the Alignment Rotation mode, the axis of rotation is perpendicular to the rotation lever you define by clicking on another object in the drawing.

Figure 8.28 The Mode bar for the 3D Rotation tool.

Figure 8.29 Don't confuse the 3D Rotation tool (left) with the Flyover tool (right), which resembles it.

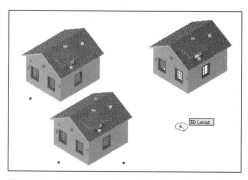

Figure 8.30 Click somewhere in the drawing area to set the pivot point for the rotation of objects. The pivot doesn't have to be on the objects themselves.

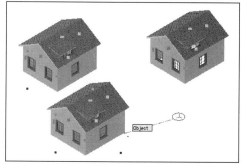

Figure 8.31 Click again to create the handle that you use to drag the objects around the pivot.

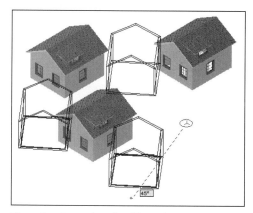

Figure 8.32 As you drag the objects, they are previewed.

4. In the drawing area, click on the point you want to set as the rotation point for the object (**Figure 8.30**).

The axis of rotation will be at this point and will be either perpendicular to the working plane or to the line between this point and the next one you click, depending on the Rotation mode you chose in Step 3.

5. In the drawing area, click again to define the handle by which you rotate the object (**Figure 8.31**).

You can snap to corner points on the object if you have disabled Constrain Working Plane (or if the points happen to lie on the working plane).

6. Drag the handle and click again to set the rotation of the object (**Figure 8.32**).

If you are in Rotate and Duplicate mode, a copy of the object will be placed.

If you are in Alignment Rotation mode, you will see the object previewed only when you have snapped to a point in the drawing. The object won't be rotated if you click the mouse without locking onto an alignment point.

✔ Tips

■ As usual in the 3D editing environment, you may need to temporarily switch to a non-oblique view (press 2, 4, 5, 6, or 8 on the keypad) to disable Constrain Working Plane and then go back to the view in which you were working.

■ When you use a 2D tool in the 3D environment, the pointer will still snap to the 2D grid (even if the 3D space is rotated and you can't see the grid) when the Snap to Grid constraint is active. This is sometimes a little disorienting.

You can also rotate 3D objects by means of commands from the menu.

Use the 2D command to rotate the object around its own center on an axis perpendicular to the screen plane. This is pretty straightforward if you are viewing the object straight on. If it is at an angle to the view, however, the relationship between a rotation on the view axis and the orientation of the object in the 3D space is harder to previsualize.

VectorWorks provides a separate Rotate 3D command that opens a dialog box where you set all the parameters for a more controlled rotation of the object around an axis determined by either the Ground plane or the active working plane.

To rotate objects with the Rotate 3D command:

1. Select the objects you want to rotate.

2. Choose Tool > Rotate > Rotate 3D.
   The Rotate Object in 3D dialog box opens (**Figure 8.33**).

3. Under the Rotation Axis heading, choose either the *x*-, *y*-, or *z*-axis of the Ground plane or the *i*-, *j*-, or *k*-axis of the working plane.
   The first option under Rotation Center will toggle back and forth between Ground Plane Center and Working Plane Center as you change coordinate systems for the Rotation Axis.

4. In the Rotate Object in 3D dialog box, select the center of the rotation by clicking one of the radio buttons under Rotation Center.

5. Type a value for the Rotation Angle in the field provided.

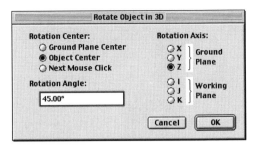

Figure 8.33 Use the Rotate Object in 3D dialog box to set the angle and the axis of rotation for the selected objects.

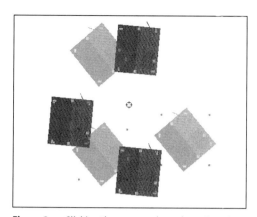

Figure 8.34 Clicking the mouse where the pointer is shown with the settings above rotates the houses 45 degrees counter-clockwise.

6. Complete the rotation by doing one of the following:

If you have chosen either Next Mouse Click as the rotation center, click OK to close the dialog box. Then click in the drawing area to set the center of the rotation

or

Click OK to close the dialog box. The rotation will be completed with the settings you have chosen (**Figure 8.34**).

✔ Tip

■ The Next Mouse Click option chooses a point on the screen plane. To rotate about a point in the 3D space, you can either set up an alternate working plane centered at that point or use the 3D Rotate tool from the 3D Tools palette.

The 3D Mirroring tool

Another way of moving an object around in space is to mirror it. At first blush, mirroring might seem the same as rotating it, but it isn't. Think about mirroring text: rotating it 180 degrees turns it upside down; mirroring it makes it read backward (**Figure 8.35**). Furthermore, the 3D Mirror tool (like the 2D one) can flip objects at angles other than 180 degrees.

The 3D Mirror tool operates in two modes, one that just mirrors the object, and one that duplicates the object before mirroring it. In the normal use of the tool, the object is mirrored parallel to the working plane across a line defined by the mouse. The Mode bar also contains a button that mirrors the object across the working plane, duplicating it in the process if that mode is selected.

To mirror objects parallel to the working plane:

1. In the drawing area, select the objects to be mirrored.

2. On the 3D Tools palette, click the 3D Mirror tool. (**Figure 8.36**).

3. On the Mode bar, click 3D Mirror mode button

    or

    Click the 3D Mirror and Duplicate button (**Figure 8.37**).

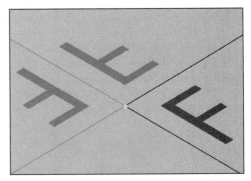

Figure 8.35 Text mirrored 180 degrees across the axis is backwards; text rotated around the origin is only upside down.

Figure 8.36 The 3D Mirror tool.

Figure 8.37 The 3D Tool Mode bar offers two modes plus a button that mirrors the selection across the working plane.

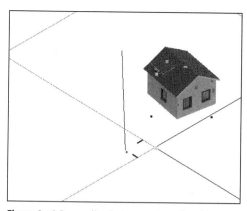

Figure 8.38 Draw a line between where the object is and where you want it to appear.

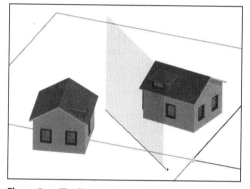

Figure 8.39 The line you draw with the 3D mirror tool is projected onto the working plane to define the plane across which the selected object is mirrored.

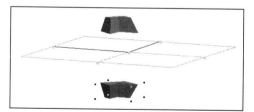

Figure 8.40 The Mirror Across Working Plane button instantaneously (more or less) flips the object over the working plane.

4. In the drawing area, click to define the starting point of the line across which the object is to be mirrored.

The line defining the edge of the plane that serves as the mirror is drawn as you move the mouse (**Figure 8.38**).

5. Click again to complete the line.

The object is mirrored across the projection of the line onto the working plane and the line disappears (**Figure 8.39**).

If you chose the Mirror and Duplicate mode, the selected object remains where it is and a copy of the selected object is placed.

To mirror an object across the working plane:

1. Select the objects you want to mirror.

2. On the 3D Tools palette, click the 3D Mirror tool.

3. On the Mode bar, click the 3D Mirror mode button to move the original object across the working plane

or

Click the 3D Mirror and Duplicate button to move a copy of the original object across the plane.

4. On the Mode bar, click the Mirror Across Working Plane button (**Figure 8.40**).

The objects are mirrored across the working plane. If you are in Mirror and Duplicate mode, a duplicate of the selection is moved and the original is left in place.

THE 3D MIRRORING TOOL

Reshaping 3D objects

Surprisingly, most 3D objects are modified not with the 3D Reshape tool, but with the 3D Selection tool—or even the 2D Selection tool.

The 2D Selection tool treats 3D objects as collections of 2D lines and points on the screen plane without regard to their true positions in the 3D space. When you move a point you may be changing all its coordinates in the ground plane or working plane systems, depending on the view in which you happen to be working.

To reshape a 3D object with the 2D Selection tool:

1. Click the 2D Selection tool on the 2D Tools palette.

2. With the 2D Selection tool (either by clicking or with the Marquee or Lasso mode), select only the vertices you want to move (**Figure 8.41**).

3. With the 2D Selection tool, click on one of the selected vertices and drag it (with the other selected vertices) to a new place in the drawing area (**Figure 8.42**).

   Release the mouse to complete the reshaping operation (**Figure 8.43**).

✔ Tips

■ Select the vertices you want to move and then choose Tools > Move > Move or press Command-M (Mac) or Ctrl-M (Windows) to move the selection in the screen plane with the Move Selection dialog box that opens (**Figure 8.44**).

■ Choose Tools > Move > Move 3D or press Command-Option (Mac) or Alt-Ctrl-M (Windows) and use the Move 3D Selection dialog box to move selected vertices relative to either the Ground plane or the working plane (**Figure 8.45**).

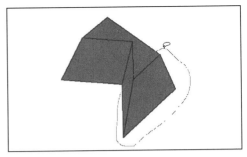

Figure 8.41 You can select the point you want to move with the marquee, the lasso, or by clicking.

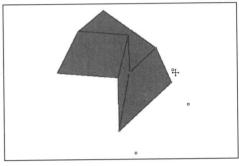

Figure 8.42 Click one of the selected vertices and drag it—with the rest of the selection—to a new location.

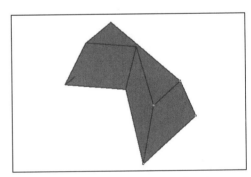

Figure 8.43 Release the mouse to complete the reshaping.

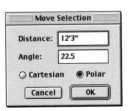

Figure 8.44 You can make a selection realtive to the screen plane with the mouse and then move it with the Move dialog box.

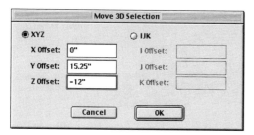

Figure 8.45 Alternatively, you can move the selection in the 3D space with the Move 3D Selection dialog box.

Figure 8.46 The shape of the pointer tells whether Constrain Working Plane is active; the arrow pointer replaces the cross when it is.

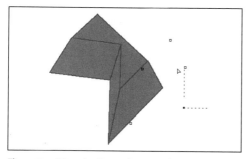

Figure 8.47 When the Constrain Perpendicular constraint is selected, selections move only along the *k*- (or *z*-) axis.

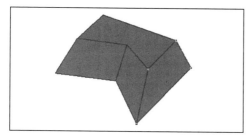

Figure 8.48 Release the mouse to complete the reshaping of the mesh.

To reshape a 3D mesh object with the 3D Selection tool:

1. Select the vertices you want to move.

   You can use either the 2D or 3D Selection tool for this.

2. On the 3D Tools palette, click the 3D Selection tool.

3. On the Constraints palette, do one of the following:

   Activate Constrain Working Plane to lock the selected vertices to their current *k* coordinates

   or

   Disable Constrain Working Plane to allow the vertices to be snapped to other points in the drawing area or to be moved onto the working plane.

4. Click one of the selected vertices and drag it to its new location.

   If Constrain Working Plane is active, the pointer will turn into an arrow without a tail when it snaps to the vertex.

   If Constrain Working Plane is not active, the pointer will become the cross with big ends when it snaps to the vertex (**Figure 8.46**).

5. Hold down the mouse as you drag the vertex (and all the other vertices selected along with it) to a new location.

   If Constrain Working Plane is active, you won't be able to click to any point not on the working plane.

6. Press R to engage the Constrain Perpendicular constraint and drag the object perpendicular to the working plane, changing only its *k* (or *z*) coordinate (**Figure 8.47**).

   Release the mouse to complete the reshaping (**Figure 8.48**).

✔ Tip

- When you undo a reshaping operation done with the 3D Selection tool, the object jumps to a new place in the drawing area. This would appear to be a bug, and I don't have a work-around for it (**Figure 8.49**).

The 3D Reshape tool is really three tools that self-select automatically depending on the object selected. Each has its own Mode bar configuration. The basic version works for cones, spheres, hemispheres, and extrusions, and gives you a way to grab an object by its handles and adjust its height or diameter (**Figure 8.50**).

The 3D Reshape tool also works on 3D polygons; you can move, add, or remove vertices by changing modes in the Mode bar (**Figure 8.51**).

Finally, the 3D Reshape tool becomes a NURBS editing tool when a NURBS curve or an Extrude Along Path object is selected (**Figure 8.52**).

The tool doesn't work on meshes, on tapered or multiple extrusions, or on sweeps. It also doesn't work with plug-in objects that are controlled from the Object Info palette, or with complex 3D objects created with the Add, Subtract, and Intersect commands (see below).

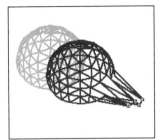

Figure 8.49 When you pull the side of the hemisphere and then undo the action, the objects snaps back from its original position as if you'd let go of a rubber band. It's a bug.

Figure 8.50 The 3D Reshape tool.

Figure 8.51 When you select a 3D polygon. the mode bar adds modes for adding and subtracting vertices.

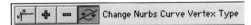

Figure 8.52 Select a NURBS object to reshape and the Mode bar has options for not only adding and removing vertices, but for changing a vertex from a curve vertex to a corner vertex and back again.

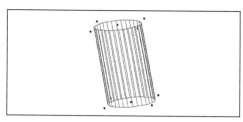

Figure 8.53 When the 3D Reshape tool is active a selected extrude displays a handle on each of its end surfaces.

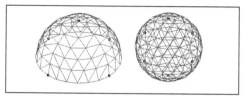

Figure 8.54 Spheres and hemispheres have handles around their equators and at their poles.

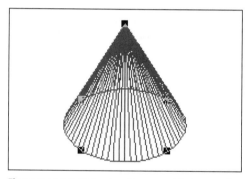

Figure 8.55 A cone has handles around its base and one at its apex.

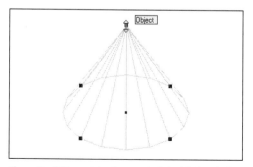

Figure 8.56 The pointer is a vertical double-headed arrow when it snaps to a center handle on a selected object.

To modify an extrude, cone, sphere, or hemisphere with the 3D Reshape tool:

1. On the 3D Tools palette, click the 3D Reshape tool.

2. Click the object you want to modify.

   In the case of an extrude, the object will have four handles for each end surface and, if it is viewed obliquely, an extra handle in the center of each face (**Figure 8.53**).

   A sphere or hemisphere will have handles on four sides and on the top. A sphere has an additional one on the bottom (**Figure 8.54**).

   A cone has four handles around its base and another at the apex (**Figure 8.55**).

   When the pointer snaps to the center handle, it will change to a different double-headed arrow than the one generally used to move vertices. (**Figure 8.56**).

continues on next page

RESHAPING 3D OBJECTS

3. Do one of the following:

To change the length of an extrude, drag one of the center handles (**Figure 8.57**).

To change the height of a cone, drag the apex handle; to change its diameter, drag one of the handles on the base (**Figure 8.58**).

To change the diameter of a sphere or hemisphere, drag any of its handles (**Figure 8.59**).

4. Click again to complete the reshaping operation.

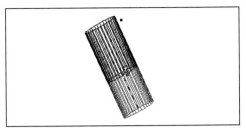

Figure 8.57 In oblique views (and with the object itself viewed obliquely to the line along which it was extruded) the length of an extrude can be modified by grabbing one of its end handles and dragging it.

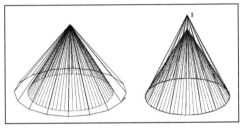

Figure 8.58 You can change the diameter of a cone by dragging one of its base handles. Drag its apex handle to change its height.

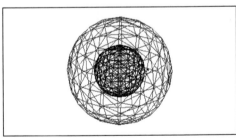

Figure 8.59 The handles on the edges of the sphere or hemisphere and those at the top and bottom all increase or decrease the diameter of the object from its center.

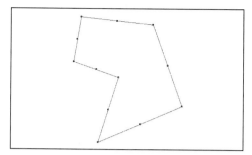

Figure 8.60 When you reshape a 3D polygon, each segment has two endpoint and a midpoint handle which you can move. You can delete vertices and points at either the vertex or the midpoint.

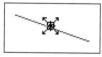

Figure 8.61 The cursor for the 3D Reshape tool is a four-headed assemblage of arrows when it snaps to a point.

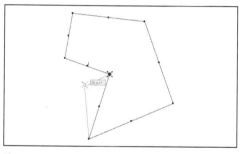

Figure 8.62 With the Add 3D Poly Vertices mode selected, click and drag either a vertex or a midpoint to add and locate a new vertex.

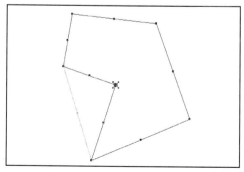

Figure 8.63 Click on the vertex you want to remove with the Delete 3D Poly Vertices mode selected.

To reshape a 3D polygon:

1. On the 3D Tools palette, click the 3D Reshape tool.

2. In the drawing area, click the 3D polygon you want to edit.

   Handles will appear at the vertices and at the midpoints of each segment and the Mode bar will show three buttons (**Figure 8.60**).

3. On the Mode bar, click the Move 3D Poly Vertices button to move individual vertices

   or

   Click the Add 3D Poly Vertices button to add additional vertices at existing vertex points or segment midpoints

   or

   Click the Delete 3D Poly Vertices button to remove vertices from the polygon.

4. With the Move 3D Vertices button selected on the mode bar, click the vertex or segment midpoint you want to move and drag it to a new position.

   The pointer will become a four-headed arrow when it snaps to a vertex or midpoint (**Figure 8.61**).

   Click again to complete the movement.

5. With the Add 3D Poly Vertices button selected, click on either a vertex or a midpoint to create a new vertex and drag it where you want it (**Figure 8.62**).

   The pointer will become a four-headed arrow when it snaps to a vertex or midpoint.

   Click again to complete the movement.

6. With the Delete 3D Poly Vertices button selected, click on a vertex to remove it (**Figure 8.63**).

   The pointer will become a four-headed arrow when it snaps to a vertex.

To reshape a NURBS or Extrude Along Path object:

1. On the 3D Tools palette, click the 3D Reshape tool.

2. In the drawing area, click the NURBS or Extrude Along Path object you want to edit.

   Handles will appear at the vertices of the NURBS curve and the Mode bar will show four buttons (**Figure 8.64**).

3. With the Move NURBS Curve Vertices button selected on the mode bar, click the vertex you want to move and drag it to a new position (**Figure 8.65**).

   The pointer will become a four-headed arrow when it snaps to a vertex.

   Click again to complete the movement.

4. With the Add NURBS Curve Vertices button selected, click on a vertex to create a new vertex and drag it where you want it (**Figure 8.66**).

   The pointer will become a four-headed arrow when it snaps to a vertex.

   Click again to complete the movement.

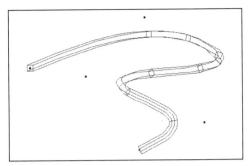

Figure 8.64 The handles of the NURBS curve underlying the Extrude Along Path object are displayed when the 3D Reshape tool is selected.

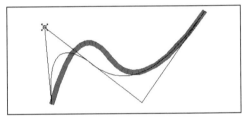

Figure 8.65 As you move a vertex of the Extrude Along Path object, the new shape of the NURBS curve is previewed.

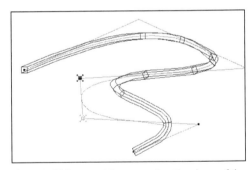

Figure 8.66 As you add a new vertex, the shape of the NURBS curve is previewed.

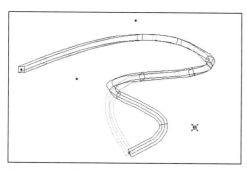

Figure 8.67 Click on one of the vertices in the Delete NURBS Curve Vertices mode to simplify the curve of the extrude.

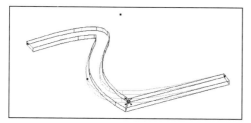

Figure 8.68 Click a vertex when the 3D Reshape tool is in the Change NURBS Curve Vertex Type mode to toggle the vertex back and forth between a curve point and a corner point.

5. With the Delete NURBS Curve Vertices button selected, click on a vertex to remove it (**Figure 8.67**).

The pointer will become a four-headed arrow when it snaps to a vertex.

6. With the Change NURBS Curve Vertex Type button selected, click a vertex to toggle it between a curve vertex and a corner vertex (**Figure 8.68**).

The pointer will become a four-headed arrow when it snaps to a vertex.

✔ Tips

- Select an Extrude Along Path object and choose Organize > Edit Group or press Command-[(Mac) or Ctrl-[(Windows) to edit the profile or the path. Choose which one you want to work with in the dialog box that opens.

- Sometimes you will find that the tool won't select vertices that aren't on the object. You can then use the Edit Group approach to modify the NURBS object and return to the layer to complete the edit.

RESHAPING 3D OBJECTS

Combining Objects

Once we have created the building blocks for more complex 3D objects, we can begin to combine them in a variety of ways. 3D objects can be added and subtracted and intersected much the way we add, clip, and intersect 2D objects (see Chapter 3, "Modifying 2D Shapes").

These Boolean operations can be performed on any overlapping 3D solids within a single layer (but not on 3D polygons or NURBS objects).

To add 3D objects:

1. Select the objects you want to add (**Figure 8.69**).

2. Choose Model > Add Solids (**Figure 8.70**).

   The objects are combined into a single object (a Solid Addition) the attributes (including class assignment) of the of the object furthest back in the stack (**Figure 8.71**).

Figure 8.69 All the Boolean operations begin with selecting the objects you want to combine.

Figure 8.70 The Add, Subtract, and Intersect Solids commands are all found under Model on the Menu bar.

Figure 8.71 When you add solids, you get a single object with the class and attributes of the object furthest back in the stack.

Figure 8.72
Subtracting solids requires you to tell the application from which object it is to subtract a part overlapped by the others.

Figure 8.73 A solid subtraction is what's left of the underlying object when you remove the overlapping parts of the other selected objects.

Figure 8.74 The intersection of a set of solids is the part they all have in common.

To subtract 3D objects:

1. Select the objects you want to combine by subtraction.

2. Choose Model > Subtract Solids.

   A dialog box opens in which you select the object from which the others will be subtracted (**Figure 8.72**).

3. In the dialog box, use the arrow buttons to choose which object will be the one from which the others are subtracted.

   As you change the selection in the dialog box, the object is highlighted in the drawing area.

4. Click OK to complete the subtraction (**Figure 8.73**).

To intersect 3D objects:

1. Select the objects to be combined.

2. Choose Model > Intersect Solids.

   The resulting solid is the volume shared by all selected objects and has the class and other attributes of the backmost object selected (**Figure 8.74**).

COMBINING OBJECTS

Converting Objects to Other Types

Just as you can convert a 2D object from one kind of object to another (from a polyline to a polygon or from a rectangle to a group of four lines, say) you can transmute 3D objects from one kind to another. And you can cross back and forth between the 2D and 3D realms as well, turning 2D polylines into NURBS objects, for example, and 3D polygons into their two-dimensional projections on the screen plane.

But as we saw with 2D conversions, once you break up a shape into its component parts, you can't always reverse the process. Converting a 3D polygon into a NURBS curve and then converting that into 3D polygons yields a group of polygons with only a single dimension: 3D lines. When you've broken a solid into lines or polygons, it can't be reconstructed except by the Undo command.

Converting an object to a mesh allows you to move individual vertices or selected vertices to create solids that would be much more difficult to define by other means.

To convert an object to a mesh:

1. Select the 3D object—sweeps, primitives, solid additions, and so forth—you want to convert.

   (This command doesn't work with 2D objects.)

2. Choose Model > Convert to Mesh.

   The object is converted and now can be reshaped point by point. The number of vertices used to define the new object is a function of the 3D Conversion Resolution setting on the 3D tab of the VectorWorks Preferences dialog box (**Figure 8.75**).

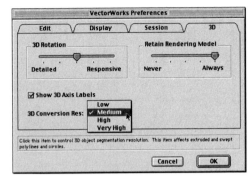

Figure 8.75 When you convert an object to mesh, the fineness of the mesh depends on the 3D Conversion Resolution setting in the Preferences.

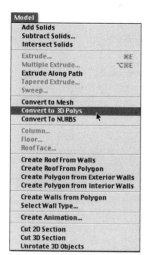

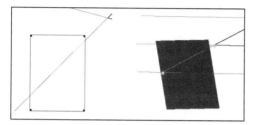

Figure 8.76 Convert objects by choosing the Convert to 3D Polygons command from the Model menu.

Figure 8.77 A 2D polygon in the screen plane becomes a 3D polygon somewhere in the space. It's location depends on the view in which it was converted.

To convert an object to 3D polygons:

1. Select the object you want to convert.

   You can break down complex 3D solids into polygons that can be edited individually. You can also convert a 2D object into a 3D polygon.

2. Choose Model > Convert to 3D Polygons (**Figure 8.76**).

   A 3D object is converted into a group of 3D polygons that you can ungroup and move individually. The number (and conversely, the size) of the individual polygons is controlled by the 3D Conversion Resolution on the 3D tab of the VectorWorks Preferences dialog box.

   A 2D object is converted into a single 3D polygon situated somewhere in the 3D space (**Figure 8.77**).

Some objects can be converted into NURBS curves. These include 3D polygons, and most 2D objects (but not text objects or loci). NURBS curves are often used as paths along which a profile can be smoothly extruded. They can also be used to simply represent a curved contour in space.

To convert an object to a NURBS object:

1. Select the 2D object or 3D polygon you want to convert.

2. Choose Model > Convert to NURBS.

   The object is converted to one or a group of NURBS curves.

To convert a 3D object to lines:

1. Select the 3D objects you want to convert.

2. Choose Tool > Convert to Lines (or, Convert Copy to Lines—see Chapter 3, "Modifying 2D Shapes").

   A dialog box with three radio buttons opens that lets you specify how to deal with the lines that represent surfaces which would be hidden in the rendered object (**Figure 8.78**).

3. In the unnamed dialog box, choose one of the following options:

   Click the Wireframe Rendering radio button to convert all the lines visible in the wireframe rendering to 2D line objects (**Figure 8.79**).

   Click the Hidden Line Rendering radio button to convert only those lines you see in the current view. If none of the edges are hidden by fill, the effect will be the same as choosing Wireframe Rendering. (**Figure 8.80**).

   Click the Dashed Hidden Line Rendering radio button to convert the lines representing visible surfaces into line objects with a solid line attribute and those that represent the hidden surfaces as dashed lines with their color grayed out (**Figure 8.81**).

4. Click OK.

   The object is converted to a group of lines according to the settings in the dialog box.

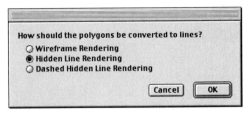

Figure 8.78 When you set out to convert a 3D object to 2D lines, a dialog box opens so you can specify exactly how you want the hidden lines handled.

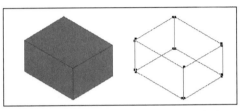

Figure 8.79 You can convert an object to lines in three ways; the first just draws the wireframe as it would appear in the selected view.

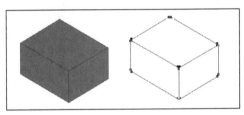

Figure 8.80 Choose the Hidden Line Rendering option to create lines only where you see them.

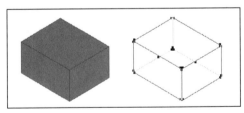

Figure 8.81 A Dashed Hidden Line Rendering converts hidden lines to dashed lines according to the settings in the Document Preferences.

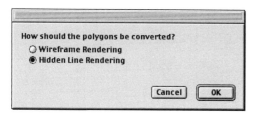

Figure 8.82 There are two modes for converting a 3D object to 2D Polygons.

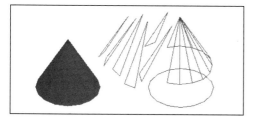

Figure 8.83 Choose the Wireframe option for reducing a 3D object to polygons to create only polygons.

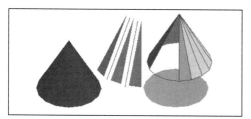

Figure 8.84 Choose the Hidden Line option for reducing a 3D object to polygons to create both lines and polygons.

Convert a solid to 2D polygons if you want to treat it as a 2D illustration, which you can easily manipulate plane by plane.

To convert a 3D object to 2D polygons:

1. Select the 3D objects you want to convert.

2. Choose Tool > Convert to Polygons (or, Convert Copy to Polygons–see Chapter 3, "Modifying 2D Shapes").

    A dialog box with two radio buttons opens that lets you specify how to deal with the lines that represent surfaces that would be hidden in the rendered object (**Figure 8.82**).

3. In the unnamed dialog box, choose one of the following options (note that the names of the options aren't particularly accurate reflections of what they actually do):

    Click the Wireframe Rendering radio button to convert the selected object to a group of polygons. (**Figure 8.83**).

    Click the Hidden Line Rendering radio button to create both lines and polygons. (**Figure 8.84**).

4. Click OK.

    The object is converted to a group of polygons according to the settings in the dialog box.

CONVERTING OBJECTS TO OTHER TYPES

Converting to Groups

Another way of making 3D objects more editable–or editable in different ways–is to deal with them as *groups*.

Most 3D objects in the VectorWorks lexicon can be resolved into to a collection of 3D polygons and then, if necessary, into 2D polygons and lines. Paradoxically, with a solid primitive, you first convert it into a group, which you then ungroup into a collection of 3D polygons.

Boolean objects are unaffected by the Group command. However, they are returned to the objects from which they arose by the Ungroup command. But you can't go the other way and create a Boolean object by grouping two solid objects.

The 3D Primitive PIOs are deconstructed as follows by either the Group or Ungroup command:

♦ Spheres, hemispheres, cylinders, toruses, ellipsoids, and cones become Sweep objects that can be turned into 3D polygons with a second Ungroup command.

♦ Box objects are dissolved into extrusions.

♦ Pyramids become multiple extrusions.

To convert a primitive object to a group:

1. Select the object you want to convert.

2. Choose Organize > Convert to Group or press Command-K (Mac) or Ctrl-K (Windows).
   The object is converted to a group of 3D polygons.

✔ Tip

■ Extrude Along Path objects break down into NURBS surfaces. And they can be further broken down into 2D lines, but the Convert to Polygons command creates only lines, and not polygons.

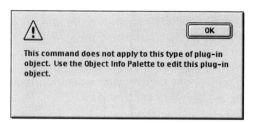

Figure 8.85 You can't edit Plug-In objects as groups.

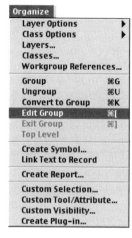

Figure 8.86 You can choose the Edit Group from the command menu or from the keyboard.

Figure 8.87 When you enter a sweep (left) to edit it, you see a profile and, in some cases, the locus around which the profile is revolved (right).

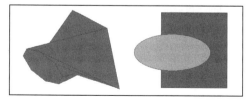

Figure 8.88 To edit an extrude, choose Edit Group and then modify the components of which the object was created. Sometimes you can untwist multiple extrudes; sometimes not.

Entering and Editing 3D Objects

The Edit Group command works in the 3D milieu pretty much the way it works in two dimensions. It lets you enter objects and tunnel down to whatever subgroups make them up, with one exception: When you try to edit a plug-in object, an alert message will pop up and direct you to the Object Info palette (**Figure 8.865**).

To enter and edit a 3D object:

1. Select the object to be modified.

2. Choose Organize > Edit Group or press Command-] (Mac) or Ctrl-[(Windows) (**Figure 8.86**).

   The selected object is displayed ungrouped in its own window (assuming you have not selected the Show Other Objects While In Groups option in the Vector-Works preferences).

   ◆ Enter a Sweep object to edit its profile and the distance between the profile and the center of revolution (**Figure 8.87**).

   ◆ Enter an Extrude object (including Tapered and Multiple extrudes) to edit its sections (**Figure 8.88**).

continues on next page

- ◆ Enter an Extrude Along Path object choose either the path or profile to edit in a separate window (**Figure 8.89**). You then edit the selected element individually.
- ◆ Enter a Boolean solid (a solid addition, subtraction, or intersection) to edit any of the solids from which it was constructed (**Figure 8.90**).
- ◆ Enter a Group created from individual objects by the Group command to work on the objects individually. (**Figure 8.91**).

3. Select objects within the original selection that are themselves groups or other kinds of 3D objects that can be edited with the command and choose Organize > Edit Group again.

Figure 8.89 Before you can use the Edit Group command with an Extrude Along Path object, you have to specify whether it's the path or the profile you want to modify.

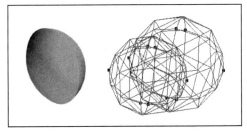

Figure 8.90 Entering a Boolean solid (in this example, a Solid Intersection) magically returns it to its original components (two spheres).

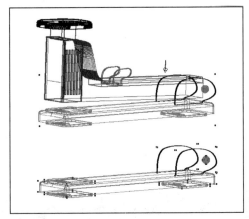

Figure 8.91 Entering a group lets you temporarily ungroup it to modify individual members.

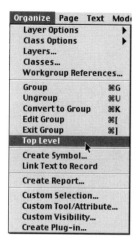

Figure 8.92 You can navigate to the correct level within the group on the command menu.

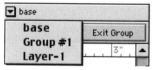

Figure 8.93 Use the Level drop-down menu on the Data Display bar to navigate within (or out of) the edit window. You can also use the Exit Group button at the right to move up one level at a time.

4. Edit the 2D and 3D objects and choose Organize > Exit Group or press Command-] (Mac) or Ctrl-] (Windows) to move up to the next level of the group

or

Choose Organize > Top Level to return directly to active level of the drawing (**Figure 8.92**)

or

Use the Level drop-down menu on the Data Display bar to go back to the top level or to another level within the edit window (**Figure 8.93**).

ARCHITECTURAL APPLICATIONS

VectorWorks is a very effective general-purpose 2D drawing tool, and pretty useful for general purpose 3D modeling. But it is with the specifically architectural functions that the program really struts its stuff. Designed with architects in mind, VectorWorks's unique layer structure shows its value, and the concept of hybrid symbols its power. And if you have RenderWorks installed, most of the textures that are provided with the package are directly applicable in the architectural design environment.

Setting up an Architectural Drawing

VectorWorks used to come with a collection of templates for architectural drawings. These files included prefab class and layer structures as well as a drawing border and title block. The latter has been replaced by the Drawing Border plug-in object which is a very flexible tool for creating a variety of borders and title blocks fitted to any size drawing sheet (**Figure 9.1**).

As a starting point, you can also use the NW House.mcd file that comes with the application (look in the Samples folder). Note that the classes and layers in this drawing aren't those of the AIA standards provided in the application's Standards folder and provided in the Layer Options and Class Options dialog boxes that open when you choose to set up a new layer or class (see Chapter 5, "Using Layers and Classes").

When you set up an architectural drawing, the settings for Z ($\Delta Z/\pm Z$ controls the default wall height) is critical only if you are going to be constructing 3D models by linking layers. The z value you give a layer in the Layers Setup dialog box has no apparent effect in the individual layer; the Ground plane always has a z coordinate of 0. But the values you establish for each of your layers controls how its contents are stacked in an assembled linked layer so that the third floor sits neatly on top of the second (see Chapter 10, "Worksheets, Reports, and Presentations").

Each floor of a multi-story building can reference its own Ground plane if the layer Z settings are correct. Many architects assign several layers to each floor of a building. One layer contains the slab, another the walls, and yet another the dimensions and notes. This way, when it comes time to assemble a model using the Layer Link command, you can quickly select the elements you want to display.

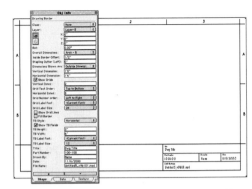

Figure 9.1 The Drawing Border plug-in creates a title block and border to your specifications. You can save it as a symbol or make it part of your template for future use.

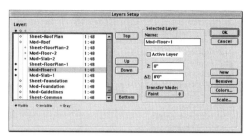

Figure 9.2 A typical layer structure includes several layers for each floor: a Mod-Slab layer for the floors, a Mod-Floor layer for the walls and other design features, and a Sheet-Floor Plan layer for notes and dimensions.

Figure 9.3 If you create new layers starting from the bottom, each will stack on top of the others.

To configure the Z settings for a typical floor:

1. Choose Organize > Layers or Layers on the Layers drop-down menu on the Data Display bar.

   The Layers Setup dialog box opens (**Figure 9.2**).

2. In the Layers Setup dialog box, select the layer you want to modify from the layers list.

   The layer will be highlighted

3. In the Selected Layer pane, type a value in the Z edit box to establish the basic height of the floor relative to some zero elevation.

   The $z=0$ height is usually the nominal grade or the level of the first floor; the foundation is then below that in the negative numbers.

4. In the $\Delta Z/\pm Z$ edit box, enter the default value for the wall height.

   You can create walls of any height in the layer, but the Z and $\Delta Z/\pm Z$ values for this layer will automatically set those for other layers you create. When you create a new layer, it will have a default Z that places it at the top of the walls in the layer below (in the 3D space) and its default $\Delta Z/\pm Z$ will be the same as the one for the floor below (**Figure 9.3**).

5. Complete creation of the layer as described in Chapter 5.

✔ Tip

- Begin setting up your layers from the bottom and work up from there; the z values for successive layers will be set automatically. Change these as necessary.

SETTING UP AN ARCHITECTURAL DRAWING

315

Drawing Walls

The wall is the basic element in a VectorWorks architectural drawing. Once you have the walls in place, you can go ahead and deploy other design features that are either within them (doors and windows) or that refer to them for their own locations. You can create a roof directly from the walls and they can also serve as the starting point for the floor.

You must first define the wall's characteristics. Since VectorWorks creates walls as hybrid objects, you need to define both its 2D symbolic form (seen only in Plan view) and its 3D appearance, which only have their width in common.

A wall's two-dimensional appearance is set as if it were just an ordinary double line in two dimensions (see Chapter 2, "Creating 2D Shapes"). Its 3D attributes are controlled by either the Attributes palette or the Textures tab on the Object Info palette (if you have RenderWorks installed), depending on the way the layer is rendered.

VectorWorks stores ten preset wall types that you can choose from the Select Wall Type submenu of the Model menu (**Figure 9.4**). While it might appear that you can edit these wall types, don't be fooled; this option is now available only as part of the Architect package, which Nemetschek sells separately.

Walls are always drawn on the Ground plane. You must be in Plan view to use either the Wall tool or the Create Wall dialog box.

To set a wall style:

1. On the Walls palette, choose either the Wall tool or the Round Wall tool (**Figure 9.5**).

2. On the Mode bar press the Wall Preferences button (**Figure 9.6**).

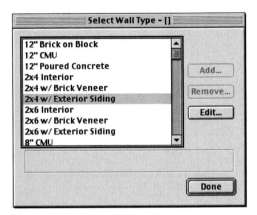

Figure 9.4 The presets for the Wall Types are fixed, but they are still a good starting point.

Figure 9.5 The Walls palette has separate tools for straight and round walls, as well as for editing walls once you've drawn them.

Figure 9.6 The Mode bar has the same four control line modes for walls that it has for double lines. The Preferences button looks the same, but it opens a different dialog box.

DRAWING WALLS

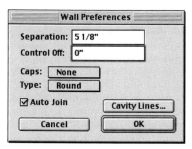

Figure 9.7 You can also start from scratch and define your wall style using the Wall Preferences dialog box.

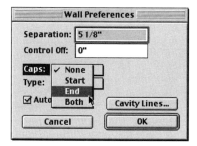

Figure 9.8 The Caps pop-up menu controls which ends of a run of wall will have caps.

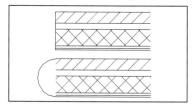

Figure 9.9 Wall caps can be either flat (top) or round (bottom) in Plan view, but they are all flat in 3D.

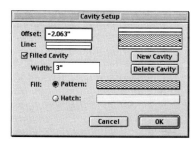

Figure 9.10 The Cavity Setup dialog box is the same one you see when you configure double lines.

The Wall Preferences dialog box opens (**Figure 9.7**). You will recognize its similarity to the Double Lines Preferences dialog box (see Chapter 2, "Creating 2D Shapes").

3. In the Wall Preferences dialog box, type the width of the wall in the Separation field and the distance from the center line to the control line in the Control Off field.

4. From the Caps pop-up menu, select the cap configuration you want to apply to the wall (**Figure 9.8**).

5. From the Type pop-up menu, choose a Flat or Round style for the caps chosen in Step 4 (**Figure 9.9**).

Caps, if any, are placed only on unjoined ends of wall objects.

6. Check the Auto Join checkbox if you want new walls to connect to existing ones when you snap them.

Otherwise, you will need to use the Wall Join tool to do it in another step.

7. Click Cavity Lines to open the Cavity Setup dialog box— the same one used to configure Double Lines—(**Figure 9.10**) and go through the procedures outlined in the section on Drawing Double Lines in Chapter 2 to define the appearance of the wall in Plan view.

Click OK to close the Wall Preferences dialog box.

DRAWING WALLS

317

Once the wall is configured, you can go ahead and draw it. The process of drawing a wall is identical to drawing a double-line polygon; it's just the result that differs. Walls are always drawn in Plan view. When you use the Wall tool, VectorWorks will always use the $\Delta Z/\pm Z$ value set for the layer as the height of the wall; you can change this parameter later.

To draw a wall:

1. From the Walls palette, choose the Wall tool.

   If the palette is not on the desktop, open it by clicking its name to place a checkmark in front of it on the Palettes menu.

2. On the Mode bar, select the Control Line mode you want to use (**Figure 9.11**).

   This is the same as the Double Line tool methodology.

3. Click in the drawing area to place the first point on the control line that defines the placement of the wall itself.

   As you drag the pointer, the wall is previewed.

4. Click again at each vertex of the control line. (**Figure 9.12**).

   Terminate the wall by either clicking again at the starting point or by double-clicking. The caps are placed only after the wall is complete (**Figure 9.13**).

   The wall is placed in the active layer and class.

Figure 9.11 The control line for a wall can be (from left to right) the top, center, or bottom line or a custom line within the confines of the wall.

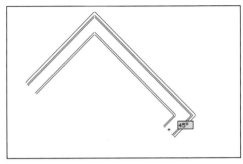

Figure 9.12 As is so often the case, drawing a wall begins with placing its starting point.

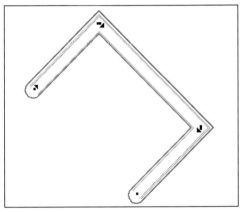

Figure 9.13 The caps are placed on the ends of the run after you complete it.

DRAWING WALLS

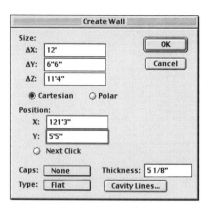

Figure 9.14 The Create Wall dialog box.

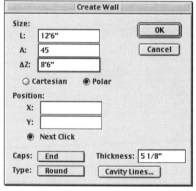

Figure 9.15 The polar coordinate option allows you to specify the wall by length and angle. This is often the most straightforward approach.

✔ Tips

- Creating walls with the dialog box limits you to a single wall segment.

- Wall caps are strictly a 2D phenomenon. The settings you choose have no effect on the 3D presentation of the wall.

To create a wall from the dialog box:

1. On the Walls palette, double-click the Wall tool.

   The Create Wall dialog box opens (**Figure 9.14**). .

2. Set the size of the wall by clicking the Cartesian radio button and entering values in the $\Delta X/\pm X$ (x dimension), $\Delta Y/\pm Y$ (y dimension), and $\Delta Z/\pm Z$ (height) fields

   or

   Click the Polar radio button and enter values in the L (length), A (angle), and $\Delta Z/\pm Z$ (height) fields (**Figure 9.15**).

3. Define the location of the starting point of the wall by entering its X and Y coordinates in the fields under Position

   or

   Click the Next Click radio button to place the wall's starting point with a mouse click after you close the dialog box.

4. From the Caps pop-up menu, choose how you want to terminate the wall objects you create .

5. From the Type pop-up, choose either Round or Flat for whatever wall caps are drawn.

6. Set the wall thickness by typing a value into the Thickness box.

7. Click Cavity Lines to open the Cavity Setup dialog box to configure the Plan view appearance of the wall.

8. Click OK to create the wall.

   If you chose to position the wall by Next Click, click in the drawing area to set the wall's starting point and create the wall.

   The wall is placed in the active layer and class.

Yet another—and quite effective—way of creating walls is to start with a 2D polygon and then use the Create Walls from Polygon command.

To create walls from a polygon:

1. Select a polygon (**Figure 9.16**).

2. Choose Model > Create Wall from Polygon. The Create Wall from Polygon dialog box opens (**Figure 9.17**).

3. In the Wall position pane of the dialog box, click the radio button next to Center, Inside, or Outside to indicate the how the wall to be created should relate to the polygon.

4. Use the Assign to class drop-down menu to choose which class the wall will join.

5. In the Use existing wall style pane, click Yes to create the wall using whatever settings are current; click no to create a wall with the thickness set in step 6, but without cavity lines.

6. In the Use existing wall thickness pane, either click Yes

   or

   Click No and enter a new value in the Thickness edit box.

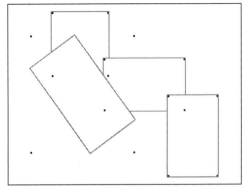

Figure 9.16 Laying out a building with polygons is fast and flexible. You can use all the editing tools for polygons to get the building blocked out before you go 3D.

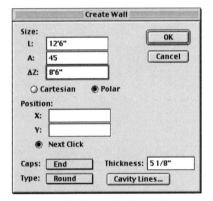

Figure 9.17 The Create Wall from Polygon dialog box.

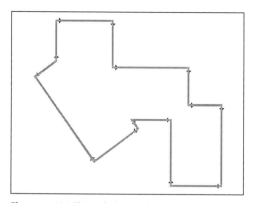

Figure 9.18 Voilà! A whole set of walls is created from the polygon.

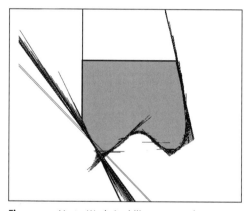

Figure 9.19 VectorWorks's ability to approximate fancy curved walls with the Create Walls from Polygon command is not without its limitations. If you choose too many short sides, the failure can be spectacular.

7. In the Use existing wall height to use the $\Delta Z/\pm Z$ for the layer as the wall height

   or

   Click No and enter another height in the edit box.

8. Check the Delete Source Poly checkbox to replace the polygon with the wall; otherwise the 2D polygon will still be there after the wall is drawn.

9. Click OK to create the wall in the active layer (**Figure 9.18**).

   If you are in Top or Plan view, the wall will coincide with the polygon. If you are in another view, the wall will be placed on the Ground plane with the coordinates the polygon has on the screen plane.

✔ **Tip**

■ There's a limit to how close to a curve you can come with the polygon from which you create a set of walls. At some point, the software breaks down and the walls appear to turn into fractals (**Figure 9.19**).

Creating Curved Walls

Except for their shape, round walls are just like their straight relatives. Their heights, widths, and cavities are determined by the same settings; they lie on the Ground plane; and they can be joined to straight walls or to other curved walls.

You create round walls in two basic ways: use the Round Wall tool or its correlate dialog box, or use the fillet tool to draw a curved wall between two straight walls. Unlike straight walls, however, round walls are drawn one at a time. They mimic the Arc tool from the 2D Tools palette, whereas the Wall tool is analogous to the Polygon tool.

To draw a round wall:

1. On the Walls palette, click the Round Wall tool.

2. On the Mode bar, choose one of the four control line options as you would for a Wall or for a Double Line (**Figure 9.20**).

3. On the Mode bar, click the Preferences button to open the Wall Preferences dialog box (the same one used for Walls). Change the settings as required and click OK to return to the drawing.

4. On the Mode bar, click one of the arc creation modes (see Chapter 2, "Creating 2D Shapes").

5. In the drawing area, click to set the first point of the arc that defines the Round Wall (**Figure 9.21**).

6. Complete the arc (and the Round Wall) according to the mode you have selected (**Figure 9.22**).

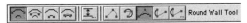

Figure 9.20 The control line options for round walls are analogous to those for straight ones.

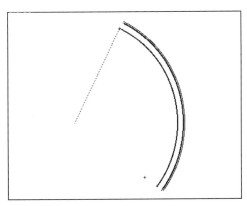

Figure 9.21 Round walls are drawn by creating the arc that the wall uses as its control line.

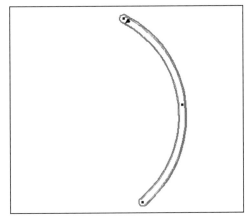

Figure 9.22 When you finish defining the arc that controls the path of the round wall, the object is created.

CREATING CURVED WALLS

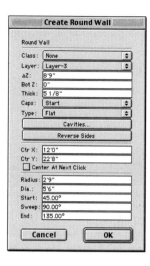

Figure 9.23 Double-click the Round Wall tool to open the Create Round Wall dialog box.

Round walls can also be created by a dialog.

To create a Round Wall using the dialog box:

1. Double-click the Round Wall tool on the Walls palette.

   The Create Round Wall dialog box opens; it looks suspiciously like the Object Info palette (**Figure 9.23**).

2. In the Create Round Wall dialog box, set the class and layer into which you want the new wall placed.

3. In the Create Round Wall dialog box, set the height of the wall in the ΔZ/±Z field and the wall's offset above the Ground plane in the Bot Z edit box.

   Set the wall thickness in the Thick field.

4. Configure the end caps by setting which ends of the wall will have caps in the Caps drop-down menu and their style in the Type drop-down menu.

5. Click Cavities to open the Cavities Setup dialog box and configure the lines and fills between the lines representing the width of the wall.

   The default condition for Round Walls created from the dialog box is no cavity lines or fills.

6. Click Reverse Sides to put the outside of the wall (were the wall drawn in the "normal" clockwise direction) on the inside.

7. In the Ctr X and Ctr Y fields, type the x and y coordinates for the center point of the wall's arc

   or

   Check the Center At Next Click checkbox to defer locating the object until after the dialog box is closed.

continues on next page

CREATING CURVED WALLS

8. In the pane at the bottom of the dialog box, define the arc of the control line for the Round Wall.

You can set either the radius or the diameter (they're obviously interrelated); Round Walls are always defined by their center lines when created by way of the Create Round Wall dialog box.

Set the two of the three values for Start, Sweep, and End (the three values are also interrelated). The angles are measured counter-clockwise from the horizontal and 0 degrees is shown in the dialog box as 360.

9. Click OK to close the dialog box.

If you have checked the Center At Next Click checkbox, you have to click to set the center of the arc; otherwise, the wall will be placed with its center at the coordinates you chose in the dialog box.

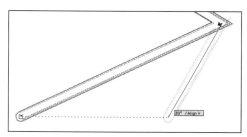

Figure 9.24 You can edit the location, direction and length of an individual wall as if it were a line.

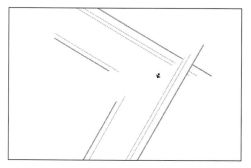

Figure 9.25 Use the Wall Join tool to clean up the mess that repositioning a wall leaves behind.

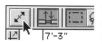

Figure 9.26 It's easier to move a wall by its corner without rescaling it if you first disable the interactive scaling mode.

- The 3D Selection tool moves a wall in the 3D space, but doesn't reshape it. Use the 3D constraints to help control the movement relative to the Ground plane.

Editing Wall Objects

Because VectorWorks creates walls with flat tops at the layer's $\Delta Z/\pm Z$ height and bottoms firmly planted on the Ground plane, you will often find it necessary to go back and modify them. Houses built on uneven ground, for example, need to have the bottom edges of the walls adjusted to conform to the terrain. With gabled roofs, you must make the end walls peaked to keep out bad weather and bats.

Once you have placed a wall, even if it was drawn as part of a continuous run, it is selected and edited as an individual object.

To modify a wall's length and position:

1. Set the view to Plan view and select the wall you want to edit.

2. With the 2D Selection tool, drag either of the endpoints to a new position when the pointer becomes a double arrow (**Figure 9.24**)

   or

   Drag the entire wall with the arrow pointer or with the cross pointer at an end or center point.

✔ Tips

- When you move the endpoint of a wall, you will probably have to go back and clean up its intersection with the wall to which it is joined. (**Figure 9.25**).

- Disable the Interactive Scaling mode by releasing its button on the Mode bar to keep the 2D Selection tool from reshaping the wall when all you want to do is move it (**Figure 9.26**).

- The 2D Selection tool will move walls (but not reshape them) in any view, but in oblique views you may find it hard to control exactly what's going on in the *x*, *y*, and *z* directions.

The 3D Reshape tool is the workhorse in the wall editing department. Use it to adapt ordinary rectangular walls to a variety of purposes.

To modify the vertical profile of a wall (round or straight):

1. Select the wall you want to reshape.

2. Click the 3D Reshape tool on the 3D Tools palette.

   The Mode bar shows that you are in the Reshape 3D Walls mode and the wall has additional handles at its corners (**Figure 9.27**).

3. On the Mode bar, click the Add Vertex button (**Figure 9.28**).

4. Click on one of the wall's vertices to create a new vertex and drag it to a new location (**Figure 9.29**).

   The pointer becomes a four-headed arrow when it snaps to a vertex.

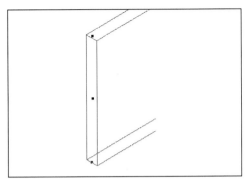

Figure 9.27 The handles at the corners of the wall are for adding vertices and moving the corners of the wall.

Figure 9.28 The 3D Reshape tool automatically goes into the Reshape 3D Walls mode when a wall is selected.

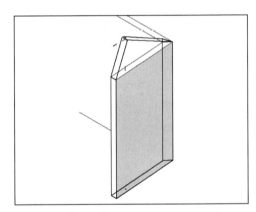

Figure 9.29 Choose the Add Vertex mode and drag a vertex to a new position to add wall peaks or to adjust the bottom edge of a wall.

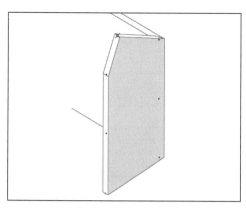

Figure 9.30 The Remove Vertex mode will only select vertices added to the wall, not the basic four corners.

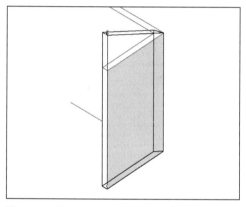

Figure 9.31 You can move any vertex when you select the Move Vertex mode.

Figure 9.32 The Data Display bar is a good way to control the placement of wall peak vertices. Set the Ratio to 0.5 if you need to keep the peak centered over the wall.

Figure 9.33 The Data Display bar for Round Walls offers somewhat less control than the one for straight walls.

5. On the Mode bar, click the Remove Vertex button, then click one of the wall peaks to remove the vertex (**Figure 9.30**).

The pointer becomes the four-pointed arrow when it snaps to one of those vertices.

You can't delete the original corner vertices that define the basic wall.

6. On the Mode bar, click the 3D Reshape mode button.

7. Click on one of the walls vertices and drag it to its new position (**Figure 9.31**).

The pointer becomes a double-headed arrow when it snaps to a corner vertex. It becomes a four-headed arrow when it snaps to a vertex added with this tool.

✔ Tips

■ Wall surfaces are always planar; you can't move a vertex to warp a wall out of its own plane. Likewise, the vertices of round walls always lie on an arc that defines the curvature of the wall.

■ Use the Data Display bar to control the placement (or movement) of a new vertex on a straight wall (**Figure 9.32**).

You can set the offset relative to the ends of the wall or lock the value in the Ratio field. You can set the height of a peak by locking the Z value to the desired measurement.

■ On round walls, the Data Display bar only allows you to set the height of an additional vertex (**Figure 9.33**).

EDITING WALL OBJECTS

Some editing can be also be done in the Object Info palette.

To edit walls from the Object Info palette:

1. Select the walls you want to modify.

2. On the Object Info palette, change the wall's class and layer by selecting from the names on the Class and Layer drop-down menus (**Figure 9.34**).

3. Change the height of the wall by entering a new value for ΔZ/±Z.

4. Change the wall's vertical position by entering a new value in the Bot Z field.

5. Add or remove caps on the ends of walls and change their styles by changing the selections in the Caps and Type menus.

6. Modify the cavity lines by clicking the Cavities button to open the Cavities Setup dialog box where you can change the appearance of the wall in Plan view.

7. Click Reverse Sides to flip the wall's inside to the outside (**Figure 9.35**).

8. Click the Cartesian coordinates button and change the ΔX and ΔY values that control the length and direction of the wall

    or

    Click the Polar coordinates button and change the wall's length (L) and angle (A).

9. Click one of the three reference points on the Segment Position (this refers to the centerline of the wall) and change its X and Y coordinates to move the whole wall.

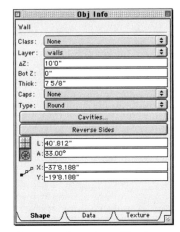

Figure 9.34 Once the wall has been drawn, you can modify important variables such as its *z* and ΔZ/±Z values in the Object Info palette.

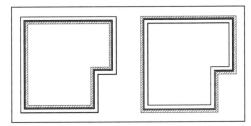

Figure 9.35 Being able to flip walls inside out is very handy when you have drawn your walls counter-clockwise (left) so that the inside winds up on the outside.

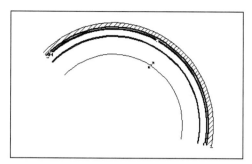

Figure 9.36 Round walls are edited like arcs; drag the midpoint handle to change the radius of the curve.

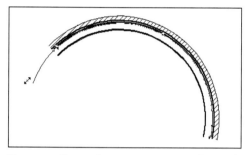

Figure 9.37 Change the sweep parameters of a round wall by dragging the endpoints around the arc.

Round walls can be modified in much the same way rectangular walls can be.

To change the radius and sweep of a round wall:

1. Set the view to Plan and select the Round Wall you want to change.

2. On the 2D Tools palette, click the 2D Selection tool.

3. Click the midpoint of the wall and drag it inward or outward to change the wall's radius (**Figure 9.36**).

   The pointer will become a double-headed arrow when it has snapped to the control point. The pointer cue will read Arc End.

4. Click one of the endpoints of the wall and drag it around the arc to change the sweep of the wall (**Figure 9.37**).

   The pointer will become a double-headed arrow when it has snapped to the control point. The pointer cue will read Arc End.

✔ Tip

- You can also use the 3D Reshape tool to modify the arc that defines the wall, but unless you are in Top view, you may have trouble seeing exactly what is happening. The pointer cue will be Object when it has snapped to a handle at either the midpoint or one of the endpoints of the wall.

Joining Walls

When you create straight walls, you can draw them as if you were drawing a 2D polygon; each automatically connects to the one before it until you double-click to end the series or bring it back to its own staring point.

When walls aren't already connected, you will often want them to be. As is the case with most of these operations, you will probably recognize the analogy to the various ways of joining lines into polygons and polylines.

To join two walls:

1. On the Walls palette, click the Wall Join tool (**Figure 9.38**).

2. On the Mode bar, choose a mode as follows:

   Choose Standard Join mode to intersect the walls according to their geometry and to join their outside boundaries. This mode extends walls to form an intersection, but doesn't trim them (**Figure 9.39**).

   Choose Butt Join mode to intersect walls without breaking the outside lines of the walls. The first wall clicked is butted up to the other wall.

   Choose Standard Corner Join mode to bring the walls to a corner intersection by mitering the walls so that both the outside lines and the cavities are joined.

   Choose Corner Butt Join to trim the walls to an intersection but run the first wall clicked into the second.

3. Click the first wall.

   A wall is highlighted as you bring the pointer over it.

4. Click on the second wall to complete the joint.

   A dotted line is drawn between the two wall before the joint is made (**Figure 9.40**).

Figure 9.38 The Wall Join tool on the Walls palette.

Figure 9.39 The Wall Join tool has four modes of operation.

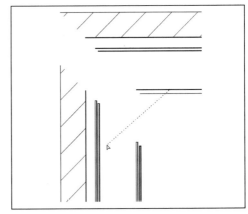

Figure 9.40 When you bring the pointer near a wall, it is clearly highlighted.

Figure 9.41 The Fillet tool on the Walls palette is the same one you find on the 2D Tools palette.

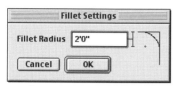

Figure 9.42 Enter the fillet radius in the Fillet Settings dialog box which opens when you click the Fillet Preferences button on the Mode bar.

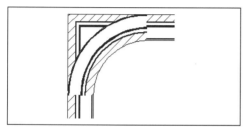

Figure 9.43 The basic fillet mode draws a circular wall at the intersection of two walls with the attributes of the walls it is connecting.

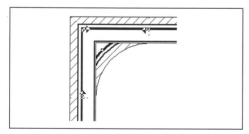

Figure 9.44 The Fillet and Split mode puts in a circular wall and slices the original walls where they meet it.

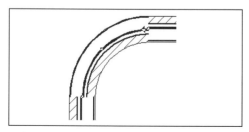

Figure 9.45 The Fillet and Trim mode is just the Fillet and Split mode with the extra pieces of the original wall automatically deleted.

You can also use the Fillet tool to join walls with a section of Round wall. This works only between two straight walls with the same cavity lines.

To join walls with a fillet:

1. On the 2D Tools palette or the Walls palette, click the Fillet tool (**Figure 9.41**).

2. On the Mode bar, click the Preferences button to open the Fillet Settings dialog box and type the radius of the fillet in the Fillet Radius field (**Figure 9.42**).

   The fillet radius controls the inside radius of the wall created.

3. On the Mode bar, choose one of the three modes:

   Choose Fillet mode to create a round wall to conform to the intersection (or the projected intersection) of two walls (**Figure 9.43**).

   Choose Fillet and Split mode to create the wall while extending walls that don't reach the round wall and trimming the ones that overlap. The trimmed pieces are left in place in the drawing (**Figure 9.44**).

   Use the Fillet and Trim mode to place the round wall and extend and trim the straight walls the meet it neatly (**Figure 9.45**).

4. In the drawing area, click the two walls.

   The fillet wall is placed and the straight walls are trimmed according to the mode chosen above.

✔ Tip

- If the fillet wall is inverted, use the Reverse Sides button in the Object Info palette to set it right

JOINING WALLS

The Wall Heal tool does two things: it fills in the breaks that are left in the outside lines of a wall (in its 2D manifestation) when you remove a wall that was joined to it; and it resquares the ends of a wall after it has been mitered to make a joint. It also removes end caps.

Use Wall Heal with care, since it unjoins the joints you have made.

To heal a wall:

1. On the Walls palette, click the Wall Heal tool.

   The pointer becomes a small cross.

2. Click to start a marquee around the area of the wall (or you can do several walls at a time) and click again to complete it (**Figure 9.46**).

   The gaps and clipped ends are returned to their native states (**Figure 9.47**).

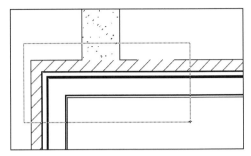

Figure 9.46 Draw a marquee around the areas of the wall that need healing.

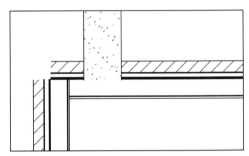

Figure 9.47 The Wall Healing tool straightens out mitered wall ends and closes gaps created by wall joints that have been moved.

JOINING WALLS

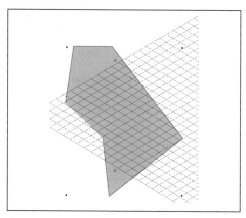

Figure 9.48 Any open or closed shape can be turned into a floor slab.

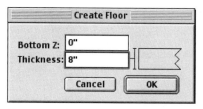

Figure 9.49 All you need to do to create a floor is specify the thickness and the height of the floor above the Ground plane.

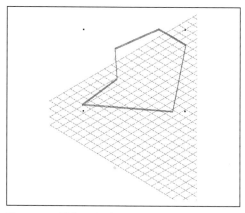

Figure 9.50 Click OK in the Create Floor dialog box and the floor is created.

Floors

Floors are pretty simple, since they are usually flat slabs parallel to the Ground plane. Even cutting holes in them so virtual people can pass from floor to floor is easy.

To create a floor:

1. Select a shape in form of the floor (**Figure 9.48**).

   You can either draw a shape or select the walls that enclose the area of the floor and then choose Model > Create Polygon from Interior Walls (the floor will sit inside the walls) or Model > Create Polygon from Exterior Walls (the floor will take its dimensions from the outside surfaces of the walls).

2. Choose Model > Floor.

   The Create Floor dialog box opens (**Figure 9.49**). The layer doesn't need to be in Plan view.

3. In the Create Floor dialog box, type the bottom height of the floor in the Bottom Z field and the thickness of the slab in the Thickness field.

4. Click OK to create the slab.

   Whether the shape was closed or not, the floor will be created as if it were (**Figure 9.50**).

To edit a floor:

1. Select the floor slab you want to edit.

2. Choose Organize > Edit Group, or press Command-[(Mac) or Ctrl-[(Windows) The floor slab is temporarily returned to its original state.

3. Modify the shape with the 2D drawing tools or by drawing other 2D shapes and adding them to it or clipping them out of it (**Figure 9.51**).

4. Click the Done button on the Mode bar to return to the drawing (**Figure 9.52**).

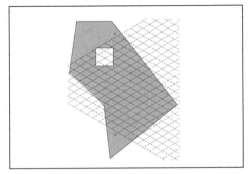

Figure 9.51 In the edit mode, you can add to a shape or clip it.

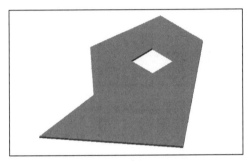

Figure 9.52 Returning to the layer, the shape cut out of 2D polyline is now a hole in the slab.

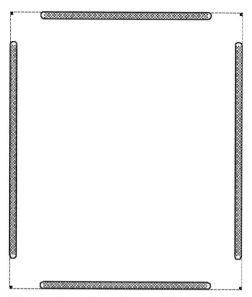

Figure 9.53 As an alternative to creating a roof from the walls, use a polygon (or a rectangle). Especially useful if the walls don't fully enclose the area.

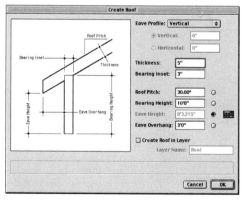

Figure 9.54 The Create Roof dialog box looks complicated, but don't be put off. It's a shortcut to an object that would be much more labor-intensive by other means.

Roofs

Once the walls and the floors are in place, chances are you will want to put a roof over them all. VectorWorks's Roof function is a remarkably "smart" little utility that creates a basic roof from a single dialog box.

You can then go back and modify individual faces of the roof in a variety of ways to meet the vast majority of your design needs. Gabled roofs, dormers, skylights, and roofs with faces at different pitches are modifications of the basic roof created from the dialog box.

You can use either a polygon or the polygonal area enclosed by the walls you have already drawn as the basis for the roof.

To create a roof:

1. Select either a set of walls completely enclosing the area over which you want to place a roof

    or

    Select a polygon defining the area you want to roof. You can use the Create Polygon commands (mentioned in the section on Floors above) to create a polygon from the walls or, if the walls were originally created from a polygon, use that one. (**Figure 9.53**).

2. Choose Model > Create Roof from Walls or Model > Create Roof from Polygon according to the selection above.

    The Create Roof dialog box opens (**Figure 9.54**).

3. In the Create Roof dialog box, set the basic parameters of the roof by typing the thickness into the Thickness field and the angle of the roof from the horizontal in the Roof Pitch edit field.

continues on next page

ROOFS

4. In the Create Roof dialog box, define how the roof sits on the walls by typing values into the Bearing Inset and Bearing Height fields.

5. In the Create Roof dialog box, set the eave profile by choosing a style from the Eave Profile drop-down menu (**Figure 9.55**).

The diagram on the left side of the dialog box changes to reflect the choice of profiles

If you have chosen Double, click either the Vertical or the Horizontal radio button and type the dimension for that surface (see the diagram on the left side of the dialog box). The other eave profiles set their own dimensions based on the roof's thickness and pitch.

6. Check the Create Roof in Layer checkbox and assign the roof to either an existing layer or a new layer that will be created when you type a heretofore unused name in the field.

7. Click OK.

The dialog box closes and the roof is created in the layer to which you have assigned it (**Figure 9.56**).

✔ Tips

■ Use a polygon to define the roof in situations where the walls don't completely enclose an area.

■ Click the radio button to the right of Roof Pitch, Bearing Height, Eave Height, or Eave Overhang. These fields are interrelated; fixing any three defines the fourth. It is common to leave the Eave Height to be defined by the other parameters.

■ The Roof function doesn't support Round walls. Create a 2D polygon version of the slab and use that to generate the roof.

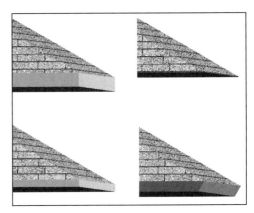

Figure 9.55 There are four basic profiles to choose from (clockwise from upper left): Vertical, Horizontal, Double, and Square Cut.

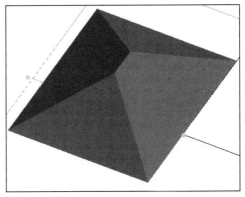

Figure 9.56 The basic roof created by the Create Roof command is the starting point for more complex roofs or, more often, a finished object.

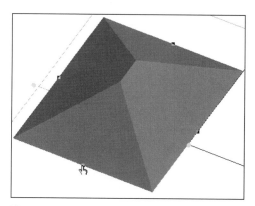

Figure 9.57 Use the 2D Selection to click on the handle of the roof face you want to modify.

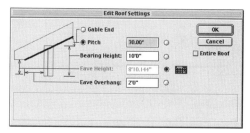

Figure 9.58 The Edit Roof Settings dialog box is where you can change the settings for some of the parameters controlling the selected roof face or the whole roof. It's also where you go to turn a pitched roof face into a gable.

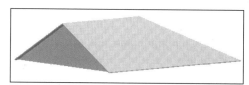

Figure 9.59 Clicking the Gable End radio button in the Edit Roof Settings dialog box flattens out the selected roof face to create a gable. You'll may still need to add a peak to the wall.

Roofs can be edited one face at a time or all at once.

To edit a roof:

1. Select the roof you want to edit.

2. Click the handle at the edge of the face you want to modify (**Figure 9.57**).

   The pointer changes to a pointing finger when it snaps to a roof handle.

   The Edit Roof Settings dialog box opens (**Figure 9.58**).

3. In the Edit Roof Settings dialog box, check the Entire Roof checkbox if you want to change the settings for the entire roof; otherwise only the selected roof face is affected.

4. In the Edit Roof Settings dialog box, click the Gable End to remove the selected roof face or select Pitch to leave the face in place.

5. In the Edit Roof Settings dialog box, type a new value into the Pitch, Bearing Height, Eave Height, or Eave Overhang field.

   If you have chosen to convert the selected face to a gable, the Pitch field will be disabled.

6. Click OK to close the dialog box and change the roof settings (**Figure 9.59**).

ROOFS

You can use the 2D Reshape tool to modify a roof object. You can move individual vertices or extend roof faces by dragging them. You can work in any view, but Plan view seems to produce the most predictable results.

To reshape a roof with the 2D Reshape tool:

1. On the 2D Tools palette, click the 2D Reshape tool.

2. Click on the roof you want to reshape.

    The vertices of roof as a polygon are displayed.

3. On the Mode bar, click the Add Vertices button and add additional vertices to the roof by clicking on an existing vertex or midpoint and dragging the new vertex to its correct location (**Figure 9.60**).

    The pointer becomes the arrow with two black boxes when it snaps to a vertex or segment midpoint.

4. On the Mode bar, click the Delete Vertex button and remove vertices as required (**Figure 9.61**).

    The pointer becomes the arrow with an open box when it snaps to vertex

5. On the Mode bar, click the Move Handle button and drag vertices or midpoints wherever they need to go (**Figure 9.62**).

    The pointer becomes the familiar double-headed arrow when it snaps to a vertex or segment midpoint.

✔ Tips

■ Drag a marquee around multiple vertices and midpoints to move them as a unit. Hold down the Option/Alt key to lasso a selection of handles.

■ Neither the Change Vertex Type nor the Hide/Show Edges mode works with roof objects.

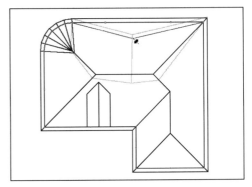

Figure 9.60 The 2D Reshape tool lets you add vertices to a roof just as you would to a 2D polygon.

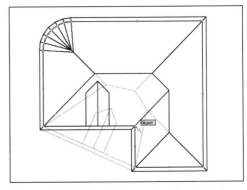

Figure 9.61 The Delete Vertex mode of the 2D Reshape tool forces the roof edge to take the shortest distance between the points either side of the deleted one.

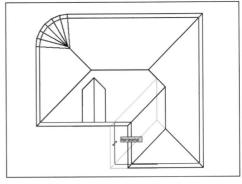

Figure 9.62 You can drag vertices or midpoints to reshape the roof in two dimensions.

ROOFS

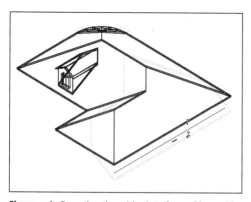

Figure 9.63 Dragging the midpoint of a roof face with the 3D Reshape tool extends or retracts the edge without affecting the pitch.

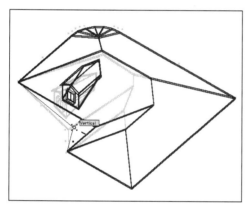

Figure 9.64 You can move a vertex by dragging it to a new place with the Move Vertex mode selected.

The 3D Reshape tool can also be used on roof objects; it has the advantage of moving vertices parallel to the ground plane regardless of the view, but when you grab the midpoint of a roof face, it moves only perpendicular to the Ground plane.

To reshape a roof using the 3D Reshape tool:

1. On the 3D Tools palette, click the 3D Reshape tool.

2. In the drawing area, click the roof you want to modify.

   The roof will show handles at the vertices and at the midpoints of its surfaces.

3. On the Mode bar, click the Reshape mode button and drag the midpoint handle of a surface to change the extension of that plane of the roof along the pitch angle (**Figure 9.63**).

   The pointer will become a vertical double-headed arrow when it snaps to the handle.

   Changing the length of the face changes the bearing height of the roof.

4. On the Mode bar, click the Reshape mode button and drag a vertex handle to move it parallel to the working plane (**Figure 9.64**).

   The pointer becomes a four-headed arrow when it snaps to a vertex.

   continues on next page

ROOFS

5. On the Mode bar, click the Add Vertex mode button, click on either a vertex or a midpoint, and then drag the new vertex to its new position (**Figure 9.65**).

6. On the Mode bar, click the Delete Vertex mode button and then click on the vertex of the roof you want to delete (**Figure 9.66**).

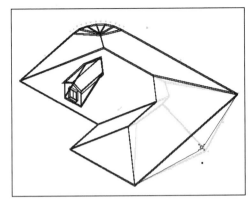

Figure 9.65 Click on a vertex to create a new one and drag it to a new location.

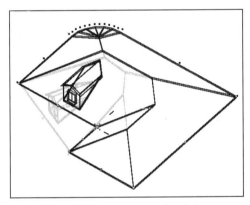

Figure 9.66 In the Delete Vertex mode, click on an existing vertex to remove it. The roof is reshaped.

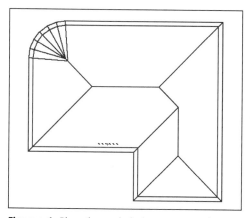

Figure 9.67 Place the symbol where you want the front of the dormer and click.

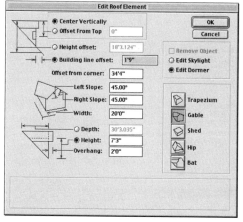

Figure 9.68 The Edit Roof Element dialog box opens when you place the symbol on the roof.

Roof Elements

Dormers and skylights are referred to as *roof elements*. You can add them by simply placing a window symbol on the roof and assigning the parameters to the dormer or skylight in the dialog box that opens automatically when you place a 3D symbol on a roof.

To create a roof element:

1. Place the layer in Plan view.

2. Using either the Object Browser or the Resources palette, select a symbol or plug-in object.

   It can be any 3D or hybrid symbol or plug-in, but windows—as opposed to things like stoves or staircases—are the most usual choice.

3. On the 2D Tools palette, click the 2D Symbol Insertion tool if it was not already selected by the Object Browser.

4. In the drawing area, click on the roof where you want to put the dormer or the skylight (**Figure 9.67**).

   The Edit Roof Element dialog box opens (**Figure 9.68**).

   The symbol automatically aligns with the roof edge.

continues on next page

ROOF ELEMENTS

5. In the Edit Roof Element dialog box, click either Edit Skylight or Edit Dormer to define the basic type of roof element you are creating.

If you choose Edit Skylight, the dialog box is quite simple and you need to specify only the location of the element and whether or not the symbol (only if it is a purely 3D one) that defines its opening should appear or not (**Figure 9.69**).

6. If you clicked the Edit Dormer radio button, start by choosing the dormer style from the selection pane (**Figure 9.70**).

7. Position the symbol on the face of the dormer by clicking either the Center Vertically radio button or the Offset From Top radio button and entering a value in the edit box (**Figure 9.71**).

8. Position the dormer between the edge and the peak of the roof, clicking either the Height offset or Build line offset radio button and then typing the distance into the associated field (**Figure 9.72**).

9. Configure the dormer using the other edit boxes according to the type of dormer you have selected.

Each dormer type has its own set of parameters (roof slopes, widths, overhangs, and so on) (**Figure 9.73**).

10. Click OK to close the dialog box and create the dormer or skylight.

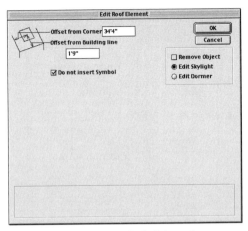

Figure 9.69 Choosing the Edit Skylight option simplifies the dialog box.

Figure 9.70 VectorWorks comes with five pre-packaged dormer styles from which to choose.

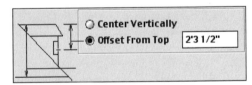

Figure 9.71 You can set the position of the window in the dormer manually or just tell VectorWorks to center it.

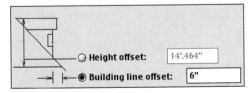

Figure 9.72 Move the dormer up or down from the roof edge by setting one of these parameters.

ROOF ELEMENTS

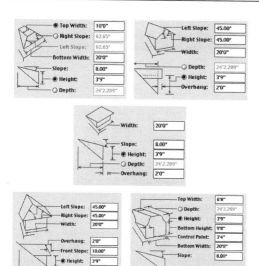

Figure 9.73 Each style of dormer has a different set of parameters that control its dimensions.

Figure 9.74 To reshape a dormer, click its handle with the 2D or 3D Selection tool.

To edit a roof element:

1. In the drawing area, select the roof to which the element is connected.

2. Using either the 2D or 3D Selection tool, click the handle at the base of the element (**Figure 9.74**).

    The pointer changes to the pointing finger when it snaps to the handle.

    The Edit Roof Element dialog box opens.

3. In the Edit Roof Element dialog box, make whatever changes you need to and click OK.

    The dialog box closes and the changes are made.

✔ Tips

- Once you have place a symbol or plug-in object into a roof element, you can no longer edit it. You can edit the symbol by editing another instance of it in the drawing file, but you are stuck with the PIO in its default configuration.

- The changes you make to a roof element aren't displayed until the view is re-rendered. To force a re-rendering, choose the rendering mode again from the View menu. When the dialog box asks if you want to re-render everything, answer OK.

ROOF ELEMENTS

The basic roof construction algorithms in the VectorWorks package will probably serve your purposes in at least 90 percent of your work. But sometimes you have to break the roof down into individual *roof faces* that can be moved and edited independently of one another.

To work with individual roof faces:

1. Select the roof you want to break down.

2. Choose Organize > Ungroup, or press Command-U (Mac) or Ctrl-U (Windows). In the alert box that opens, click Yes to ungroup the roof (**Figure 9.75**).

 The roof dissolves into a collection of roof faces. A dormer becomes an assemblage of walls with a roof made of 3D polygons.

 The Edit Group command doesn't work with roofs. The Create Group command breaks the roof all the way down into 3D polygons, which is probably overkill.

3. Select the roof face you want to edit.

4. Choose Organize > Edit Group.

 The roof face is presented as a polyline that you can edit like any other polyline (see Chapter 3, "Modifying 2D Shapes") (**Figure 9.76**).

5. Edit the polyline and click Exit Group. The view returns to the layer view with the roof modified.

6. Edit the walls and polygons that make up the dormers as usual.

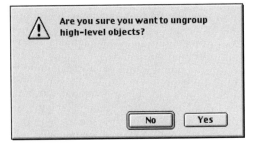

Figure 9.75 Ungrouping a roof is not reversible. Proceed with caution...

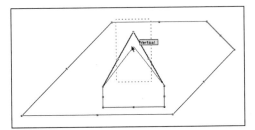

Figure 9.76 In the edit layer, a roof face is an easily editable polyline or polygon. You can change its outline or the shape of any cutouts.

ROOF ELEMENTS

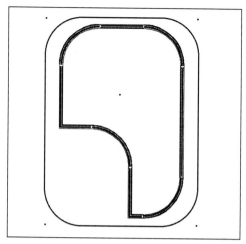

Figure 9.77 Select a 2D shape for the roof surface.

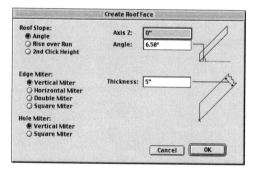

Figure 9.78 The Create Roof Face dialog box.

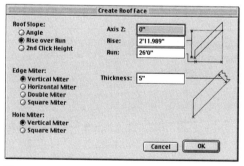

Figure 9.79 Instead of setting the roof's slope by specifying an angle, you can set it by specifying the amount it rises over a given horizontal run.

You can work the other way and create roof faces from 2D shapes. When you do, you aren't limited to polygons as you are with the commands that make a whole roof in one shot, so round or even polyline roofs are possible. This is usually the easiest way to develop an irregularly shaped roof or one at an angle to the run of a wall.

To create a roof face from a 2D shape:

1. In Top or Plan view, draw the shape representing the projection of the roof face (not the shape of the roof face itself) onto the Ground plane (**Figure 9.77**).

2. With the shape selected, choose Model > Roof Face.

   The Create Roof Face dialog box opens (**Figure 9.78**).

3. In the Create Roof Face dialog box, set the slope of the roof face by clicking the Angle radio button and entering an angle in degrees in the Angle field

   or

   Click the Rise over Run radio button and enter the amount the roof increases in height (Rise) over some horizontal distance (Run) (**Figure 9.79**).

continues on next page

ROOF ELEMENTS

4. Choose an Edge Miter condition from the four radio buttons and set its dimensions in the edit boxes (**Figure 9.80**).

5. Under Hole Miter, click either Vertical Miter or Square Miter to set the edges of holes in the roof face perpendicular to the Ground plane or to the roof face, respectively (**Figure 9.81**).

6. In the Axis Z field, type the height above the ground plane at which the axis you will define below in Step 9 will lie.

7. In the Thickness field, type the roof's thickness.

8. Click OK.

The dialog box closes and the pointer becomes a small arrow.

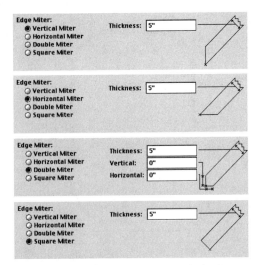

Figure 9.80 Choose the Edge Miter type in the Create Roof Face dialog box.

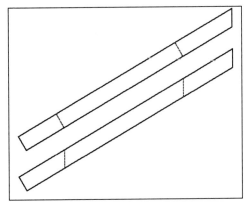

Figure 9.81 Holes in roof surfaces can be either vertical (bottom) or square (top) to the surface.

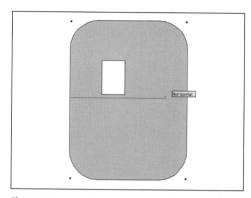

Figure 9.82 Draw the horizontal axis that lies at the Z height entered in the Axis Z field in the dialog box.

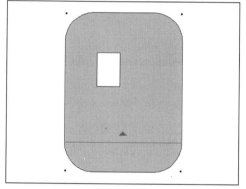

Figure 9.83 Complete the roof face by specifying the direction in which the surface rises. In 2nd Click Height mode, the distance between this click and axis is the run against which the rise is measured.

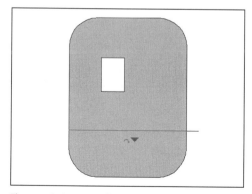

Figure 9.84 You can adjust a roof surface's axis while it is in Plan view.

9. Click to set the first point of the horizontal axis at the *z* height set in Step 6 and click again to complete the axis (**Figure 9.82**).

An arrow head will appear on one side of the axis line.

10. Move the pointer to put the arrow pointing up the slope of the roof (set in Step 3) and click to complete the creation of the roof face (**Figure 9.83**).

✔ Tips

■ When a layer is in Plan view, select the 2nd Click Height radio button in the Roof Slope section and enter the rise in the dialog box. Then specify the run by the distance between the axis you draw in Step 9 and the click in Step 10 that defines the slope direction.

■ You may have to adjust the settings in the Attributes palette to make the new roof surface visible in the drawing.

To edit a roof surface:

1. In Plan view, select the roof surface you want to edit.

The horizontal axis and slope arrow are displayed.

2. Move the axis by dragging it by its middle handle.

3. Change the alignment of the axis by dragging one of its endpoints.

4. Change the direction of the surface's slope by clicking on the arrow when the pointer becomes a curved arrow, dragging to the opposite side of the axis so that the arrow flips, and clicking again (**Figure 9.84**).

ROOF ELEMENTS

Using Symbols and Plug-ins in Walls

One of VectorWorks's strongest selling points is the ease with which you can integrate doors, windows, and other standard architectural features into walls, then modify them as the design evolves. Both symbols and plug-in objects automatically create breaks in walls and fit themselves in just the way you hope they would.

You can use the Object Info palette to control PIOs in a wide variety of ways, altering their dimensions and graphic attributes. Symbols are more firmly tied to the original archetype in the drawing file. This is both an advantage and a disadvantage; symbols don't have the flexibility of PIOs, but changing the symbol definition changes all the instances in the file. This makes global revision of a door or window style a piece of cake.

VectorWorks provides a few sample plug-in objects and symbols in the Object Libraries folder that installs with it. You can also avail yourself of symbols in the sample files in the Resources folder, notably NW House.mcd.

For a general discussion of symbol placement, see Chapter 6, "2D Symbols and PIOs."

To place a symbol in a wall:

1. Put the layer into Plan view.

2. Using either the Object Browser or the Resources palette, select a symbol or plug-in object.

   It can be any 3D or hybrid symbol or plug-in, but windows and doors—as opposed to things like plants or stoves or staircases—are the most usual choices.

3. On the 2D Tools palette, click the 2D Symbol Insertion tool if it was not already selected by the Object Browser.

Figure 9.85 The Mode bar has two groups of buttons. The first group controls the overall function of the tool; the second moves the insertion point.

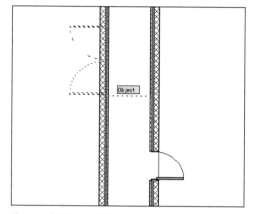

Figure 9.86 Use the Offset Insertion mode to place the symbol relative to a reference point defined by a mouse click.

4. On the Mode bar, choose an insertion mode from the three buttons at the left:

Choose Standard Insertion mode to place the selected symbol with the point defined by a mouse click (**Figure 9.85**).

Choose Offset Insertion mode if you want to click a reference somewhere in the drawing area and then enter the distance from that point to the actual insertion point in the wall in the dialog box that opens.

Click the Symbol Pick Up mode button to select a symbol by clicking one of its instances in the drawing and then place it using the Standard Insertion Mode.

5. On the Mode bar, choose an insertion mode button that moves the symbol's insertion point along the x-axis as follows:

Click the Align Symbol Left button to temporarily shift the insertion point of the symbol all the way to the left edge of the symbol.

Choose the Align Symbol Center mode to move the insertion to the horizontal center of the symbol.

Choose the Align Symbol Right mode to put the insertion point on the right edge of the symbol.

Click the last button to use the insertion point as it exists in the symbol definition.

6. In the drawing area, click on the wall to define the insertion point

or

If you have chosen the Offset Insertion mode, click anywhere in the drawing area to set the reference point from which the insertion point will be measured.

When you set a reference point, VectorWorks projects a line from it parallel to the wall in which the symbol is placed and measures along that line (**Figure 9.86**).

continues on next page

Using Symbols and Plug-ins in Walls

7. In the drawing area, move the mouse to set the orientation of the symbol in the wall.

The dashed symbol will jump from one quadrant to another as the mouse is moved. Click to choose the correct alignment.

If you are in the Offset Insertion mode, enter the distance along the wall from the click to the actual insertion point in the Enter Offset dialog box that opens (**Figure 9.87**). Then click OK.

The symbol is placed in the wall.

You can place an array of equally spaced symbols in a wall. This is often useful for placing windows or even doors in a large building. This tool works somewhat like the 2D Duplicate Along Path tool.

To duplicate a symbol in a wall:

1. On the Resources palette, choose the symbol or plug-in object you want to use.

Using the Object Browser to choose a PIO sometimes creates unnecessary problems; it's best to stick with the Resources palette method.

2. On the Walls palette, choose the Duplicate Symbol in Wall tool (**Figure 9.88**).

3. On the Mode bar, click either the Flip Symbol Mode button or the Don't Flip Symbol Mode button (**Figure 9.89**).

Flip Symbol mode flips the symbol across a line perpendicular to the wall from its normal position. Right-hand doors become left-hand doors.

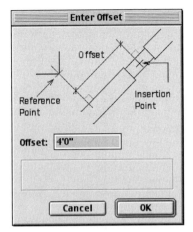

Figure 9.87 Once you have placed the symbol in the wall and set its orientation, you can enter the distance from the reference point to the symbol's insertion point in the Offset field of the Enter Offset dialog box.

 Figure 9.88 Choose the Duplicate Symbol in Wall tool on the Walls palette to place a symbol in a regular linear array in the wall.

Figure 9.89 The Mode bar for the Duplicate Symbol in Wall tool has two modes for the handedness of the insertion and a preferences button.

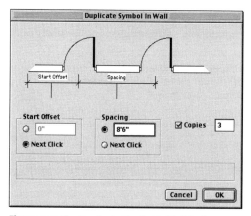

Figure 9.90 The Duplicate Symbol in Wall Preferences dialog box includes a nice explanatory diagram.

4. On the Mode bar, click the Duplicate Symbol in Wall Preferences button.

   The Duplicate Symbol in Wall Preferences dialog box opens (**Figure 9.90**).

5. In the Start Offset pane of the Duplicate Symbol in Wall Preferences dialog box, choose the Next Click radio button to place the insertion point of the first symbol where you click on the wall

   or

   Click the radio button next to the edit box and enter the distance (measured from the starting point of the wall) to the first insertion point in the field.

6. In the Spacing Offset pane of the Duplicate Symbol in Wall Preferences dialog box, choose the Next Click radio button to define the spacing between symbol insertion points by the second click of the mouse

   or

   Choose the radio button next to the edit field and enter the spacing between symbol insertion points in the field

7. Check the Copies checkbox and enter the maximum number of copies of the symbol to be placed in the wall (fewer will be placed if there isn't enough room for them all)

   or

   Leave the Copies checkbox unchecked and the number of copies will be determined by the available space on the wall.

8. Click OK to close the dialog box.

   The pointer becomes a small cross.

9. In the drawing area, click on the wall in which you want to place the symbols.

   If you have opted to set the Offset by first click, this click will place the first insertion point; otherwise it only identifies the target wall.

continues on next page

USING SYMBOLS AND PLUG-INS IN WALLS

10. Click again in the drawing area to define the direction in which the symbols will propagate down the wall and to complete the insertion (**Figure 9.91**).

This click also sets the spacing between symbols, if you didn't set it in the Duplicate Symbols in Wall dialog box.

The side of the wall on which you click determines whether the symbols are oriented to the inside or the outside of the wall (**Figure 9.92**).

✔ Tips

■ The Duplicate Symbols in Wall doesn't support round walls, unfortunately.

■ If you duplicate a plug-in object, the new instances will be treated as symbols. You can edit them as such and whatever modifications you make will be applied to all the other instances of the symbol, but not to objects that were originally placed as PIOs. The current symbol definition will, however, become the default presentation of the PIO.

To reposition a symbol in a wall with the Object Info palette:

1. Select the symbol you want to reposition.

2. In the Object Info palette, click the Insert pop-up menu and select either Right Edge or Left Edge to move the insertion point from its default on the centerline (**Figure 9.93**). (Right and Left are considered when viewing the wall from the top and proceeding from its starting point toward its endpoint.)

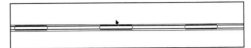

Figure 9.91 Click to define the direction (and in some cases, the spacing) in which the symbols are distributed in the wall.

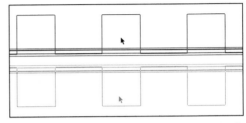

Figure 9.92 The line of symbols flips from one side of the wall to the other as you bring the pointer across it.

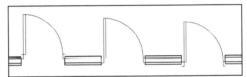

Figure 9.93 Shift the position of the symbol relative to the wall centerline from Insert pop-up menu in the Object Info palette.

USING SYMBOLS AND PLUG-INS IN WALLS

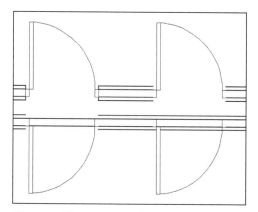

Figure 9.94 There are four styles of wall break from which to choose in the Break pop-up menu in the Object Info palette.

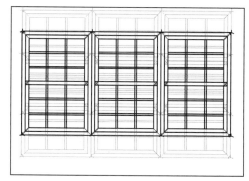

Figure 9.95 The Height field controls the vertical position of a symbol relative to its normal insertion point.

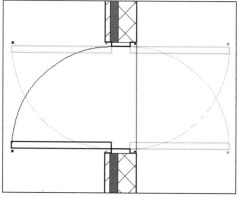

Figure 9.96 The Flip button cycles a symbol through its four possible orientations.

3. From the Break pop-up menu, choose a break style to control the presentation of the symbol in the wall in Plan view (other views aren't affected).

Full break with caps draws the wall with a cut all the way through where the symbol is placed. The ends of the wall are capped where they have been cut.

Full break without caps cuts the wall all the way, but doesn't cap the ends.

Half break breaks only the outside line of the wall opposite the side from which the symbol extends

No break doesn't interrupt the wall (**Figure 9.94**).

4. In the Height field, type the distance above or below (enter a negative value) the default height of the symbol insertion (**Figure 9.95**).

5. Click the Flip button to successively flip the symbol into each quadrant around its insertion point (**Figure 9.96**).

continues on next page

USING SYMBOLS AND PLUG-INS IN WALLS

6. Click the Position button to open the Position Symbol in Wall dialog box, click one of the six spots representing the corners and the ends of the centerline of the wall and type a distance from that point to the insertion point of the symbol in the Offset field (**Figure 9.97**).

7. Click Replace to open the Symbol Replace dialog box where you can select a symbol from the resources palette (**Figure 9.98**).

✔ Tips

- In Plan view, you can drag a symbol with the 2D Selection tool either along the axis of the wall or out of the wall to break its association with the wall. The pointer becomes the double-headed arrow when it snaps to the symbol in the wall, but it will not reshape the symbol (**Figure 9.99**).

- The Symbol Replace dialog box lets you choose a symbol from the Resources palette to replace the one selected in the drawing, but not to replace a symbol with a plug-in object.

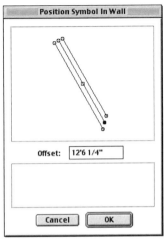

Figure 9.97
The diagram in the Position Symbol in Wall dialog box represents the insertion point of the symbol in the wall. You can select either end of the wall and the centerline or one of the corners for your reference point.

Figure 9.98 Use the Symbol Replace dialog box to choose any symbol in the file's resources to replace the symbol selected in the drawing.

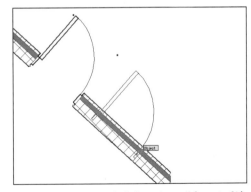

Figure 9.99 Drag a symbol along the wall (or out of it) with the 2D Selection tool in Plan view.

USING SYMBOLS AND PLUG-INS IN WALLS

354

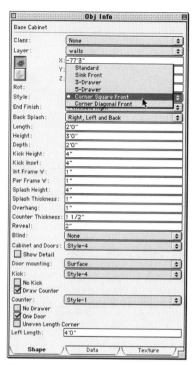

Figure 9.100 As an example, the Object Info palette for the Base Cabinet plug-in object offers six styles which you can then customize by dimension and finish.

Other Architectural Symbols and PIOs

Chapter 6 introduced plug-in objects as a subject of general interest. VectorWorks doesn't provide much support for other disciplines, but it offers a pretty good selection of basic PIOs for architectural design, including office planning.

If you are coming to VectorWorks 9 from an earlier version of the software, you would be well advised to import the resources that the new version has left behind; they include a large repertoire of built-in symbols for architectural objects. While you can generate most of them from the PIOs in version 9, you can save yourself some time and effort by resorting to the ready-mades that used to be part of the package.

Probably the most important plug-in objects you get with VectorWorks are the ones that create doors and windows. The ones for cabinets and the set for office furniture are quite flexible, capable of generating a complete repertoire of generic casegoods (**Figure 9.100**). These PIOs don't draw detailed objects—for that you need to treat them as design objects in their own rights—but they are quite adequate for laying out an architectural project.

OTHER ARCHITECTURAL SYMBOLS AND PIOS

There is also a pair for stairways, one for straight stairs and one for spiral ones (**Figure 9.101**). And there is even a PIO that creates a campanile (with a bell or clocks, if that is your heart's desire), but you may not have much occasion to use it.

The VectorWorks application also supplies a number of static symbols for architectural use (chairs and tables, stoves and sinks, trees and trucks, etc.). You'll find these within the NW House.mcd drawing file as well as in the Object Libraries folder (**Figure 9.102**).

If you have created an object with a plug-in and you want to duplicate it throughout the drawing, consider creating a symbol from it. The symbol can be either 3D or hybrid (see Chapter 6, "2D Symbols and PIOs").

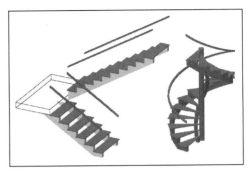

Figure 9.101 The two stairway PIOs create stairs with variable dimensions, riser styles, and finishes.

Figure 9.102 There are enough static symbols to get you started on almost any design project, and you can easily modify these to generate your own symbol libraries.

WORKSHEETS, REPORTS, AND PRESENTATIONS

10

At various points in the design process, it becomes necessary to take what you have done and put it into a readily communicable format. While you are at work on a project and everything is in flux, you may not want to take the time to do the things required for a presentation, but there comes a time when you will want to use some of VectorWorks's capabilities for display.

Dimensions

One of the most obviously necessary sets of tools is the one that puts dimensions into the drawing. While you are at work, the interactive nature of the application generally obviates the need to actually dimension objects, but when you print out a drawing or want to show a project to someone not quite so conversant with the software as you, dimensions are a fine thing indeed.

VectorWorks supports a variety of dimensional standards recommended by the AIA (American Institute of Architects), ASME (American Society of Mechanical Engineers), SIA (Société Suisse des Ingénieurs et Architectes), and other, similar bodies. You can modify any of these standards to create your own custom standard as well (**Figure 10.1**).

Keep in mind that dimensioning is strictly a 2D activity. It's hard to snap to some 3D objects and even if you can, when you rotate a view, the two dimensional dimensions don't stay with their intended objects. (**Figure 10.2**).

To set up the dimension tool:

1. Choose File > Preferences > Document Preferences.

   The Document Preferences dialog box opens (**Figure 10.3**).

2. On the Dimensions tab of the Document Preferences dialog box, click the Associate Dimensions checkbox to lock dimensions to their objects.

   A dimension can be associated with an object so that resizing the object automatically updates the dimension. This doesn't work, however, if the dimensions are in a different layer (as is common practice) than the objects to which they refer.

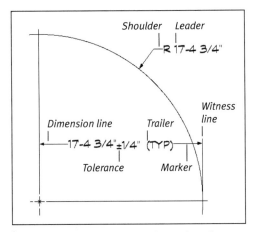

Figure 10.1 Dimensions consist of a number of parts.

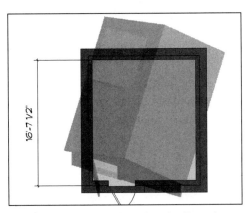

Figure 10.2 When you rotate a view, the dimensions don't follow.

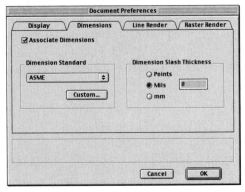

Figure 10.3 The Dimensions tab on the Document preferences dialog box.

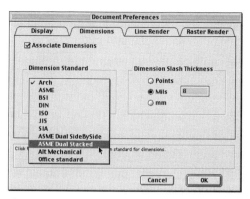

Figure 10.4 The Dimension Standard pop-up menu holds custom standards as well as the ones provided by Nemetschek.

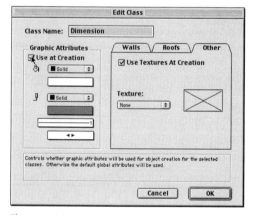

Figure 10.5 Setting the class attributes and checking the Use at Creation checkbox helps keep your dimensions consistent.

Constrained linear dimension tool

Unconstrained linear dimension tool

Radial dimension tool

Angular dimension tool

Centermark tool

Tape measure tool

Revision cloud tool

Protractor tool

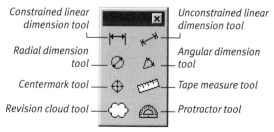

Figure 10.6 The Dimensioning palette.

3. On the Dimensions tab of the Document Preferences dialog box, Choose a standard from the Dimension Standard pop-up menu. (**Figure 10.4**).

4. On the Dimensions tab of the Document Preferences dialog box, set the Dimension Slash Thickness.

Slash thickness is the width the slash that some (notably the Architectural) dimension standards use as markers

Click OK to close the dialog box.

5. Set the Class Attributes (see Chapter 5, "Using Layers and Classes") for the Dimension class according to your needs and check the Use at Creation checkbox so the dimensions will be consistent throughout the drawing. (**Figure 10.5**).

Set the Fill to Solid (usually white) if you want to the text to stand out against the background and to break the extension lines when the text is in the dimension line.

6. Open the Dimensioning palette by choosing Palettes > Dimensioning (**Figure 10.6**).

7. Choose Text on the Menu bar and set the font, size, and style for the dimension.

8. On the Constraints palette, make sure the Snap to Object constraint is selected.

DIMENSIONS

There are many ways to dimension a drawing. The object of the dimensioning is to specify the locations and sizes of important features in a way that facilitates the realization of your design. How you do this is largely a matter of personal preference or office practice.

Dimensions parallel to the axes

Sometimes it makes sense to define all the measurements but their x and y distances from one point in the drawing—as you might if you were drilling a pattern of holes on a milling machine, for example. Other times, the best way is to give the dimensions as a series of independent values that will save the craftsperson the trouble of figuring it all out on site (**Figure 10.7**).

To dimension objects along the *x*- and *y*-axes:

1. On the Dimensions palette, click the Constrained-Line Dimensioning tool.

2. On the Mode bar, click the Constrained Linear mode button (**Figure 10.8**).

3. In the drawing area, click the first point that will define the dimension.

4. Click the second point the that defines the dimension.

   The witness and dimension lines are previewed.

5. Drag the dimension to the desired distance from the original points.

   If the points you set are aligned neither horizontally nor vertically, the dimension will jump to either the *x*- or the *y*-axis as you drag the cursor in that direction (**Figure 10.9**).

6. Click to set the dimension's position and orientation (**Figure 10.10**).

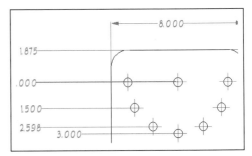

Figure 10.7 Choose your dimensioning scheme with an eye to how the object will be made as well as to what looks nice on the page.

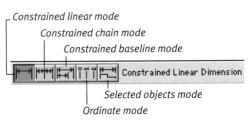

Figure 10.8 The Constrained Linear Dimension tool operates In five distinct modes.

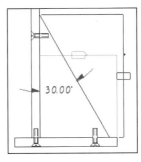

Figure 10.9 As you drag the dimension to its final resting place, VectorWorks will try to figure out whether you want the x or the y distance.

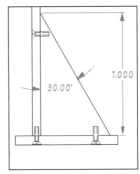

Figure 10.10 Once you have the dimension where you want it, click to make its placement final.

DIMENSIONS

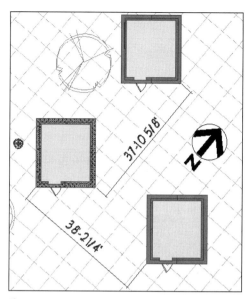

Figure 10.11 Rotating the grid is an easy way to free the dimensions of the tyranny of the paper's vertical and horizontal.

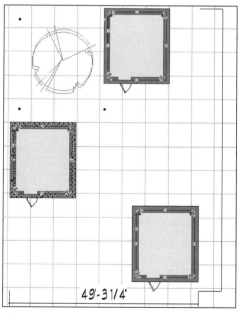

Figure 10.12 Automatic dimensioning can be applied to multiple objects as well as single ones.

✔ Tip

- When you rotate the grid, the orientation of constrained dimensions becomes the *i*- and *j*-axes instead of the standard x and y coordinate system (**Figure 10.11**).

To dimension an object automatically:

1. Use either the 2D or the 3D Selection tool to select the object to be dimensioned.

   You can select a set of objects; VectorWorks will draw a dimension for either the height or the width of the bounding box that includes them all (**Figure 10.12**).

2. Click in the drawing area.

   The dimension lines will preview as follows:

   A horizontal dimension will be shown if you click within the area selected or if you click above or below the selection

   A vertical dimension will preview if you click outside the selection to the left or right or if you click within it while you hold down the Option/Alt key.

3. Drag the dimension where you want it and click again to complete the operation.

When you have lots of dimensions along an axis, they can be *chained* together to streamline the operation. All the dimensions will be aligned; this can be a good thing—it makes things look nice and even—but if there isn't enough space between the points, the dimensions all crowd together and are illegible.

To create a chain of dimensions:

1. On the Dimensions palette, click the Constrained-Line Dimensioning tool.

2. On the Mode bar, click the Constrained Chain mode button.

3. Click the starting point of the chain. The cursor becomes a bombsight.

4. Click the second point of the chain. The witness and dimension lines are previewed.

5. Drag the cursor away from the object to define the distance between it and the dimension and to choose along which axis the dimensions are measured. Click to lock both those parameters (**Figure 10.13**).

6. Continue clicking points in the chain. As you continue, the distances between successive points are dimensioned as part of the chain (**Figure 10.14**).

7. Double-click the last point to complete the operation.

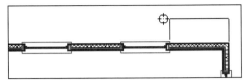

Figure 10.13 Once you've set the first distance in the chain, drag the pointer away to set the distance between the dimensions and the object.

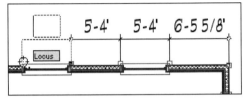

Figure 10.14 Keep clicking points to add to the chain. Double-click to stop.

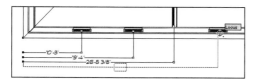

Figure 10.15 Baseline dimensions are all taken from the first click and each is stacked about a centimeter out from the one before it.

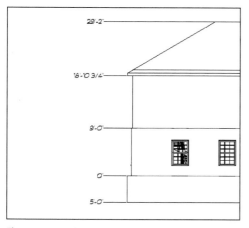

Figure 10.16 Ordinate dimensions do away with the dimension lines and place the text at the end of the witness line.

Another variation on the same theme is *baseline dimensioning*, which measures a series of points from the first point clicked and spreads the dimensions at a fixed distance from one another as they progress across.

To create a string of baseline dimensions:

1. On the Dimensions palette, click the Constrained-Line Dimensioning tool.

2. On the Mode bar, click the Constrained Base-Line button.

3. Click the starting point to set the baseline.

4. Click the second point of the chain.
   The witness and dimension lines are previewed.

5. Drag the cursor away from the object to define the distance between it and the dimension and to choose along which axis the dimensions are measured. Click to lock both those parameters.

6. Continue clicking points in the chain.
   As you continue, each point is dimensioned from the baseline and the dimension is stacked above the preceding one (**Figure 10.15**).

7. Double-click the last point to complete the operation.

✔ Tip

■ There is yet another more mode that amounts to a combination of baseline and chain dimensioning. *Ordinate dimensioning* generates a witness line labeled .000 (but no other dimension lines) with the first click. Each successive click places a parallel witness line with the distance between it and the .000 line displayed (**Figure 10.16**).

Unconstrained Dimensions

Sometimes translating your dimensions into x-y coordinates is counterproductive and the drawing is easier to understand when the dimensions follow a more intuitive route. These are called *unconstrained dimensions* and their tool has three modes.

To place an unconstrained dimension:

1. On the Dimensions palette, click the Unconstrained Dimension tool.

2. On the Mode bar, click the Unconstrained Linear Dimension button (**Figure 10.17**).

3. Click the first point to which you want to anchor the dimension (**Figure 10.18**). At this point, the angle of the dimension is still up for grabs.

4. Click the second point of your dimension. The dimension is drawn directly between the two points (**Figure 10.19**).

5. Drag the dimension parallel to its original line and click to place it and complete the operation (**Figure 10.20**).

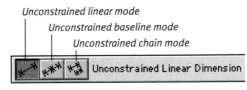

Unconstrained linear mode
Unconstrained baseline mode
Unconstrained chain mode

Figure 10.17 The Mode bar for unconstrained dimensions has three modes, and they're analogous to the ones for constrained dimensions.

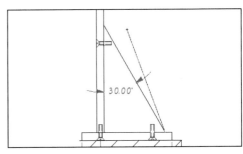

Figure 10.18 An unconstrained dimension is begun by clicking the first point and dragging toward the second.

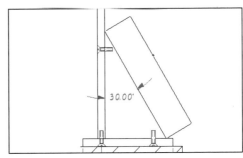

Figure 10.19 Click the second point and drag away to set the distance from the object.

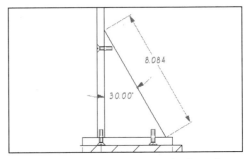

Figure 10.20 Click again to complete the dimension.

DIMENSIONS

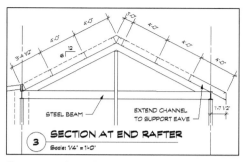

Figure 10.21 Chained unconstrained dimensions help the roofers figure out where to place the purlins.

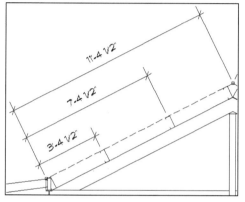

Figure 10.22 Unconstrained baseline dimensions are like constrained ones but–obviously–unconstrained.

To create chained dimensions at an angle to the axes:

1. On the Dimensions palette, click the Unconstrained Dimension tool.

2. On the Mode bar, click the Unconstrained Chain Mode button.

3. Click on the first point (the one from which all the others will be measured).

4. Click on the second point and drag the cursor to situate the dimension line.

5. Click on each successive point to be dimensioned.

   The distance to that point from the one before it is recorded as a dimension aligned with the first dimension in the chain.

6. Double-click the last point to complete the chain (**Figure 10.21**).

To place unconstrained dimensions from a baseline:

1. On the Dimensions palette, click the Unconstrained Dimension tool.

2. On the Mode bar, click the Unconstrained Baseline Mode button.

3. Click on the first point (the one from which all the others will be measured).

4. Click on the second point and drag the cursor to situate the dimension line.

   The baseline is established at the first point, perpendicular to the line between it and the second point.

5. Click on the third point to draw a new dimension parallel to the first one.

   Each succeeding dimension is from the baseline to a witness line from the point clicked.

6. Double-click the last point to stop the operation (**Figure 10.22**).

Arcs and Angles

The ability to effectively describe arcs and angles is another important feature of the VectorWorks dimensioning palette. Any of the Radial Dimension tools works on any circular curve, but you can't use them to dimension ellipses or the Bézier and Cubic Spline segments of polylines, and unfortunately their use is limited to 2D objects.

To dimension a circle or arc:

1. On the Dimensioning palette, click the Radial Dimension tool (**Figure 10.23**).

2. On the Mode bar, click one of the dimensioning modes as follows:

   Choose Interior Diametrical Dimension mode to place a dimension line through the center of the curve with markers at each end. The position of the text depends on the final mouse click (**Figure 10.24**).

   The Exterior Diametrical mode places arrows outside the circle.

   Interior Radial mode draws an arrow from the center to the circumference and gives the dimension as the radius

   The Exterior Radial option draws a line to the outside of the arc and dimensions the uses the arc's radius as the dimension.

3. On the Mode bar, choose either Left Hand Shoulder or Right Hand Shoulder mode to set the direction that the leader to the text will point (**Figure 10.25**).

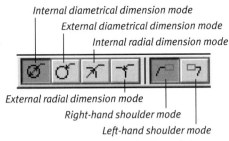

Internal diametrical dimension mode
External diametrical dimension mode
Internal radial dimension mode
External radial dimension mode
Right-hand shoulder mode
Left-hand shoulder mode

Figure 10.23 The Mode bar for the Radial Dimension tool has two groups of buttons.

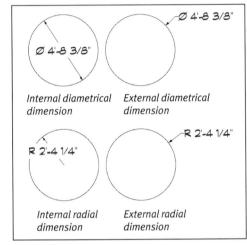

Internal diametrical dimension   External diametrical dimension

Internal radial dimension   External radial dimension

Figure 10.24 The mode bar lets you choose radial or diametrical dimensioning with arrows facing in or out.

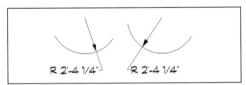

Figure 10.25 The leader lines can go either right or left. Hold down the Option/Alt key to force the leader left.

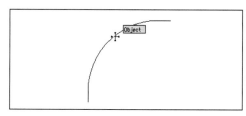

Figure 10.26 Start a radial dimension by clicking on the arc that you want to measure.

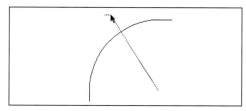

Figure 10.27 Drag to preview the dimension.

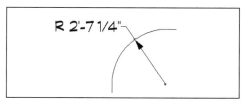

Figure 10.28 When you have the dimension where you want it, click to complete it.

4. In the drawing area, click on the curve to be dimensioned (**Figure 10.26**).

The cursor becomes a cross with thickened ends when it has snapped to the curve (**Figure 10.27**).

5. Drag the cursor to position the dimension text and click to place the dimension (**Figure 10.28**).

✔ Tips

- To dimension a spherical surface of a 3D object, you have to draw a 2D circle (it can be invisible or you can remove it after the dimension has been placed) and dimension that instead. The Circle by 3 Points tool is useful here.

- You can't dimension arcs when they are part of a Group object, but you can go into the Edit Group routine and dimension them. The dimensions will still be there when you exit the group, but they will be part of the group.

- Some dimension standards (Architectural, for one) don't use shouldered leader lines for arcs.

You can easily dimension the angle between any two straight lines or between a line and a reference line defined with the mouse. The lines can be line objects or they can be segments of other 2D objects. Sorry, this tool doesn't work for 3D objects.

To dimension the angle between two objects:

1. On the Dimensioning palette, click the Angular Dimension tool.

2. On the Mode bar, click the Angular Mode button (**Figure 10.29**).

3. Click on the first line defining the angle you are dimensioning.

   The cursor changes from the small cross to the big one when it has identified either of the lines between which it will measure the angle.

   As you drag the cursor to the second line, a dotted line is previewed (**Figure 10.30**).

4. Click on the second line.

   An arc is struck between the two objects (**Figure 10.31**).

5. Drag the cursor to position the arc and click again to complete the dimension.

   Moving the arc inside or outside the angle selects and interior or exterior angle (**Figure 10.32**).

Angular mode

Figure 10.29 The mode bar for angular dimensioning has only two buttons.

Angular dimension from reference line mode

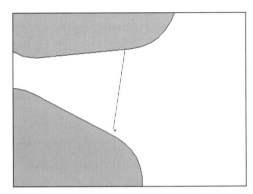

Figure 10.30 Drag the pointer from the first line to the second.

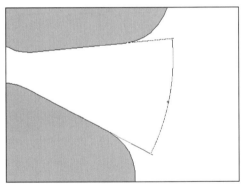

Figure 10.31 When you click on the second line, an arc is struck. Drag it to where you want the dimension placed.

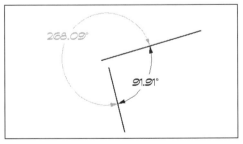

Figure 10.32 Drag the arc to the other side of the vertex to place and exterior angle dimension.

DIMENSIONS

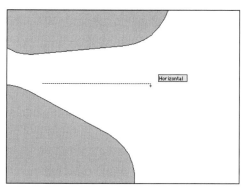

Figure 10.33 Click and drag the reference line from which the angle to the object will be measured.

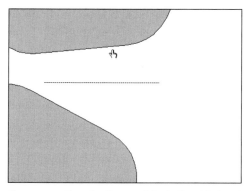

Figure 10.34 Move the finger pointer to the object and click again.

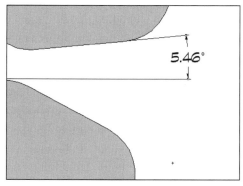

Figure 10.35 The angle dimension is placed between the reference line and the object.

Use the Angular Dimension From Reference Line mode to display the angle between an object and some direction in the space without adding an extra line to represent it. This if often used to show the angle from the vertical or the horizontal, but you can use any angle you wish.

To dimension an angle between a line and a temporary reference line:

1. On the Dimensioning palette, click the Angular Dimension tool.

2. On the Mode bar, click the Angular Dimension From Reference Line Mode button.

3. In the drawing area, click and drag the line to which you will refer the object to be dimensioned (**Figure 10.33**).

   The cursor will be a small cross and the line will be sketched in as you draw.

4. Click again to set the line.

   The cursor will turn into a pointing finger until it finds an object to which you can snap the angle (**Figure 10.34**); then it becomes the big cross with the fat ends.

5. Click on the line you want to dimension.

   An arc is struck between it and the reference witness line.

6. Drag the dimension where you want it and click again to complete it (**Figure 10.35**).

✔ Tip

■ Use the Angle Snaps constraint to create a reference line oriented to not only the usual 30 and 45 degree angles, but to an Alternate Coordinate System or to angles relative to a rotated grid. You can also lock the angle of the line you draw using the Data Display bar (see Chapter 4, "Drawing With Constraints").

DIMENSIONS

Editing dimensions

Once dimensions are drawn, they often need some adjustment. Some of this is done in the drawing area by dragging either the text or the endpoints of the witness lines; other changes are effected from the Object Info palette.

To edit a dimension graphically:

1. In the drawing area. select the dimension you want to modify.

2. With the 2D Selection tool, click the dimension text and drag it either closer or further from the object or drag it along the dimension line to move it within the witness lines or outside them (**Figure 10.36**). This doesn't affect the value of the dimension.

3. With the 2D Selection tool, click the end of the witness line next to the object and drag it to a new location (**Figure 10.37**). The dimension will change to reflect the new distance between the witness lines; dimensions that were associated with an object will no longer be so.

4. With the 2D Selection tool, click one of the witness lines and drag the whole dimension away from the object. This breaks the association of the dimension with the object.

✔ Tip

- Hold down the Option/Alt key to force external radial dimensions to turn their leaders to the left instead of to the right per the default. There is also a Leader to Left checkbox in the Object Info palette that you can use to the same end.

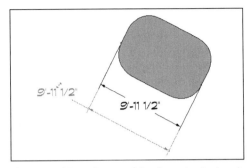

Figure 10.36 Once the text of the dimension is placed, you can drag it wherever you want in the drawing area without changing its value.

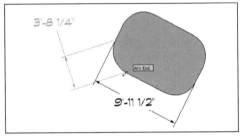

Figure 10.37 When you drag a witness line, the value of the dimension will change to reflect its new location.

DIMENSIONS

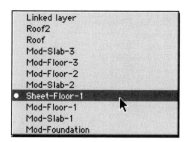

Figure 10.38 You can change the class and layer settings of a dimension just as if it were any other object.

To modify a dimension by way of the Object Info palette:

1. Select the dimension to be modified.

2. On the Object Info palette, change the class and layer settings as required (**Figure 10.38**).

   Normally, dimensions are always created in the Dimension class and placed in the active class.

3. From the Dimension Standard pop-up menu, choose a different dimension standard from those available in the drawing file.

4. Enter a value in the Dimension Off set field to control the distance between the dimension and its reference points on the object.

5. In the Text Offset field, set the relationship between the dimension line and the text.

6. Choose an orientation for the text in the Text Rotation pop-up menu.
   - ◆ Horizontal dimensions are always aligned with the x-axis.
   - ◆ Aligned dimensions set the text baseline at the same angle as the dimension lines.
   - ◆ The Hor/Vert setting sets all text horizontal unless the dimension is vertical; then the text is aligned vertically.

7. In the group of checkboxes under the Text Rotation pop-up menu, set the parameters for the display of the dimension as follows:
   - ◆ Check the Auto Position Text checkbox to center the text in the dimension.
   - ◆ Check the Flip Text checkbox to move text that sits on one side of the dimension line to the other; it also reverses the order of the tolerance and the basic dimension.
   - ◆ Check Arrows Inside if that's what you want; otherwise the arrows are outside the witness lines pointing inward.

continues on next page

DIMENSIONS

8. Use the Precision pop-up menu to control the way dimensions are rounded (**Figure 10.39**). VectorWorks stores values to ten places, so you are not throwing away precision when you choose not to flaunt it.

9. Check the Box Text checkbox to enclose the dimension text in a box

or

Leave the Show Dimension Value checkbox checked (as it is by default) unless you want just the leader displayed. (That would allow you to replace the automatically generated dimension with a text object of your own.) (**Figure 10.40**)

10. In the Leader and Trailer fields, enter whatever letters or symbols you want to place before or after the actual dimension.

By default, radial dimensions are preceded by "R" and diametrical ones by "Ø." You can also use this function to add such text as "2 PLACES," "REF" or "TYP" after a dimension.

11. On the pop-up Tolerances menu, choose the style of tolerance appropriate to your drawing and enter the values in the edit boxes that are presented for each option (**Figure 10.41**).

✔ Tips

■ If the selected dimension is an angle and the Interior Arc checkbox is checked, the arc will be dimensioned as an angle of less than 180 degrees; otherwise, the external angle will be displayed.

■ If the selected dimension is an arc, the Leader To Left checkbox forces the leader from the dimension to the left; otherwise it will go to the right.

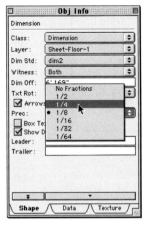

Figure 10.39 The Precision pop-up menu controls the rounding of the dimension display and the choice of decimal or minutes and seconds for angles.

Figure 10.40 Some standards box the text in a dimension.

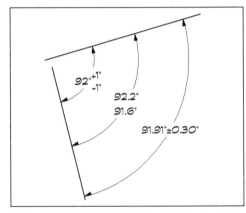

Figure 10.41 VectorWorks supports all the standard approaches to tolerancing dimensions. (This screen is from the U.S. edition of the software.)

Other goodies on the Dimensioning palette

The Dimensioning palette has a few other useful tricks up its virtual sleeve.

The Center Mark tool places a standard center mark at the center of any circular arc (**Figure 10.42**). Choose it and click on the arc when the cursor becomes a big cross. It also works with rectangles, rounded rectangles, and ellipses.

Draw even a ragged a freehand outline around an area and the Revision Cloud tool turns it into traditional fluffy revision cloud (**Figure 10.43**).

The Tape Measure tool measures the distance from one click to the next one and keeps track of the total distance you have traversed until you double-click to end the measurement. The distances are displayed on the Data Display bar.

The Protractor tool measures the angle between two objects or the angle defined by three clicks. Its result is also displayed on the Data Display bar.

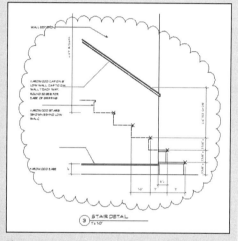

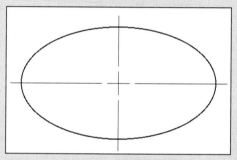

Figure 10.42 Center marks can be placed on rectangles and ellipses as well as on true arcs.

Figure 10.43 Revision clouds are used to highlight changes made after the first issue of a drawing.

Sections

Architects and other designers often present complex objects (from houses to steam turbines) by cutting through them along carefully chosen planes to expose their inner workings. Sometimes you will see a cut through a whole building; other times, sections are used to give a clearer exposition of a detail (**Figure 10.44**).

Section views often hatch the surfaces that have actually been cut to distinguish them from the ones beyond the cutting plane. Sometimes, standard hatch patterns are used to indicate what kind of material the "knife" has cut through (**Figure 10.45**).

There are two section commands. The 2D Section command produces a group of lines that represent what you would cut through if you cut the object along a plane defined by the line you draw. One major advantage of the 2D Section over the 3D one is that VectorWorks is much better at dimensioning 2D objects than 3D ones.

The 3D Section command draws the section as a group of 3D Polygons that you can rotate to view from different angles. The result can also be rendered with all the options available in any other situation, although selecting the polygons for each fill or texture can be a bit of a chore.

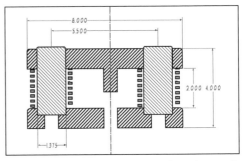

Figure 10.44 Sections are used to explicate the overall architecture of a building as well as individual details.

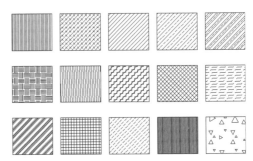

Figure 10.45 Standard hatch patterns represent everything from cork to concrete in sectioned objects.

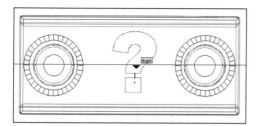

Figure 10.46 The arrow by the section line points the direction in which the viewer is looking.

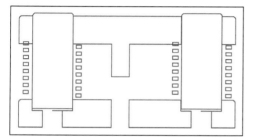

Figure 10.47 A 2D section is a collection of lines.

To cut a 2D section:

1. Choose Model > Cut 2D Section.

2. In the drawing area, click to start the cut line.

   The cursor will be a small cross and the line will be previewed as you draw it.

3. Click again to finish the line.

   An arrow will be displayed on one side of the line, but will move from one side to the other as you move the cursor (**Figure 10.46**).

4. Click to complete the section (**Figure 10.47**).

   It will be drawn in a new layer as a group of lines. In many cases, you can enter the group and use the Compose Curve command to form objects that you can then define with whatever hatches, patterns, or fills best clarify the structure of the object sectioned.

3D sections are cut the same way 2D sections are.

To cut a 3D section:

1. Choose Model > Cut 3D Section.

   The view will be rendered as a wireframe, if it was not already so.

2. In the drawing area, click to start the cut line.

   The cursor will be a small cross and the line will be previewed as you draw it.

3. Click again to finish the line.

   An arrow will be displayed on one side of the line, but will move from one side to the other as you move the cursor.

4. Click to complete the section.

   It will be drawn in a new layer as a group of 3D polygons. You can rotate a 3D section to whatever angle displays it most clearly (**Figure 10.48**).

✔ Tips

- Sections don't have to be cut along the axes.

- You will probably notice that cutting through a VectorWorks model reveals a hollow inside and that the application creates surfaces rather than a true solids. But you can cut pieces of objects away with the Subtract Solids command without revealing this sordid truth.

- Repeat the procedure on a completed section to cut along other planes and expose more of the internal structure of the objects (**Figure 10.49**).

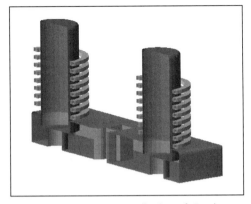

Figure 10.48 3D sections are collections of 3D polygons that can be rendered and rotated at will. Note, however, that what appeared solid is revealed to be only a shell.

Figure 10.49 Since 3D sections are themselves 3D objects, you can cut them into sections as well.

Figure 10.50 Setting the perspective to 1.50 gives a radical presentation to an otherwise mundane object.

Perspective

Perspective renderings do not, strictly speaking, provide any more information than orthogonal drawings; and you lose the ability to take measurements from the drawing. But the trade-off is that you can convey a sense of the experience of an object that a rectilinear projection can't impart. Taken to a more extreme level, you can create images that are more striking than realistic (**Figure 10.50**). This is usually more useful on the sales and marketing side of the operation than on the design side.

The degree of perspective is denoted by the equivalent focal length of a camera lens. Short lenses tend to give extreme perspectives by exaggerating the difference between objects seen at different distances; long lenses flatten out the view. (VectorWorks doesn't let you choose a lens longer than 100 mm, but that's reasonably close to orthogonal.)

Viewing 3D objects in the perspective projection is sometimes confusing. What you see on the screen depends not only on the magnification and orientation of the working plane relative to the screen plane, but in equal degree on the perspective settings for the effective focal length of the lens and the angle between the direction of view and the screen plane.

To set the perspective of the layer view:

1. Choose View > Perspective and select one of the presets (Narrow, Normal, or Wide) from the menu (**Figure 10.51**)

    or

    Choose View > Perspective > Set Perspective. The Set Perspective dialog box opens (**Figure 10.52**).

2. In the Set Perspective dialog box, type a value in the Perspective field and click OK.

    The layer is placed in perspective view and the degree of perspective is whatever you set in the dialog box.

3. Use the 2D or 3D Selection tool to drag the corners of the perspective window in or out to hide or show objects in the layer (**Figure 10.53**).

You can also vary the perspective dynamically using the Translate View tool.

To change the perspective of a layer:

1. With the layer in Perspective projection, click the Translate View tool on the 3D Tools palette (**Figure 10.54**).

    The cursor becomes a four-headed arrow.

2. Hold down the Option/Alt key and

    Drag the cursor *left* to shorten the lens and increase the effect of the perspective

    or

    Drag the cursor to the *right* and flatten out the perspective by increasing the focal length of the virtual lens.

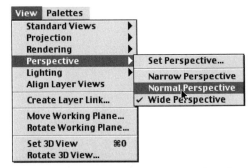

Figure 10.51 Choose a standard perspective from the list under the View menu.

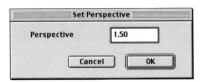

Figure 10.52 Alternatively, enter a value in the Set Perspective dialog box.

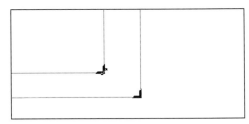

Figure 10.53 Perspective views are drawn within a picture frame that you can reshape by dragging its corners.

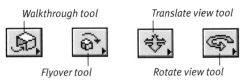

Figure 10.54 There are four tools that you can use singly or in combination to get a better look at the drawing.

PERSPECTIVE

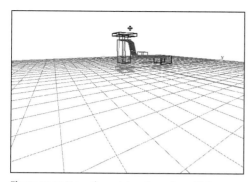

Figure 10.55 Move the pointer above the middle zone to move in closer to the object.

Perspective views differ from their orthogonal counterparts in which the distance between the object and the viewer makes no difference. Think of orthogonal views as perspectives seen from infinite distance with an infinitely long lens, so moving in or out makes no difference.

To move in or out in a perspective view:

1. While in perspective projection, click the Walkthrough tool on the 3D Tools palette. The cursor becomes a four-headed arrow.

2. Starting with cursor in the center of the window, hold down the mouse button and drag it up to move into the drawing or down to move away (**Figure 10.55**).

To move the view point up or down:

◆ Select the Translate View tool and drag the cursor *up* to move the viewpoint up or *down* to move it down relative to the view horizontal plane

 or

◆ With the Walkthrough tool selected, click the Down arrow on the Mode bar to move the horizontal plane down (effectively raising the viewer) or click the Up arrow to move the viewer down

 or

◆ Select the Walkthrough tool from the 3D Tools palette and hold down Option/Alt as you drag the cursor up or down

 or

◆ Select the Flyover tool from the 3D Tools palette and drag the cursor up or down as you hold down the Option/Alt key.

PERSPECTIVE

✔ Tips

■ The Walkthrough tool is unique in this group of tools in that it is position sensitive rather than motion sensitive. Clicking outside the center of the window will move the image; the other tools operate when they are moved in the appropriate direction. Watch out where you have the cursor when you click.

■ Select the Translate View tool and click in the middle of the window to display the current settings for Viewer Z (the height of the viewpoint above the ground plane) as well as the settings for Viewer X and Y in the Data Display bar (**Figure 10.56**).

■ Select the Rotate View tool and click in the drawing area without moving the cursor to display the angular orientation of the view in the Data Display bar.

■ When the view gets so twisted around that you can't find a way to get it into a useful orientation with the mouse, try reverting to the Standard View menu. The Walkthrough tool has a button for Front view on its Mode bar; the 3D Selection tool has them for Top, Front, Right, and Right and Left Isometric views (**Figure 10.57**).

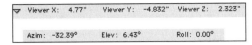

Figure 10.56 The Translate View tool Data Display bar (top) and the one for the Rotate View tool (below) give readouts of the orientation of the viewer relative to the scene.

Figure 10.57 The mode bar for the 3D Selection tool has buttons for standard views that will return you to familiar territory when you've gone over the edge with the view tools.

Figure 10.58 Tilting the camera 30 degrees up or down can do some pretty strange things to the perspective.

When you move the viewpoint up or down, you will probably need to adjust the angle at which the "camera" is tilted so that the objects don't disappear from view.

To change the angle of the view relative to the screen plane:

1. While in perspective projection, click the Walkthrough tool on the 3D Tools palette.

   The cursor becomes a four-headed arrow.

2. Starting with cursor in the center of the window, hold down the Option/Alt key and the mouse button and drag the cursor *left* to tilt the camera up or *right* to move it down (**Figure 10.58**)

   or

   On the Mode bar, click the Viewer Looks Down button to set the camera angle lower or the Viewer Looks up button to raise it.

Rotating Objects in Space

There are two distinct rotational movements in the perspective space; the Rotate View tool spins the view around the origin of either the Ground plane or another working plane or around a selected object. The Walkthrough tool spins the view by turning the viewer–always perpendicular to the screen's horizontal plane.

To freely rotate objects in the space:

1. On the 3D Tools palette, click the Rotate View tool

   Select the center of rotation on the Mode bar as follows:

   Select an object and click Rotate About Object Center mode (**Figure 10.59**)

   or

   Click the Rotate Around Ground Plane Center Mode button

   or

   Click Rotate Around Working Plane Center to rotate the objects around that point.

2. Drag the cursor along the horizontal centerline of the window toward the left side of the window to rotate the objects clockwise around a vertical axis through the selected center of rotation.

   Drag the cursor to the right to rotate the objects counter-clockwise (**Figure 10.60**).

3. Drag the cursor along the vertical centerline of the window to rotate the objects around a horizontal axis through the selected center of rotation (**Figure 10.61**).

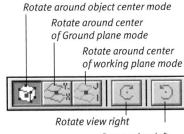

Rotate around object center mode
Rotate around center of Ground plane mode
Rotate around center of working plane mode
Rotate view right
Rotate view left

Figure 10.59 The Mode bar for the Rotate View tool has one set of buttons to set the center or rotation and another pair that rotates the view right or left around that center.

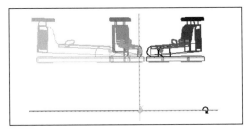

Figure 10.60 Dragging along the horizontal axis spins the object on the screen's vertical axis.

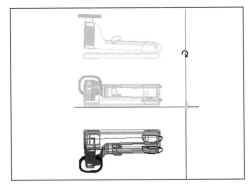

Figure 10.61 Dragging the pointer vertically rotates the object on the horizontal axis.

PERSPECTIVE

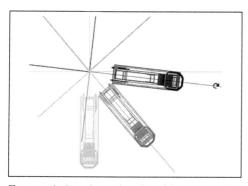

Figure 10.62 Dragging at the edge of the screen spins the object around the screen's z-axis.

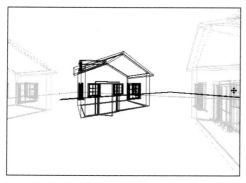

Figure 10.63 Drag the pointer horizontally to simulate turning your head in the view.

4. Drag the cursor along one of the edges of the window to rotate the objects around the z-axis of the screen plane through the selected center of rotation (**Figure 10.62**).

✔ Tip

■ Dragging the cursor diagonally in the drawing area rotates the view on two axes at once.

■ Use the Flyover tool to rotate the view with less freedom, but better control. Dragging horizontally rotates the view around the screen z-axis. Dragging vertically rotates the view around the screen x-axis.

To rotate objects around the viewpoint:

1. While in perspective projection, click the Walkthrough tool on the 3D Tools palette. The cursor becomes a four-headed arrow.

2. Drag the cursor from the center of the window toward the left to rotate the images around the viewer's position in a clockwise direction. Drag right to rotate them counterclockwise (**Figure 10.63**).

PERSPECTIVE

Walkthroughs and Flyovers

When you aren't using the Walkthrough and Flyover tools to orient the view for a specific shot, use them by themselves to navigate freely through the view. Walkthroughs require you to be in perspective projection; for flyovers it's optional.

The Walkthrough tool is used by itself to simulate the experience of walking through the objects in a perspective layer—though not quite at the Pixar level, it must be admitted. In its unmodified modes, Walkthrough lets you (in the metaphor of a camera) move in and out and pan right and left. The Flyover lets you buzz around and over and under the objects in a similar way.

To fly around a view:

1. In any 3D view, click the Flyover tool on the 3D Tools palette.

   The cursor becomes a circulating arrow.

2. On the Mode bar, choose a center or rotation as follows:

   Click Rotate About Object Center mode to use a selected object as the center of rotation (**Figure 10.64**)

   or

   Click the Rotate Around Ground Plane Center Mode button

   or

   Click Rotate Around Working Plane Center to rotate the view around that point.

3. In the drawing area, move the cursor left or right to rotate the view around the screen vertical axis through the selected center of rotation

   or

   Move the cursor up or down to tilt the view around the screen horizontal axis passing through the center defined in Step 2.

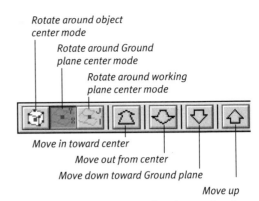

Rotate around object center mode

Rotate around Ground plane center mode

Rotate around working plane center mode

Move in toward center

Move out from center

Move down toward Ground plane

Move up

Figure 10.64 The Flyover tool offers three options for a center of rotation and four buttons use can use to move around the object if you don't (for some reason) want to use the pointer to navigate.

4. Move the viewpoint up or down by holding down the Option/Alt key as you drag the cursor vertically

or

By clicking the Move Down Toward Ground Plane Mode or Move Up From Ground Plane Mode buttons on the Mode bar

5. In a perspective projection, move into or out of the view by holding down Option/Alt as you drag the cursor horizontally

or

Use the Move In Toward Center and Move Outward From Center buttons on the Mode bar.

To walk through a view:

1. While in a layer in perspective projection, click the Walkthrough tool in the 3D Tools palette.

The cursor becomes the four-headed arrow.

2. Adjust the eye level and orientation of the viewer as follows:

Move the viewpoint up or down the (Viewer Z) by holding the Option/Alt key as you press the mouse with the cursor above or below the center of the window. Or use the Raise (or Lower) Ground Plane buttons on the Mode bar.

Raise or lower the viewer's gaze (pitch) by holding the Option/Alt key as you press the mouse with the cursor to the left or right of the center of the window.

3. Move the viewer into the view by dragging the cursor up from center, move back out by dragging down.

4. Turn the viewer by moving the cursor to the left or right of the neutral zone.

✔ Tips

■ For better or worse, the Walkthrough tool lets you walk through walls and other otherwise impermeable objects.

■ You can also adjust the viewer's eye level by switching over to the Translate View tool.

PERSPECTIVE

Layer Links

You may already have noticed that regardless of how you set up the Z values for your individual layers, when you view the first and second floor layers in the same window, they lie right on top of one another.

Don't jump in there and start moving things around within their layers–you'll make your life miserable when you need to modify the design. The VectorWorks answer is to create a new display layer with *links* to the working layers. The relationships between the layers will be displayed correctly in the new layer and the composite will automatically update whenever you make changes in any of the working layers.

To create a layer link:

1. Open the Layers dialog box and create a new layer.

    Give the new layer a distinctive name; set the Z value to 0 so that you can use this linked layer to create others, but don't worry about the ΔZ/±Z setting. The scale should be selected so that the model will fit in the drawing area (**Figure 10.65**).

2. Choose View > Create Layer Link.

    The Create Layer Link dialog box opens (**Figure 10.66**).

3. In the Create Layer Link dialog box, select the names of the layers you want to link.

    Hold down the Command (Mac) or Ctrl (Windows) key to select more than one.

4. Click Link.

    The dialog box closes and 3D images of the selected layers are placed according to their x-y locations in their own layers and stacked in the z-axis according to their Z values in the Layers dialog box (**Figure 10.67**).

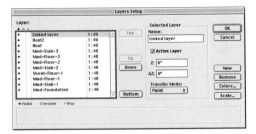

Figure 10.65 It's usually a good idea to start with a clean layer for your layer links.

Figure 10.66 Setting up a new layer for a layer link is just a varlant on setting up any other layer.

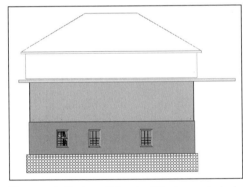

Figure 10.67 The layer link gets all the layers stacked up into a model–if you set the Z values in the Layers dialog box correctly.

All layer links are by default locked in position and, even when unlocked, can be modified only in their original layers.

✔ Tips

- Unlocking and moving layer links doesn't move them in their own layers.

- To remove a layer link, select it, unlock it, and delete it. The original layer is unaffected.

- You can add lights and other features to the layer into which you have linked other layers.

Rendering

The basic information in a drawing is all contained in the dimensioned wireframe rendering of its objects. Designers render their drawings in a variety of ways. Even without creating 3D models, you can use different colors or shades of gray to make your intentions clear. Adding distinctive patterns or hatches adds another level of information.

If you take the time to create a 3D model, you can go further in the direction of photorealism and render surfaces with light and shadow (not to mention perspective). Then, if you own the RenderWorks package, you can add hidden line renderings, more realistic shadowing, and textures.

Rendering is done a layer at a time and only 3D objects are affected.

To render a layer:

◆ Click View > Rendering on the Menu bar and select the rendering mode from the list (**Figure 10.68**). (If RenderWorks isn't installed, many of the options will be unavailable and grayed out.)

✔ Tip

■ Note that patterns are applied to 3D objects only in wireframe and polygon renderings and hatches only in Plan view. Renderings in RenderWorks or OpenGL (a popular 2D and 3D graphics application programming interface) use the background color as a solid fill in the absence of a texture. Textures are used in both the OpenGL and RenderWorks rendering modes, but only fully realized in Final Quality RenderWorks.

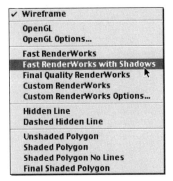

Figure 10.68 The Rendering menu has fewer options without the RenderWorks package (right), but you can still do some interesting things.

Figure 10.69
Individual textures are stored in drawing files you can enter without opening via the Resources palette.

Figure 10.70
Select a texture and click Import (or just double-click it) to bring it into the current file.

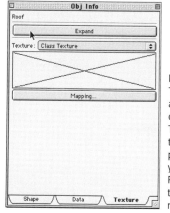

Figure 10.71
Textures are applied to objects from the Texture tab of the Object Info palette. But if you don't have RenderWorks, that tab will be missing.

To texture an object:

1. On the Resources palette, navigate to the location of the texture file you want to use and click Enter to expand it (**Figure 10.69**).

   Select the texture you want and click Import to add it to the resources of the current drawing file (**Figure 10.70**).

   RenderWorks comes with an assortment of textures in the Textures file it installs in the VectorWorks folder, but additional ones may be available in other drawing files at your disposal.

   Once you import a texture, it is available for use on any texturable object in the drawing file.

2. Select the object to be textured.

3. On the Object Info palette, click the Texture tab (**Figure 10.71**).

continues on next page

RENDERING

4. Click the Expand button at the top of the tab to texture different surfaces differently on roofs and walls (**Figure 10.72**).

A roof can have one texture for its top surface and another ("Sides") for its dormers (**Figure 10.73**).

A Wall can have different textures inside and out and a third one assigned to its center.

Most objects are assigned only a single texture.

5. Choose a texture from the Texture pop-up menu (**Figure 10.74**).

6. Click the Mapping button to open the Edit Mapping dialog box that controls how the texture is actually applied to the surface (**Figure 10.75**).

7. In the Edit Mapping dialog box, select the Map Type from the pop-up menu at the top and set the scale of the texture in the Scale edit box.

Hybrid objects have their own preset map types and the menu will be grayed out.

8. Adjust the offsets and the rotation of the texture pattern using either the edit boxes or the graphic controls under the preview window.

Use the view controls below and to the right of the preview window to rotate the view do you can see what you're doing.

9. Click OK to close the dialog box and impose the texture on the object.

It's not difficult to get the texture settings to create some pretty bizarre effects; click Default to get back to the starting point if you find you've gone to far afield.

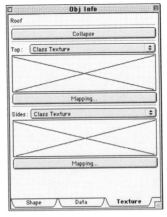

Figure 10.72 Expand the texture tab to more closely control which surfaces get which textures. Or collapse it and apply the texture to all the surfaces uniformly.

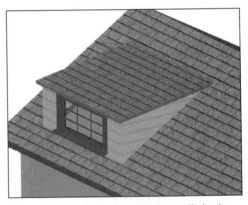

Figure 10.73 The dormer has shingles applied to its top surface and siding on its walls.

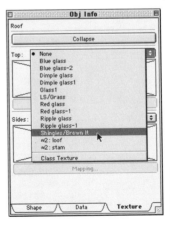

Figure 10.74 Drag down the menu to select the texture.

RENDERING

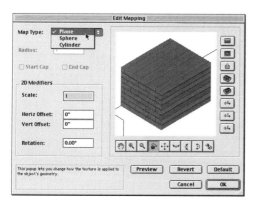

Figure 10.75 The Edit Mapping dialog box lets you scale and rotate the texture rather just accepting it as is.

Textures and fills in PIOs

Plug-in objects have their own approach to rendering. Many present pop-up menus for their various parts on the Shape tab of the Object Info palette when they are selected (**Figure 10.76**). Each of these menus contains a list of styles that are modified in the Classes dialog box. Once a style has been selected in a PIO Object Info palette, it is added to the Class list where you can assign it whatever attributes you want, including textures (**Figure 10.77**).

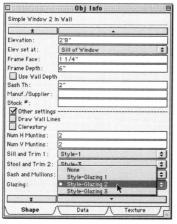

Figure 10.76 The textures or fills within a plug-in object are controlled from the Object Info palette.

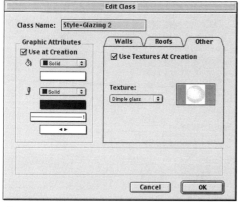

Figure 10.77 Adjust the Styles and Glazing Styles in the Edit Class dialog box.

RENDERING

Lighting

It just won't do to render a view and leave the lighting to chance. By default, the only light in a layer is the Layer Ambient which has a default value of 25 percent of its full brilliance. You will find that it casts a pretty dim light on your design. While you can adjust the brightness to make it easier to the objects in the layer by choosing View > Lighting > Set Layer Ambient, there are more dramatic—and informative—ways to light a scene. Remember that shadows are important visual clues to an object's shape.

Lights are just like other 3D objects in that they are created in a layer and are members of a class. They have a location in space, although they have no size or attributes.

To set the default light:

1. On the 3D Tools palette, click the Light tool (**Figure 10.78**).

   The cursor becomes a small cross and the Mode bar shows three modes and a Light Preferences button (**Figure 10.79**).

2. On the Mode bar, click the Light Preferences button.

   The Light Preferences dialog box opens (**Figure 10.80**).

3. In the Light Preferences dialog box, leave the On radio button selected (unless you want the lights you place turned off by default) and set the Brightness to the desired value; 75 percent is the default.

4. In the Light Preferences dialog box, click the color button to give the light a hue.

   The color picker opens (**Figure 10.81**). Select a color and click OK.

Figure 10.78 The Light tool is a powerful instrument for controlling what your renderings look like.

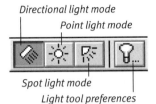
Directional light mode
Point light mode
Spot light mode
Light tool preferences
Figure 10.79 The Mode bar for the Light tool.

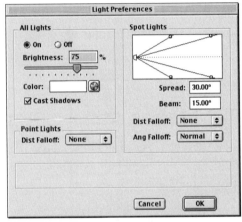
Figure 10.80 The Light Preferences dialog box sets the defaults for the Light tool.

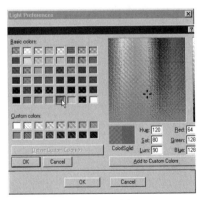
Figure 10.81 Click the color button to open the color picker and apply a gel to your light source.

LIGHTING

Figure 10.82 Setting the distance falloff to None gives a wide distribution of light from a spot.

Figure 10.83 Smooth falloff limits the illumination as a function of distance from the source.

Figure 10.84 Sharp falloff gives you a light source that has only a very local effect.

5. In the Point Lights panel, choose a setting for the Distance Falloff from the pop-up menu as follows:

None means that the intensity of illumination is independent of the distance between the source and the object (**Figure 10.82**).

Smooth means that the intensity is proportional to the distance (**Figure 10.83**).

The Sharp setting causes the intensity to fall off exponentially (**Figure 10.84**).

6. In the Spot Lights panel, adjust the Beam and Spread angles either graphically by moving the handles in the diagram or by typing values into the edit boxes below it.

continues on next page

7. Set the Distance Falloff as above. Set the Angle Falloff to control the distribution of light between the Spread and the Beam as follows:

None distributes the light evenly all the way across the Spread angle (**Figure 10.85**).

Normal concentrates the light in the beam with the intensity falling off linearly across the remainder of the Spread angle (**Figure 10.86**).

Smooth has a sharper falloff as you leave the beam area (**Figure 10.87**).

Sharp puts all the light into the beam (**Figure 10.88**).

To place a light in the drawing:

1. On the 3D Tool palette, click the Light tool.

2. On the Mode bar, choose the kind of light you want to place:

A Directional Light is an infinitely large source that produces parallel rays in one direction. It is a pretty good model for sunshine.

A Point Light is a bare bulb-type source that casts light of equal intensity in all directions.

A Spot Light is a directed beam that has controllable angle and spread.

3. In the drawing area, click to place the light.

The light will be placed like any other object in space. The illumination of Directional Lights is independent of their location, depending only on their orientation and strength.

By default, the light will be oriented at 45 degrees from the *x*-axis (azimuth) and pointed down at 35.26 degrees (Elevation). With Point Lights, these numbers don't matter. Spot lights depend on both location and orientation.

Figure 10.85 Angle Falloff gives a broader or narrower cone of light from a source. Setting the Angle Falloff to None lets the light spread out across the entire Spread setting.

Figure 10.86 Normal concentrates most the light within the region of the beam with some leakage into the Spread area.

Figure 10.87 A Smooth falloff setting yields an even more concentrated beam.

Figure 10.88 Set the Angle Falloff to Sharp to keep the beam very focused.

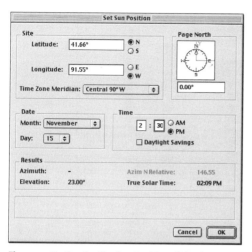

Figure 10.89 Use the Set Sun Position dialog box to create the solar conditions for a particular time and place. Architects like to use solar studies of their buildings.

Figure 10.90 Putting lights inside objects adds to the realism of the rendering.

✔ Tips

- VectorWorks will place a special Directional Light that allows you to see where the shadows of the sun fall at a given time at a given location. Choose View > Lighting > Set Sun Position to open the Set Sun Position dialog box. Fill in the blanks and a light will be placed to mimic the sun for your settings (**Figure 10.89**).

- Creating lighting fixtures with Spot or Point lights inside them can model actual lighting conditions in a design (**Figure 10.90**).

To edit a light:

1. In the drawing area, select the light you want to edit.

2. On the Object Info palette, set the class and layer and choose the radio button that turn the light on or off (**Figure 10.91**).

3. Set the brightness with either the Brightness edit box or the slider control under it.

   Set the color by clicking on the color button and adjusting the color in the picker that opens. Check the Cast Shadows checkbox if that is the desired effect.

4. Click either the working plane or the Ground plane button and enter values in the X, Y, and Z or the I, J, and K fields to position the light.

   (The position of a Directional light doesn't matter.)

5. From the Light Kind pop-up menu, choose Spot, Point or Directional.

6. For Directional and Spot lights, set the light's orientation by choosing either Pan and Tilt for spot lights or Azimuth and Elevation for directional lights or $\Delta X/\pm X$, $\Delta Y/\pm Y$, and $\Delta Z/\pm Z$ for either and entering values in the adjoining data fields (**Figure 10.92**).

   Point sources are by definition omnidirectional.

7. Set the Beam of a spot as you did when you set up the defaults.

✔ Tips

■ Set the brightness to overload by a number larger than 100 into the Brightness field.

■ You can also adjust the positions and orientations of lights graphically by grabbing the handles of the lights with the 2D Selection tool and moving them around. It's usually easiest to do this in the top, front and side views.

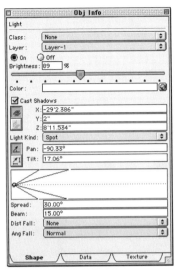

Figure 10.91 The Object Info palette for lights lets you change every parameter for both their positions and their optical qualities.

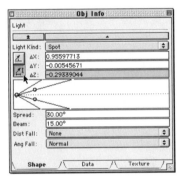

Figure 10.92 Set the orientation of the light with either xyz (above) or angular settings.

■ Render the view using the OpenGL option and you can see the effects of moving a light in real time. Other wise, you have to wait for the scene to re-render.

LIGHTING

Worksheets and Reports

The world of database management tools that VectorWorks provides may be a little beyond the scope of this book, but it's nonetheless worth touching on. If you don't need the tools you don't have to use them, but for a project of any size, the ease with which you can create parts lists and bills of materials is worth looking into.

Once you have set up the basic structure of a worksheet, you can do the kinds of database manipulation you would do with any other spreadsheet application. A selection of wall objects can be converted to an area calculation, for example, which can then be used to compute the amount of paint required to cover them.

The most expedient way to begin is to create a *record format* that associates information with the individual objects in the drawing for later retrieval. Symbols are particularly handy for this since once the record format is attached to the symbol definition, it will be associated with every symbol placed in the drawing.

To create a record format:

1. On the Resources palette, click New.

   The Create Resource dialog box opens (**Figure 10.93**).

2. In the Create Resource dialog box, select the Record Format radio button and click Create.

   The Create Record Format dialog box opens (**Figure 10.94**).

3. In the Create Record Format dialog box, type a name for the new record format in the Name field.

4. Add a field to the record format by clicking New.

   The Edit Field dialog box opens (**Figure 10.95**).

5. In the Edit Field dialog box, enter a name for the field, check the radio button for the type of data that will be in the field, and enter (this is optional) a default value.

6. When you have completed the format, click OK to close the dialog box and add the record format to the resources of the drawing file.

✔ Tips

- You don't have to use every field of the record format for every object. In general, better to err on the side of excess, but a record format can have only a single field.

- To edit a record format, select it on the Resources palette and click Edit to reopen the Edit Record Format dialog box. You can change the defaults or add or remove fields or even change the name of the record format.

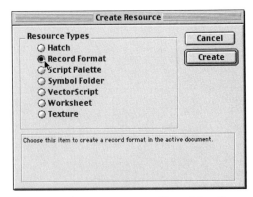

Figure 10.93 Start your new record format from the Create Resource dialog box.

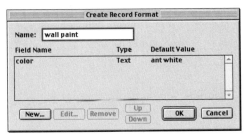

Figure 10.94 Go to the Create Record Format dialog box to set up the fields for a record format one by one.

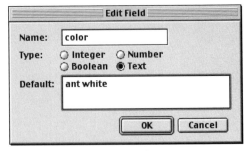

Figure 10.95 The details of each field are handled in the Edit Field dialog box.

Manuf./Supplier : Andersen
Stock # : TW3052
Color : Sandstone
Rough Opening : 3'-2 1/8" W. x 5'-5 1/4" H.
Masonry Opening : 3'-4" W. x 5'-6 5/8" H.
Egress Compliant : -
Sill Detail : -

Figure 10.96 Select the object to which you want to attach a record and click the record's checkbox on the Data tab of the Object Info palette.

Figure 10.97 Choose a symbol on the Resources palette and then click Attach to open the Attach Record dialog box.

✔ Tip

■ Attaching or removing record formats from symbol definitions affects only symbols placed after the fact. Instances of the symbol already in the drawing remain as they were until you select them and attach the record format to them.

To attach a record to an object:

1. In the drawing area, select the object with which you want to associate a record.

2. On the Data tab of the Object Info palette, select the record format you want to use and check its checkbox (**Figure 10.96**). Any object can have more than one record attached to it.

The fields of the selected record format will be displayed in the area below the list of formats. The first field will be highlighted and its default value will be shown in the box at the bottom of the palette.

3. Enter the desired value in the bottom box and continue selecting fields in the box above until you have entered as much information as required.

Skip the fields you don't need.

To attach a record format to a symbol definition:

1. On the resource palette, select the symbol to which you are attaching the record format.

2. Click Attach.

The Attach Record dialog box opens (**Figure 10.97**).

3. In the Attach Record dialog box, select the record formats you want to attach to the selected symbol and check the Attached checkbox.

The Attached Records menu displays all the available record formats with diamonds next to the ones already attached.

4. Click OK.

The dialog box closes and the record format is attached to the symbol definition in the drawing file.

WORKSHEETS AND REPORTS

To create a worksheet:

1. On the Resources palette, click New.
   The Create Resource dialog box opens.

2. In the Create Resource dialog box, select the Worksheet radio button and click Create.
   The Create Worksheet dialog box opens (**Figure 10.98**).

3. In the Create Worksheet dialog box, type a name for the new worksheet in the Name field and enter the number of rows and columns it should have in the appropriate fields.

4. Click OK.
   The dialog box closes and the new blank worksheet appears in the window (**Figure 10.99**).

To create a report:

1. Choose Organize > Create Report.
   The Create Report dialog box opens (**Figure 10.100**).

2. In the Create Report dialog box, give the report a name in the Title field
   or
   Click Options and append this report to an existing worksheet.

3. From the List all pop-up menu, select either Objects with a record or Symbols.

4. If you have chosen Objects with a record, select the record format from the Listing objects with record pop-up menu and then choose which fields will be used for columns in the worksheet (You may notice that PIOs have their own record formats that are not visible in the Resources palette)
   or
   If you have selected Symbols, the only columns to choose from are Symbol Name and Quantity.

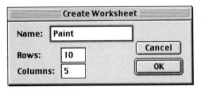

Figure 10.98 The Create Worksheet dialog box sets up the bare bones of a worksheet you can then develop into a sophisticated data management instrument.

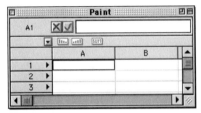

Figure 10.99 The new worksheet is nothing more than an empty canvas.

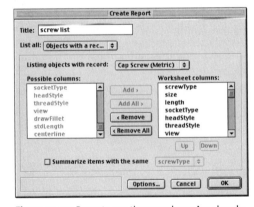

Figure 10.100 Reports use the records you've already attached to your objects to generate worksheets with whichever fields you choose as the column headings.

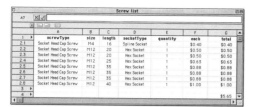

Figure 10.101 Once you click the OK button in the Create Worksheet dialog box, VectorWorks opens it on top of the drawing.

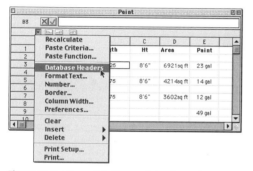

Figure 10.102 To work in the worksheet, you have to display database headers by selecting that item in the worksheet menu. Selecting it again will hide the headers.

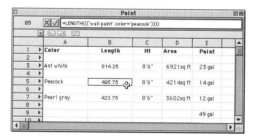

Figure 10.103 The content of each cell is determined by the formula (be it ever so simple) shown in the formula bar at the top of the worksheet.

5. Click OK.

The Report is created and opens in the window (**Figure 10.101**). It is also added to the list of Worksheets under the Window menu on the menu bar and on the Resources palette.

To perform simple calculations on the worksheet:

1. Open the worksheet in which you want to make your calculations.

2. Click the worksheet menu arrow in the upper-left corner of the worksheet and select Database Headers on the drop-down menu (**Figure 10.102**).

The database rows will be displayed.

3. In the worksheet, select the database cell for the cells you want to modify.

The formula that defines the cells it controls is displayed in the formula bar (**Figure 10.103**).

4. Type the formula that defines the data in the cells.

The formula can be anything from a word to a complex expression using logical and mathematical functions (preceded by = to let the software know it has to calculate something).

5. Press Enter or Return or click the check mark to the left of the formula field to enter the formula and calculate the results.

6. If you make changes in the drawing that effect the worksheet, click Recalculate in the worksheet dropdown menu to have them reflected in the results.

✔ Tip

■ If you're not comfortable with writing formulas into the formula bar of the spreadsheet, click the worksheet menu arrow and select Paste Function to open the Select Function dialog box and then select a function from the list (**Figure 10.104**).

You can use the same method to place the criteria the function will use to determine the values for the data cells by choosing Paste Criteria and using the Criteria dialog box to complete the formula (**Figure 10.105**).

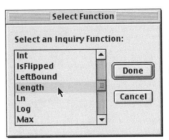

Figure 10.104 You can use the Select Function dialog box to paste functions into the formula bar if you don't know them.

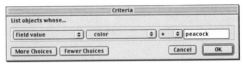

Figure 10.105 The Criteria dialog box opens when you choose Paste Criteria from the worksheet menu. Use it to fill in the selection criteria for the functions you put into the formula bar.

INDEX

INDEX